C000062651

SOULFULNESS

SOULFULNESS
The Marriage of Shamanic and Contemporary Psychology

David England

KARNAC

"The Bold Knight, the Apples of Youth, and the Water of Life" by Aleksandr Afanas'ev reproduced by kind permission of Pantheon Books, an imprint of the Knopf Doubleday Publishing Group, a division of Penguin Random House LLC.

Eight lines from *Four Quartets* by T. S. Eliot reproduced by kind permission of Faber and Faber Limited

"We are transmitters" by D. H. Lawrence reproduced by kind permission of Peters Fraser and Dunlop (PFD)

Markova, D., PhD (2000). *I Will Not Die an Unlived Life: Reclaiming Purpose and Passion*. Conari Press. Reprinted with permission.

First published in 2017 by
Karnac Books Ltd
118 Finchley Road
London NW3 5HT

Copyright © 2017 to David England

The right of David England to be identified as the author of this work has been asserted in accordance with §§ 77 and 78 of the Copyright Design and Patents Act 1988.

All rights reserved. No part of this publication may be reproduced, stored in a retrieval system, or transmitted, in any form or by any means, electronic, mechanical, photocopying, recording, or otherwise, without the prior written permission of the publisher.

British Library Cataloguing in Publication Data

A C.I.P. for this book is available from the British Library

ISBN-13: 978-1-78220-475-6

Typeset by V Publishing Solutions Pvt Ltd., Chennai, India

Printed in Great Britain

www.karnacbooks.com

CONTENTS

LIST OF FIGURES

DEDICATION AND ACKNOWLEDGEMENTS

I dedicate this book and offer my gratitude to my teachers at The Institute of Psychosynthesis, London, for their quality of training to be a psychosynthesis guide with individuals and groups; my supervisor in my early years as a fledgling psychotherapist, Becket Ender, who skilfully and sensitively guided me to a deeper appreciation of what this work is about; my teachers at Eagle's Wing College of Contemporary Shamanism for their quality of training to be a shamanic practitioner; my friend and psychosynthesis colleague Jessica Nelson and my son Ed for their support and invaluable feedback on the book—Ed also prepared the illustrations, the shamanic maps and models, which form such an important part of the book; my supervisor, Dawn Russell of Eagle's Wing, for the insightful way in which she talked through the book with me as it unfolded; my shamanic group, especially Bernhard, Gabriella, Ian, and Ivon, for their care of my soul and for the depth of work that we undertake together.

Last but not least, I thank Karnac Books for offering me the opportunity to see this book in print, and in particular to my editor Rod Tweedy.

ABOUT THE AUTHOR

David England is a psychosynthesis psychotherapist and counsellor, a shamanic guide, a workshop leader, an author, a professional story-teller, and a public speaker.

David trained at The Institute of Psychosynthesis, London, gaining a Diploma in Psychosynthesis Counselling in 1996 and an MA and Diploma in Psychosynthesis Psychotherapy in 1998. He is a registered psychotherapist with the UK Council for Psychotherapy. Since graduation, he has run a private psychotherapy and counselling practice in the Royal Borough of Windsor and Maidenhead.

In his MA thesis, David reflected on how a client who presents with a particular existential issue has an analogue in the hero or heroine of a traditional story. For example, where a client has an abandonment issue this is matched with remarkable accuracy by the story of Hansel and Gretel.

For five years, from 1999 to 2004, working alongside a psychosynthesis colleague, Simon Smith, who is the author of *Inner Leadership, Realize Your Self-Leading Potential* (2000), David undertook psychosynthesis-based business coaching and personal development work with business managers.

David's Soulfulness website is *Soulfulness.co.uk*.

For seven years, from 2005 to 2012, he worked as a course tutor at The Institute of Psychosynthesis. He is a member of the Society for Story-telling and of Equity. His storytelling work mainly includes schools, nature centres, libraries, and festivals. In September 2009, he read a paper, "Storytelling as a healing art", at a Society for Storytelling con-ference, "The quest for vision", which brought together storytellers and psychotherapists to explore where the edges of their work meet.

In Autumn 2010 and Spring 2011 he was one of the facilitators on two programmes for head teachers, "Leading for the future", run by the environmental, educational charity Commonwork, at their organic farm in Kent, in conjunction with WWF. As the programme was essentially a reflective journey around the principles of sustainability, David's role was to hold the psychological context, which involved leading daily check-ins, with poems and stories, and running a number of seminars.

David was introduced to shamanism at his foundation year summer school at The Institute of Psychosynthesis, and has retained his interest ever since. Between 2011 and 2013 he completed practitioner training at Eagle's Wing College of Contemporary Shamanism. He has since run many Soulfulness shamanic groups and shamanic journey sessions. He is a member of an ongoing shamanic group.

David is an author of two books of folk tales, Berkshire Folk Tales (England & Bilbé, 2013) and Lancashire Folk Tales (England & Bailey, 2014).

For leisure, David enjoys qigong, walking, circle dancing, films and plays.

FOREWORD

I thought I had a fairly normal childhood. It was only when I entered psychotherapy and began to think about how I was as an adult, and so commenced exploring my early years, that I started to understand the trauma of my "normal childhood".

This book is about the traumas that we suffer as infants and children during our development, how this "developmental trauma" can affect us all, and how a contemporary use of ancient shamanic healing techniques can help us to deal with afflictions that beset us, "so as to lead a more fruitful and fulfilled life" (Mulhern, 2012). The book presents Soulfulness, and its application of shamanic psychology and soul retrieval, as a practice that enhances our experience of living, and as a contemporary shamanic approach to working with trauma sufferers.

Of course, as a talking therapist myself, I recognise that psychotherapy and counselling also enhance our experience of living. I examine the ways in which the complementary approaches of psychotherapy/counselling and Soulfulness can be integrated.

I take the view that developmental trauma can affect us all. I should like to illustrate this by telling a tale: I suggest this is a universal story. The theme of the story is how we narrow ourselves down by hiding away parts of ourselves to fit with how our parents would like us to be.

Chest of drawers

Once upon a time there was a little boy. He lived with his mother and father in a nice house. He had his own bright little bedroom. And in the bedroom was a little bow-fronted chest of drawers. He kept his toys in the middle drawer.

One day he painted a picture of himself. It was so bright, and colourful, and full of life. He felt happy and excited to have painted such a lovely picture. He wrote on the picture, "This is me".

He took the picture to his mother and said, "Look, Mummy, I've painted a picture of myself. Mummy, look!" "Not now, dear," his mother replied, "I have a report to write for work tomorrow. Go upstairs and play with your toys." So, the little boy went upstairs, opened the middle drawer of his chest of drawers, took out his toys, and played with them as his mother had said.

The following day the little boy painted a picture of himself. It was not quite so bright or colourful or lively as the day before, but it was still a lovely painting. He wrote on the picture, "This is me". He went to his mother and said, "Look, Mummy, I've painted a picture of myself. Mummy, look!" "Not now, dear," his mother replied, "I have to finish the ironing. Go upstairs and play with your toys." So, the little boy went upstairs, took his toys out of the middle drawer and played with them as his mother had said.

Every day the little boy painted a picture of himself. And every day when he went to show his picture to his mother she told him to go and play with his toys, which he did. One day the little boy painted a picture of himself. His heart was sad. The picture was all grey and drab and colourless. He took the picture to his mother and said, "Look, Mummy, I've painted a picture of myself. Mummy, look!" "Not now, dear," his mother replied, "I have some letters to write. Go upstairs and play with your toys."

The little boy went upstairs to his room. He took all the grey and colourless paintings of himself that made him feel so sad and put them in the bottom drawer of his chest of drawers. He closed the drawer and never opened it again. Then he gathered together all the bright and colourful paintings of himself. He felt sorry his mother had not liked these paintings of himself. So, he put them in the top drawer of his chest of drawers. He closed the drawer and never opened it again. Then he took his toys out of the middle drawer and played with them as his mother had said.

Some years later, the little boy is a rising executive. He is well thought of. He does as he is told. He never challenges the people he works for. He does not like to be challenged by those who work for him. He still lives his life out of his middle drawer. He knows he is competent. He keeps an even keel. He does not think of himself as a creative person or an original thinker.

He is married and has a little boy of his own now, and a little girl on the way. His life is good. Only, something triggers sudden feelings of sadness, and anxiety grips him at unexpected moments. The feelings he has are like those grey forgotten images of himself from his bottom drawer, come to disturb his peace of mind.

And in the night something awakens those bright forgotten images of himself from his top drawer, so colourful, so full of vitality, which come and dance in his dreams and disturb his rest. In the daytime, as he does his work, he somehow knows that life could be so much more. It causes him unaccountable pain and distress.

And this is where we leave him. At the beginning of a journey.

INTRODUCTION

This book comprises ten chapters and an Appendix. Chapter One begins with a discussion of what the book is about. In Chapter Two, a brief background is provided of traditional shamanism, and I explain what is meant by contemporary shamanism. A description of the "Medicine Wheel" as a key model is provided in Chapter Three, where "Medicine" means wholeness and energy for life. The maps and models around the Medicine Wheel form shamanic psychology and are described in detail with a brief introduction to their psychotherapeutic application.

Chapter Four includes an account of Colin Murray Parkes' (2006) review of existing research into infants' attachment to their mothers, followed by an account of his own research into the way childhood attachment carries over into adult life. His overall conclusion is of a close correlation between a child's attachment pattern and the attachment pattern that he or she subsequently exhibits as an adult.

Alongside the description of Parkes' review of infant attachment and his research into adult attachment, this chapter shows how the Medicine Wheel maps and models provide a systematic, cognitive method of analysing a person's attachment pattern in order to build up a picture portraying the influence of their attachment pattern on their world view and on the formation of their survival personality.

In Chapter Five the role of the Soulfulness shamanic guide is explained, in holding the space for a person to make a shamanic journey, including helping them to set their intention before the journey and to integrate their experience afterwards. The guide may also hold the space for a group of people to make shamanic journeys. Emphasis is placed on the vital importance of the guide having a respectful and empathic attitude towards the person or the group.

I explain how the intention of a shamanic journey is to help the person making the journey to explore and gain insight into some aspect of their history, experience or behaviour that is of concern to them. I explain the form in which the guide induces a trance, and how this serves to relax the body, create a sense of wellbeing, and bring the mind into a quiescent state in preparation for the journey. The guide's use of the medicine drum is explained, and the way this helps a person who is journeying to maintain their trance and keep their focus upon their intention.

I explore the term "soul retrieval", which is a shamanic journey that has the specific intention of retrieving a lost part of a person's soul energy and restoring their vital essence. A shamanic journey or soul retrieval may be a deeply moving experience, hence the importance of the space being strongly and sensitively held by the guide.

Chapter Six examines developmental trauma in some detail, by drawing on ideas from four authors who address issues of trauma and its impact upon psychic development, from different perspectives: analytical psychology (Donald Kalsched, 1996); human physiology (Peter Levine, 1997); and psychospiritual psychology (Roberto Assagioli, 1965; John Firman & Ann Gila, 1997).

Several conclusions are drawn from the work of these authors: first, the effect of trauma is to cause fragmentation of consciousness. To protect against annihilation of the personality and destruction of the personal spirit, the fragments are formed into energetic structures within the unconscious, charged with the mental energy necessary to maintain repression. These energetic structures become personified, which is how we encounter them—as the protector/persecutor (Kalsched), an internalised parent, such as the harsh critic, and as a survival personality (Firman & Gila, 1997).

In an attempt to mitigate against further trauma, the traumatised person enters a trance state, which may be manifested, for example, in disturbed cognition, difficult feelings, distorted self-image, aberrant behaviour, and perhaps most of all in a fragmentation of consciousness and a distorted sense of self.

Chapter Seven provides a perspective on developmental trauma from a Soulfulness shamanic perspective, in the light of the ideas expressed in the previous chapter. The chapter considers how the impact of trauma can have a dual impact upon the psyche: something is removed from the psyche—by dissociation/soul loss—and something alien is inserted. For example, when a person is sexually abused, their self-worth and their true sense of identity may be removed and what is inserted may be depression, anxiety, and false beliefs.

Chapters Eight and Nine look at four ways of using imagination to approach the "deep psyche"—a more imaginative term for the unconscious—in psychotherapeutic work. Chapter Eight describes the principles and practice of active imagination and discusses the value of working with dreams. Chapter Nine discusses the shamanic procedures for approaching the deep psyche in psychotherapeutic work, namely the shamanic journey and soul retrieval. It identifies what these approaches have in common with active imagination and what distinguishes each approach.

The final chapter is about the integration of shamanic psychology and practice with the insights of contemporary psychology to provide an integrated approach to the treatment of traumatic symptoms. I refer to the psychotherapeutic practice described here as "psychotherapy and counselling with soul", because the thrust of the work is about helping the client to expand their experience of being alive, the expansion of soul in the direction of Self.

Drawing on the work of previous chapters, this chapter describes how the marriage of shamanic with contemporary psychology can be achieved. Both Alan Mulhern (2012) and Roberto Assagioli (1965) envisage a four stage structure for what Mulhern calls "psychotherapy with a spiritual dimension". The psychotherapeutic system developed in this chapter is based on a very similar four stage structure:

1. The guide's task is to build the client's trust in the therapy and the guide and so move together towards a psychotherapeutic alliance.
2. The guide's task is to help the client gain a thorough knowledge of their personality and a clearer understanding of their psyche, with its sufferings, vulnerabilities, defences, and strengths.
3. The guide's task is to help the client create a closer relationship and

collaboration between the conscious self and the unconscious, so as to align their consciousness to the deep psyche, allowing its healing energies to emerge.

4. The fourth stage is a journey towards the realisation of Self as a natural process of inner growth, a gradual, and often lengthy, step-by-step expansion of the personal self, the "I", and the alignment of "I" with Self.

The Appendix is a self-contained reflection on a powerful Russian folktale from the collection of Aleksandr Afanas'ev (1945), "The Bold Knight, the Apples of Youth, and the Water of Life". Like the world of the folktale, the shamanic world is a world of imagination, an inner world, a world of the psyche. We illustrate the shamanic world by reflecting on The Bold Knight folktale, which both implicitly reflects the shamanic landscape and has a powerful psychological resonance.

The reflection also reveals how, with my passion for powerful Russian folktales, I relate personally to the material. This reflection on The Bold Knight folktale provides a counterpoint to the main text of the book. It is presented in several sections, which are meant to be read little by little, to be chewed over and slowly digested.

CHAPTER ONE

What this book is about

This book aims to bring the wisdom of the ancient healing practice of shamanism together with the insights of contemporary psychology to provide an integrated approach to the treatment of traumatic symptoms. In relation to contemporary psychology, the book explores the effect of trauma on the psyche and on the personality, with reference to psychological writers on trauma from various perspectives.

In relation to shamanism, the book brings together two threads, one concerned more with practice and the other more with theory, together providing a basis for psychotherapeutic work: soul retrieval and shamanic psychology.

Shamanic psychology

In shamanism, there has existed from ancient times a well developed theoretical understanding of the working of the human psyche, consisting of a series of maps and models based around the "Medicine Wheel". This knowledge of the Medicine Wheel maps and models of human psychology has in more recent times been released into the public arena.

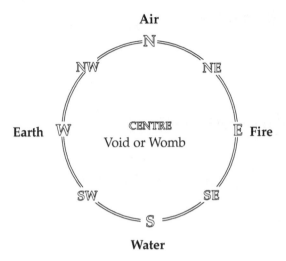

Figure 1.1. Basic Medicine Wheel.

The Medicine Wheel is arranged as a compass, with its four cardinal directions, South, West, North, and East, corresponding to the four "elements", Water, Earth, Air, and Fire. The book explains and describes the Medicine Wheel maps and models and how they can be used psychotherapeutically with clients.

Soul retrieval

The book discusses how a child's experience of an unempathic "maternal environment"—that is, the environment provided by his or her caregivers—distorts their developing psyche, altering their consciousness and distancing them from some aspects of life experience. In psychology, such alterations are termed "dissociation" and "repression". In shamanism they are termed "soul loss", the loss of a fragment of the child's soul energy. The child carries these losses into adulthood.

The shamanic procedure for restoring lost soul energy is called "soul retrieval". Soul retrieval is a key element in the contemporary shamanic practice advocated in this book. Soul retrieval provides a way of bypassing the ego to reach deeper, traumatised levels of the psyche.

In soul retrieval, the client voluntarily enters an altered state of consciousness, in which they can access their deep psychology, with a clear intention to seek insight into some particular aspect of their past history or present experience; their behaviour or some current issue of concern; or the meaning and purpose of their life. Soul retrieval is a transpersonal psychotherapeutic intervention.

I demonstrate using typical case studies how psychotherapy and counselling on the one hand and shamanic psychology and soul retrieval on the other are complementary psychotherapeutic approaches and describe how they can be integrated into a coherent and effective method of working with the symptoms of developmental trauma.

A note about terminology

My psychotherapy diploma states that I am "Entitled to Practice as a Psychosynthesis Guide with Individuals and Groups". To remove any distinctions between differing aspects of a practitioner's work, throughout this book I shall employ the term "guide" to include "psychotherapist", "counsellor", and "shamanic guide". Also, I shall employ the term "client" whenever referring to the subject of the guide's work, except where terms such as "patient" appear within quotation marks.

I shall use the term "mother" to denote an infant's maternal environment. "Mother" is taken to mean a child's primary attachment, which is not always to the child's biological mother, but may be to an adoptive mother, the father, or another carer.

Psychological context

This book's approach to shamanism is explicitly from a psychological perspective and explores the gifts that this ancient healing practice can bring to contemporary psychotherapeutic endeavour. The primary psychological context for the book is psychosynthesis (Assagioli, 1965 & 1973). Psychosynthesis holds a central place on the psychotherapeutic spectrum, and includes in its scope both psychodynamic and transpersonal approaches. However, psychosynthesis is essentially a psychospiritual psychology: it recognises "Self" as a "spiritual consciousness" acting within the human psyche. Self is distinct but not separate from any contents of the psyche, and acts within the human soul at all levels: pre-personal, personal, and transpersonal. Self is a powerful integrative principle acting within the human soul throughout life.

Through my involvement with shamanism over a long period, I have come to recognise how shamanism, in its care and concern for the Soul and its recognition of Self, is close kin to psychosynthesis. Hence, "Soulfulness", the formulation of contemporary shamanism, which is presented in this book, bears a close congruence with this psychospiritual psychology.

These two concepts, Self and Soul, the one deeply hidden and the other unavoidably manifest, are what links contemporary psychotherapeutic practice with the ancient practice of shamanism. Self and Soul are the contextual axis around which this book turns.

Foundations of Soulfulness

In order to show how Soulfulness is well founded as a way of working with symptoms of trauma, at various points throughout the book, and in varying ways, the building blocks on which it is based are considered. These include: soul, approaches to developmental trauma, shamanic psychology, the shamanic technique of soul retrieval, trance states, imagination, and energy.

Soul

Self and Soul are the contextual axis around which this book turns. So, what do I mean by "Soul"? A book about Soulfulness and Soul retrieval needs to have a clear definition of what I understand "Soul" to be.

The first definition of "Soul" in the *Shorter Oxford Dictionary* is "The principle of life in humans or animals; animate existence". Although I like the simplicity of this definition (though I prefer "being alive" to the rather formal "animate existence"), I should like to extend it a little to include our experience of being alive. Therefore, the definition of Soul in this book is, "The principle of life, being alive, and our *experience* of being alive".

What I mean by "Soul", then, is our present, whole, lived experience of ourselves. This experience changes as we grow in self-awareness and self-will, and make the Soul journey towards the realisation of our true Self. Our Soul may be so narrow we are barely aware of our own unique identity. Our Soul may be so broad and reflective we apprehend our unique identity not as an isolated entity but as a bundle of energy, interdependent with the whole of the natural universe. By soulmaking we mean the enlarging of Soul, of our lived experience of ourselves. It is a common care for Soul that links shamanism with psychotherapy and counselling.

Developmental trauma and the survival personality

The book discusses in detail how a child's experience of an unempathic maternal environment, such as in the "Chest of Drawers" story, distorts his or her developing psyche to form a restricted "survival personality", which he or she retains as they grow up. John Firman and Ann Gila (1997) write, "The survival mode is the starting place for all of us".

Shamanic psychology

The book discusses how the Medicine Wheel is used to provide the following:

1. A map of the differing elements of the human personality—body, feelings, mind, spirit, and sexuality—and the differing ways these elements make optimum use of energy when in balance. Hence, the map forms the basis for psychotherapeutic work when a client's use of energy is out of balance.
2. A map of the human life cycle. Hence, the map forms the basis for psychotherapeutic work when clients are facing existential or spiritual crises at different times of life.
3. A model of consciousness that shows how a false core belief, originating from inauthentic mirroring, impacts the personality to form a restricted survival personality and to produce a vicious or maintaining cycle. The model forms the basis for psychotherapeutic work to help a client find the will to escape the maintaining cycle.

Soul retrieval and the shamanic journey

The little boy in the "Chest of Drawers" story hides aspects of himself away: the feeling of unbearable hurt of his mother's rejection and of her failure to see his pain in the dark pictures of himself; and the creativity and vitality that she fails to honour and affirm. These losses he carries into his adulthood, as, I suggest, do we all.

In shamanism, this is called "soul loss", the loss of a fragment of our soul energy, hidden away in an unopened drawer. In psychology it is called "dissociation" (from unbearable physical and emotional experience) and "repression" (of anxiety-inducing memories unacceptable to the conscious mind).

The shamanic procedure for restoring lost soul energy is called "soul retrieval". In a soul retrieval session, we make a "shamanic journey" into our inner world of imagination in a kind of trance, a relaxed state of awareness. The journey is of a prearranged length of time and commences with a clear intention of seeking insight into some aspect of our past history, our present experience, behaviour or some current issue, or of the meaning and purpose of our life, in order to bring about change.

We make a shamanic journey, to begin with at least, in the presence of a "shamanic guide". The work of the guide in the session is to help us formulate the intention of our journey; to help us to relax; to drum for us throughout the journey; to call us back from it; to witness our account of it; and afterwards to help us bring understanding from our experience of the journey into our lives.

The book describes and explains shamanic journeying, the value of the drum, and soul retrieval, and how a soul retrieval is carried out.

Imagination

Soul retrieval is about the use of imagination (meaning what we see, hear, touch, taste, smell, in our inward perception, as well as the kinaesthetic sense of our body's movement) to help us perceive something about ourselves of which we were previously unaware. Samuel Taylor Coleridge (1817) writes, "Imagination I hold to be the living Power and prime Agent of all human Perception". A powerful statement! Nevertheless, being so intimately familiar, we easily take imagination for granted and fail to appreciate what a powerful instrument it can be.

Yet, imagination is inherent in our daily experience of being human. Imagination is a strange and mysterious phenomenon. It can disturb our dreams and fuel our anxieties. It can captivate and enthral us and engender creative insights. We cannot control imagination. It seems to have a life of its own: try holding a mental image of a black circle on a white background for thirty seconds. Yet, we can cooperate with it, set it on a course, follow its stream of images as they unfold, have some choice over the path to follow through its labyrinth. For James Hillman (1975), the imagination is "truly extraordinary ... it is always able to surprise, horrify, or break into ravishing beauty".

In its strange and mysterious way, imagination can heal our brokenness. Many therapists already use a variety of imaginative techniques as a way of working with the unconscious, including dream work, guided visualisation, and active imagination. The point here is this: the experience of working with imagination is a real experience, the insights that arise are genuine insights, and the images that emerge can, with a little effort, be comprehended by the client.

Robert Johnson (1986, p. 8) says about active imagination, "I am convinced that it is nearly impossible to produce anything in the imagination that is not an authentic representation of something in the unconscious. The whole function of the imagination is to draw up the material from the unconscious, clothe it in images, and transmit it to the conscious mind". Imagination, then, can give us an entrée into our unconscious mind.

There is something more to say about imagination: its images are often symbolic or metaphorical, and so what they communicate needs to emerge by reflecting upon them. James Hillman expresses this very succinctly when he links imagination to "soul" and "soul" to lived experience: "By soul I mean the imaginative possibility of our natures, the experiencing through reflective speculation, dream, image, and fantasy—that mode which recognises all realities as primarily symbolic or metaphorical (1975, p. xvi)".

"Because our psychic stuff is images", Hillman says, "image-making is a royal road to soulmaking (1975, p. 23)". I shall explore the power of imagination to aid soulmaking and the healing of soul.

Trance states

We are not in the same state of mind all the time. When we are relaxed, lounging in bed reading the Sunday papers, we are in a different state of mind from when we are crouching over the laptop concentrating on writing a paper. In both cases, we are aware of ourselves, but these are differing states of awareness. A therapist may be in a state of focused attention in the therapy room but when she becomes a client her mind may drift. Being in differing states of awareness at different times is part of our natural human experience.

When I hold a qigong stance for a few minutes, with my mind focused on my inner body, my face relaxes, my jaw drops, and my mouth opens. I go into a trance. I remain aware of myself and my inner body, but this is not a state of awareness I normally go into in my day-to-day life.

(Note: Qigong is the Chinese exercise system on which tai chi is based, see Eva and Karel Koskuba, 2007.)

The kind of trance we go into for a shamanic journey is a similar state of awareness to my qigong state, one in which we are deeply relaxed and inwardly focused. The guide helps us to enter the trance by using relaxing words and to maintain the trance by beating a medicine drum. The safety of the empathic relationship with the guide plus entry into a trance state serve to loosen the ego's grip sufficiently to free the psyche, so that it can travel at will wherever in imagination it needs to go to fulfil the journey's intention.

I cannot emphasise enough that in the trance we remain aware and in charge—unless we happen to fall asleep, in which case we enter a different state altogether, slumber! It is *our* journey, we remain aware as we see our journey unfold, and we are able to recall it later. The guide is there to help and guide, not to control the journey.

Energy

I struggled to write about energy. I wrote: Freud conceptualised a mental energy analogous to physical energy. Then I floundered, crossed it out and watched TV! The concept is fine, but it wasn't the concept I was struggling to express, it was the experience.

I tried again: I often find, when people speak of "energy"—I want to write "bandy about the word energy", but this sounds too harsh, angry even—I get a sinking feeling, because I don't get a sense of what they mean; right now, I see how my energy shifts, I feel I'm getting closer.

On the following morning, I went to my qigong lesson and asked my teacher about "qi", the word widely used in China to mean "energy". She told me, qi is the natural organisation of the body in movement, as exemplified by the quiet stealth of big cats.

The lesson continued, and after doing an exercise for several minutes the exercise began to be soporific, as I described it. She asked me to describe the experience further. I said that my mind became quiescent and my movements became flowing, natural, effortless. It became clear to me, "soporific" was the wrong word; with my mind quiescent for once, the repetitive exercise had induced a trance state in which I could connect with the natural, flowing energy of my body—qi. The name of the exercise was "vital energy".

And, there I have it, vital energy, which can equally be expressed as energy for life, or "lifeforce", so eloquently articulated by Dylan Thomas (1937), "The force that through the green fuse drives the flower".

Trance and trauma

This introductory chapter now comes full circle and returns to developmental trauma. The response of an animal to a threat is the familiar fight or flight, but when neither is possible the animal will enter a trance state, the freeze response. This includes humans, but whilst an animal will shake off the freeze state when the threat is passed, in humans the impact of trauma can leave us in a chronic trance state, the restricted state of awareness of the survival personality.

There is a significant contrast between the original trauma and later therapeutic work using soul retrieval: when traumatised, we enter and remain in an involuntary trance state in an attempt to mitigate against further trauma. This is the unconscious, shadow aspect of trance.

In soul retrieval, we enter a trance state voluntarily as a means of alleviating the symptoms of trauma and bringing light and healing to the soul.

In soul retrieval, we set a trance to catch a trance.

Twenty-first century spirituality

Soulfulness is a practice that enhances our experience of living and enables us to live more abundant and fulfilled lives. How so?

Twenty first-century Western society sets great store by what is scientific, practical, proven, what can be calibrated, concrete, objective. Alongside this, there is an atheistic assault upon religious belief—which is none of those things—and a decline in formal religious observance.

There is a corresponding counterbalance, which is a burgeoning interest in "spirituality". This takes a wide variety of forms: many people practise Buddhist meditation; "mindfulness meditation" is widely taught in organisations; in 2012, 14,500 people gathered at Stonehenge in the pouring rain to celebrate the Summer Solstice; the powerful green movement and the field of ecopsychology foster the idea of a living planet within which all beings are interconnected; and simply feeling a deepening awareness and sense of the natural world.

I suggest there is something in the human psyche that exerts a spiritual pull. Even the famously atheistic rationalist Richard Dawkins (2010) admits, "Irrationality is woven into the fabric of modern life. We unthinkingly indulge unscientific delusion. Half the British population now say they believe in paranormal phenomena. Over eight million of us have owned up to consulting psychic mediums".

In the same context, Richard Dawkins also makes the charmingly lyrical and spiritual statement, "Reality has a magic of its own, deeper, richer and more captivating than superstition or mysticism of any kind". I absolutely agree. I am not holding a candle for superstition or mysticism or spiritualism or new age spirituality or spiritual *belief* of any kind. I am simply suggesting that we can find reality, magic, richness—and healing—at the depth of the human soul.

To be clear, I am not an atheistic rationalist. I recognise the value for very many people of religious and spiritual belief and practice as a source of insight, solace, and spiritual growth. The point I make is that belief is not a prerequisite to spirituality or to spiritual practice and experience.

Self, soul, spirit

What is that something in the human psyche that exerts a spiritual pull? What do we mean by "spirituality"? I find it a struggle sometimes to find adequate words to communicate what I experience, but here goes. A client said to me recently, "I realise I can do plumbing," and as he said it I realised he had taught me something about "Self-realisation". Such powerful words, "I realise!" Our journey of life can be a whole series of "I realise …" statements, each one marking an expansion of our soul, our lived experience of ourselves. Each time we say "I realise …", some innate talent, or calling, or insight or higher value comes into our awareness and becomes real to us, like energy for life flowing into our Soul. D. H. Lawrence wrote:

> As we live, we are transmitters of life.
> And when we fail to transmit life, life fails to flow through us.
>
> That is part of the mystery of sex, it is a flow onwards.
> Sexless people transmit nothing.
>
> And if, as we work, we can transmit life into our work,
> life, still more life, rushes into us to compensate, to be ready

and we ripple with life through the days.

Even if it is a woman making an apple dumpling, or a man
    a stool,
if life goes into the pudding, good is the pudding
good is the stool,
content is the woman, with fresh life rippling into her,
content is the man.

Give, and it shall be given unto you
is still the truth about life.
But giving life is not so easy.
It doesn't mean handing it out to some mean fool, or letting the
    living dead eat you up.
It means kindling the life-quality where it was not,
even if it's only in the whiteness of a washed pocket-handkerchief.
("We are transmitters", 1950)

This is the lived experience of Self-realisation: life is transmitted
from what we call "Self" into and through us and we ripple with life
through the days. This is an experience that we can grasp hold of and
acknowledge.

Returning to the "Chest of Drawers" story, the aspects of himself that
the little boy hides away remain "in spirit", or to put it another way as
part of his potentiality (Note: potentiality is defined as the state or quality
of possessing latent power or capacity capable of coming into being or
action (*Shorter Oxford Dictionary*, second definition)). Each "I realise ..."
statement that a person makes marks a transmission from spirit to matter, as some potentiality is realised. This is soulmaking and the way of
Soulfulness.

So, to summarise: the "spiritual pull" is for me a pull towards Self;
the transmitting of our potentiality throughout our lives from spirit into
matter, bringing expansion to our soul, is for me a meaningful and tangible understanding of "spirituality". And Soulfulness, as a response to
the need for a contemporary spirituality, is a practice that enhances our
experience of living and enables us to live more abundant and fulfilled
lives.

Contemporary shamanism: traditional shamanism's legacy

This chapter introduces the first of the two threads brought together in this book, soul retrieval. The chapter provides a summary and a present-day perspective on traditional shamanism and its use of the shamanic trance and the practice of soul retrieval in healing people suffering from psychological, emotional or physical trauma.

Rediscovering ancient wisdom

Several writers support the general approach of bringing the wisdom of the ancient spiritual healing practice of shamanism together with the insights of contemporary psychology. Peter Levine (1997, p. 60) states that:

> Shamanistic concepts and procedures treat trauma by uniting lost soul and body in the presence of community. This approach is alien to the technological mind. However, these procedures do seem to succeed where conventional Western approaches fail. My conclusion is that significant aspects of shamanic practice are valid. When it comes to trauma, we have much to learn from the ways these traditional people practice their medicine.

Ecopsychologist Theodore Roszak (Roszak et al., 1995 , pp. 5–6) says in a passage entitled "Learning from Stone Age Psychiatry":

> I have been calling ecopsychology 'new,' but in fact its sources are old enough to be called aboriginal. Once upon a time all psychology was 'ecopsychology'. No special word was needed. The oldest healers in the world, the people our society once called 'witch doctors', knew no other way to heal than to work within the context of environmental reciprocity.

After completing her doctorate, Leslie Gray (Roszak et al., 1995, p. 173) studied for ten years with native shamans, and now practises "shamanic counselling". She says that:

> Shamanism is the oldest form of mind/body healing known to humankind. It involves the use of altered states of consciousness for the purpose of restoring well-being to those who are experiencing ill health or helplessness. Shamanism is estimated by archaeologists to be at least forty thousand years old. It's been practiced perennially—or continuously—by virtually all indigenous peoples up to today. Only in the West were its practices essentially eradicated, because of the so-called Enlightenment.

and

> The quintessential undertaking of a 'journey' to consult with spirits [is] highly adaptable to non-traditional settings. Making allies with the things in the natural world around us; talking to the stone people; acquiring an animal as a guardian spirit; Soul Retrievals— these are just some of the core shamanic practices that can be done with an individual client in an office in an urban environment.

Finally, Sandra Ingerman (1991, (p. 39)) writes, "The ancient practice of Soul Retrieval and modern psychology potentially have much to offer each other".

Shamanism

The discussion of traditional shamanism is drawn largely from *Shamanism: Archaic Techniques of Ecstasy* by Mircea Eliade (1964), which is an authoritative and meticulously detailed anthropological survey of shamanistic practices specifically in Siberian and Central Asian tribal communities as well as in other tribal societies throughout the world.

Although various forms of "shamanism" are to be found worldwide, shamanism in a strict sense is a religious phenomenon of Siberian and Central Asian tribal communities. The word "shaman" is derived from a Russian Tungus word, spelt *šaman*. From the standpoint of anthropology, shamanism and the shaman's social position in fulfilling a pre-eminent, magical role for the tribe are integral to the tribal cultures of the region, including their beliefs, myths, symbols, ceremonies, and sacrifices.

In setting out an interpretation of shamanism for the present century, the intention is not to fabricate an imitation of Russian, or any other, tribal culture, but rather to explain the essence of shamanism and to bring the wisdom of this ancient spiritual healing practice together with the insights of contemporary psychology.

In this chapter, the term "shaman" is used in the context of tribal societies and "Soulfulness shamanic guide", or just "shamanic guide" for brevity, to refer to a contemporary shamanic practitioner as envisaged in this book.

Mircea Eliade and the technique of ecstasy

Mircea Eliade (1907–1986) (pronounced Meer-cha Ay-lee-A-duh) was a professor, a writer, and a historian of religion. Amongst his religious ideas was that of drawing a clear distinction between the profane and the sacred (such as divine beings, heroes, mythical ancestors) and to regard a myth as a breakthrough of the sacred into this world, affording value, direction, and purpose. The Appendix illustrates such a breakthrough by reference to a profound Russian folktale, "The Bold Knight, the Apples of Youth, and the Water of Life".

The definition of "shamanism", which Eliade offers as its "primary phenomenon (p. 504)", is "the technique of ecstasy (p. 4)". The word "ecstasy" is normally understood to mean "rapture", but in the shamanic context it has the broader and subtler meaning of "coming out of oneself" (Greek: *ekstasis*, "put out of place", *Shorter Oxford Dictionary*). According to shamanic thinking, the shaman's mastery of the technique of ecstasy makes is possible for his soul to come out of his body and journey in the spirit world. Mastery of this technique of ecstasy is what marks out the role of shaman from other magicians and healers.

The state of ecstasy would today be referred to as a trance or an altered state of consciousness, though the technique of ecstasy is a more compelling designation, "less a trance than a state of inspiration (p. 222)".

One does not have to believe literally that the "spirit world" exists. The very term "spirit world" provides the clue: it is a place outside of everyday reality, not literal at all. At the same time, the shaman has been trained to go there; visiting the "spirit world" is part of the reality of his experience. After frequent visits to the Sky and the Underworld, he is familiar with these extraterrestrial regions. In fact, people today, like me, who have made frequent shamanic journeys, report the same experience of travelling in familiar landscapes.

Today, a shamanic guide would recognise the spirit world as the world of the imagination. For all we know, the shaman, a human being like ourselves, would recognise this too. Be that as it may, we may conjecture that, for people who have suffered sickness or misfortune, the shaman's employment of the technique of ecstasy, for it to have persisted so long and been so widespread, must have proved a powerful and effective intervention.

The shamanic universe

The shamanic universe has three cosmic regions, the Sky (or Upper World), the Earth (or Middle World), and the Underworld (or Lower World). These regions are connected by a central axis, called the World Tree. The branches of the World Tree reach up into the Sky. Its roots reach down into the Underworld. Around the World Tree, at the Centre of the World, there are openings giving access from the Earth to the Sky and from the Earth to the Underworld. With the technique of ecstasy, the shaman's soul can leave his body and ascend to the Sky or descend to the Underworld.

The shamanic universe of Sky, Earth and Underworld is not unfamiliar to us. In common speech, people refer to the sky as "the heavens" and we use the expression "seventh heaven", which carries shamanic, Judaic and Islamic references.

Deeply embedded in the human psyche, and common to most world religions, is the tacit acknowledgement of a sacred connection between the Earth and the Sky, as witnessed by steeples, towers, minarets, domes, stupas and ziggurats.

Equally, the idea of the Underworld being the domain of the dead is a motif that runs through the myths of recorded history, as well as being

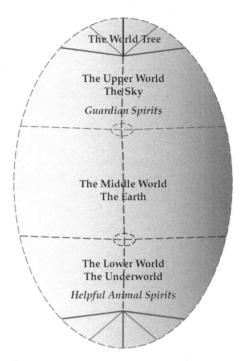

Figure 2.1. The shamanic universe.

literally where we deposit our dead. According to shamanic thinking, the Underworld is also where lost souls are imprisoned, and to the shaman visiting there it is a perilous place populated by aggressive spirits and demons.

A present-day perspective

My portrayal of the shamanic universe of Sky, Earth and Underworld is shown in Figure 2.2. A present-day shamanic guide would understand going deeply into the Underworld or high into the Sky to be about entering more profound levels of the human psyche. From this psychological perspective, the shamanic universe has close parallels with Roberto Assagioli's (1965) model of the psyche, the Egg Diagram, with its Lower Unconscious, Middle Unconscious, and Higher Unconscious:

> *The Lower Unconscious* represents our psychological past. It is the place where we repress wounds that our conscious mind is unable to cope

Figure 2.2. The shamanic universe: our inner world.

with; when, for example, the child in the "Chest of Drawers" story says, "Mummy, look at my picture of myself," and the mother repeatedly replies, "Not now, I'm busy," the child's feelings of rejection, hurt and disappointment are repressed in the Lower Unconscious. The Lower Unconscious also includes those inherent unconscious psychological activities that direct the life of the body and coordinate bodily functions, and in Lower World terms, those instinctual resourceful energies that are personified as supporters and allies—which Eliade refers to as the shaman's helpful spirits—and those traumatic wounds that are personified as the aggressive spirits and demons, which appear in dreams.

The Middle Unconscious represents our psychological present. It includes everything that is accessible to consciousness, our ordinary mental and imaginative activities, and everything we are aware of moment by moment; the flow of sensations, images, thoughts, feelings, desires and impulses that we can observe—the shifting contents of our consciousness.

The Higher Unconscious represents our psychological future. It is the place where we repress the wounding to our sense of self; when, for example, the child in the "Chest of Drawers" story says, "Mummy, look at my picture of myself," and the mother repeatedly replies, "Not now, I'm busy," the child experiences these aspects of their self-expression and creativity as unacceptable to the mother and so they are repressed in the Higher Unconscious. The Higher Unconscious is also the source of wisdom and understanding, of moral imperative and call to service, and those creative energies and intuitive insights that, in Upper World terms, are personified as wise beings or spirit guides—which Eliade refers to as tutelary or guardian spirits.

Shamanism and religion

Although shamanism is historically greatly involved in the religious life of Siberian and Central Asian tribes, it is nevertheless not a religion. Rather, it is an ecstatic technique available as part of a religious practice. Shamanism represents the esoteric aspect—and the shaman the mystics—of any particular religion in the region.

A mystic—Greek: *mustikos*, "initiated person"—, in this case the shaman, is "a person who believes in the possibility of the spiritual apprehension of knowledge not accessible to the intellect" and in "transcending human understanding". *(Shorter Oxford Dictionary)* The emphasis is on the experience by the initiate of the mystical journey and what it reveals, rather than upon adherence to religious dogma. This is congruent with my position in relation to contemporary shamanism, that the shamanic journey is an ecstatic technique available as part of a spiritual path and the practice of soul retrieval, for which religious belief is not a prerequisite.

Whilst traditional shamanism serves religious practice, contemporary shamanism serves "spirituality", as discussed in Chapter One. Contemporary shamanism is a spiritual practice that enhances our experience of living and enables us to live more abundant and fulfilled lives. Contemporary shamanism is an aid to soulmaking and the healing of soul.

Spirits

Along with the shaman's mastery of the technique of ecstasy is his fluency in conversing with "spirits", which may be souls of the dead, nature spirits, demons, mythical animals, guardian spirits, or divine beings.

Of particular relevance to shamanic guides are the shaman's helping spirits, most of which have animal forms, including bears, wolves, stags, hares, geese, eagles, owls, crows, and great worms, as well as wood spirits and earth spirits. In one case a shaman was given three assistants by his tutelary or guardian spirit, a panther, a bear, and a tiger. There is a grey horse that he rides when he ascends to the Sky, and there is a celestial Great God, who dwells in the highest sky and whose sons, daughters, messengers or servants are charged with watching over and helping human beings.

The Lord of the Underworld, Erlik Khan, is also known to the shaman. There is a spirit in the shape of a bear that protects the shaman when he descends to the Underworld, and a funerary dog that he encounters in his descent. It is a dog who guards the entrance to the realm of the dead, a well-known motif in other cultures as well; for example, Cerberus in Greek mythology.

Shamanic societies were animist: people saw every plant as having an animating and enlivening spirit. It is the spirit of a plant that knows how roots grow down and sideways and young shoots grow up. From this perspective, it is the spirit of the sunflower that follows the eye of the sun. When the plant dies its spirit dies with it. Equally, every creature has an animating and enlivening spirit. When the creature dies its spirit dies.

A present-day reflection

This way of looking is different from the scientific viewpoint from which we now observe reality. But it's just that: animism is simply a different way of looking at the natural world. We can look at a growing flower and describe its growth in biological and biochemical terms, or we can see the action of its enlivening spirit. Of course, in the laboratory it may be more suitable to take a scientific view. But, in the garden or the woods and streams it may be more appealing to see spirits, wood sprites and water sprites everywhere. Indeed, this latter approach may encourage greater empathy with the natural world of which we are a part.

Anyway, it isn't as if we have to make a choice one way or the other. We can have both at once, the biology and the enlivening spirit, and so we have the best of both—different ways of looking at the same phenomena.

Eliade has little or nothing to report on shamans' dialogues with helpful spirits, be they messengers of the gods or animal spirits. So, part of the experience of learning to make shamanic journeys is to discover what it means to meet and converse with the personages I refer to as "wise beings" and "animal allies".

The shamanic drum and rattle

The shamanic drum is indispensable to the shaman's work, as it enables him to concentrate and to enter that ecstatic state in which he can fly through the air and travel in the spirit world. The drum is seen as part of the World Tree, its shell being made from the wood of the Tree. Through his drumming, the shaman is magically projected to the Centre of the World, where he can symbolically climb up to the Sky or down to the Underworld, to undertake whatever mission he is called to carry out for the person who has sought his aid. With its role of conveying the shaman into the spirit world, the shamanic drum is also known as the "shaman's horse".

The beating of the shamanic drum enables the shaman to concentrate and to enter the state of ecstasy in which he can journey in the spirit world.

Eliade describes a shaman's rattle, "made from a gourd containing seeds or stones and fitted with a handle (p. 178)". In some traditional societies the rattle is a sacred instrument, the seeds or stones inside the rattle representing the spirits "with which the shaman enters relations". In other societies, the shamans perform on their rattles "highly stylised representations of the chief divinities whom they visit during their trances". There is thus a direct association between the shaman's rattle and the spirits with whom he converses on his journeys.

Eliade does not reveal the frequency of the drum beat. However, in contemporary shamanism it is found that a regular drumbeat of 240–245 beats per minute greatly assists a person in attaining and maintaining an altered state of consciousness; the reason may be explained by the frequency of electrical waves in the brain: 240 beats per minute (or 4hz) is at the low end of the theta frequency range (4hz to 7.5hz). Theta frequencies are said to be associated with memory access, learning, deep meditation, the threshold of the subconscious, and dreaming.

The shaman's calling, initiation, and character

The position of shaman is either inherited or is "the call of the gods and spirits". Either way, "shamanism is always a gift of the gods or spirits (p. 15)"; typically, the Supreme God will appear in a dream to call the future shaman. The future shaman reportedly exhibits bizarre conduct, variously described as frenzied behaviour, withdrawal to the forest, wounding himself with knives, epileptic seizures, an epileptoid attack or a hysterical crisis. An old shaman then undertakes to teach the novice shaman the technique of ecstasy, how to control the various types of spirits, and other shamanic techniques, traditions, and mythology.

Bizarre behaviour, psychopathology, or spiritual crisis?

Whilst the future shaman's conduct is understood to include meetings with the gods, Eliade, after considering the contention by other commentators that this behaviour is evidence of psychopathology, rejects this by pointing out that the only difference between a shaman and an epileptic is that the latter cannot deliberately enter into trance. The future shaman is cured with the help of the same spirits that will later become his helpers; cure, control and equilibrium is brought about by the actual practice of shamanism.

In considering the contention of the shaman's psychopathology from a psychodynamic perspective, John Merchant (2011) suggests a "borderline dynamic". From a psychospiritual perspective, on the other hand, the novice shaman's psychotic-like behaviour is more akin to a spiritual emergency, because he is able to work through the crisis and attain a more developed psychology, with increased concentration, energy, and mastery, as evidenced in two reports quoted by Eliade about the character of a shaman (p. 29):

1. The shaman displays keen intelligence, a perfectly supple body, and an energy that appears unbounded. His very preparation for his future work leads the neophyte to strengthen his body and perfect his intellectual qualities.
2. The perfect shaman must be serious, possess tact, be able to convince his neighbours; above all, he must not be presumptuous, proud, ill-tempered. One must feel an inner force in him that does not offend yet is conscious of its power.

Eliade describes the ceremony to determine an initiate shaman's vocation as comprising, symbolically, suffering, death, and dismemberment, and then resurrection. The initiate's life transition is only accomplished by experiencing in trance his death and dismemberment and his restoration to a new life.

A present-day psychospiritual viewpoint

At a time of spiritual crisis and change, it is common for us to suffer a fantasy of sickness, disintegration and death, as the soul in its expansion bursts through our muscle-bound mental structures. We cannot go back to the way things were, there is "something broken, twisted, hurting, forcing reflection" (Hillman, 1983). We begin the work of imagining ourselves and our lives differently. Something does indeed die in us as something new is born, so that we know ourselves anew and see our world in a different light. Here is my personal story:

> At such a time of spiritual crisis, I felt like a man with no bones, a pool of a man, this was my image of myself, and I suffered a kind of claustrophobia whereby seeing curtains closed or apples still in their paper bag brought on intense anxiety. This fantasy of dismemberment and entombment lasted for three days. Then, standing in my kitchen, I felt a strange, spontaneous, astonishing influx of energy, lasting maybe a second or maybe an hour. A couple of days after this restorative trance, on a memorial tablet in the ambulatory of Beverley Minster, I read the word 'resurgam', I am risen. I felt a thrill of excitement and relief, knowing it was true for me, I am risen.

The shaman's role

The role that the shaman performs, as distinct from other magicians and healers, is in his care for the human soul. The soul is considered to be a precarious psychic entity, readily inclined to forsake the body and thus be an easy prey to evil spirits and sorcerers.

The shaman fulfils his role of caring for the soul wherever the immediate fate of the soul is under threat, including misfortune, sickness, and death. The shaman is equipped to perform this unique role because it is his vocation; he is a sick man who has succeeded in curing himself through the shamanic initiation process and ceremony. Knowing the technique of ecstasy, being familiar with the pathways of extraterrestrial regions, being able to converse with spirits, and having the support of helpful spirits, he can safely abandon his body and descend to the Underworld or rise to the Sky.

In the case of misfortune, the shaman searches for and consults animal spirits, guardian spirits, and divine beings, in order to uncover the causes of misfortune for the person seeking his aid and help restore their fortune.

In the case of death, the shaman is the "psychopomp"; his role is to guide the dead person's soul to the Underworld.

Caring for the departed soul: a present-day reflection

The moment of a person's death is a tangible experience for those who are present with them. There is a distinct change in the dying person's body, the sudden departure of its vital spark. It isn't surprising that people through the ages have felt this sudden departure to be the soul leaving the body, as many people today still do. The ancient motif of the soul flying from the body in the form of a white bird retains a strong emotional appeal. In common speech, the term "the departed" is still used to refer to a person who has died.

As in the above discussion of spirits, death is a phenomenon that can be looked at in different ways. From the perspective of biology and public health, the body must be disposed of, a service performed by undertakers. At the same time, care for the human soul requires comfort and support for the bereaved, including some ceremony to honour and celebrate the life of the departed soul and, as it were, escort the soul safely to the next world, a service performed by priests and funeral celebrants, the present-day successors of the psychopomp.

Soul retrieval

When a person becomes gravely ill, physically, emotionally or psychologically, or when they are overtaken by grief, they seem to lose something of their vital essence. In traditional shamanism, this diminishing of vital essence is understood to be the loss of soul. So, it is the healing work of the shaman to make a journey into the spirit world to search for the person's fugitive soul, to retrieve it, and to cause it to return to reanimate the body that it had vacated. This is soul retrieval.

The story of Kubaiko

Eliade illustrates how the theme of shamanic descents to the Under-world has passed into the oral literature of the Siberian people by recounting the story of Kubaiko (p. 213):

> This is the story of a brave girl called Kubaiko, who goes down to the Underworld with the intention of bringing back the head of her brother, decapitated by a monster. After many adventures and after witnessing the torments by which various sins are punished, Kubaiko finds herself in the presence of the King of the Underworld himself, Erlik Khan. He consents to her carrying back her brother's head if she can emerge triumphant from an ordeal: she must draw out of the ground a seven-horned ram buried so deep that only its horns can be seen. Kubaiko successfully performs the feat and returns to earth with her brother's head and the miraculous water that the god has given her to restore him to life.

It is interesting to read the short, fascinating, and highly complex story of Kubaiko from a psychological as well as a shamanic viewpoint. Sometimes in folktales, Hansel and Gretel for example, brother and sister represent different aspects of the same composite person. Applying this idea shamanically, the decapitated head is a soul part that has been lost to the Underworld as a consequence of trauma. In her journey to the Underworld, the brave girl imaginatively experiences adventures, witnesses torments and punishments, then meets the king, who turns out to be an ally. He challenges her to unearth a deeply held secret before he can return her brother's head and give her the gift of miraculous water, which on her return from the journey will restore her soul.

Applying the idea of a composite person psychologically, the story suggests severe dissociation as a consequence of trauma, with the "brother" as the dissociated part and the "sister" as the part that is active in the world. The "sister" undertakes an adventurous yet peril-ous psychotherapeutic journey in which she gains insight into the tor-ments inflicted upon her for imagined sins, and takes a symptom by the horns to unearth from her unconscious a beastly secret, before emerg-ing triumphant and restored to fullness of life.

The role of the Soulfulness shamanic guide

The essential role of the shaman in traditional shamanism is his care for the human soul. The role of a shamanic guide is the same, which means helping a person to broaden and deepen their present, whole, lived experience of themselves.

Holding the space for shamanic journeys

In traditional shamanism, the shaman makes the journey to the spirit world on behalf of the one who seeks their aid. The approach advocated in this book, however, is for the shamanic guide to teach the person seeking help to make the shamanic journey for themselves, with the guide "holding the space" for them, which includes helping them to articulate a clear intention for the journey, helping them enter an altered state of consciousness, drumming for their journey, and then helping the person to integrate their experience.

Rather than receive a second hand report of a journey, to which they may or may not relate, it is more empowering for a person to experience the journey first hand and be able to relate this experience directly to their lives.

Holding the space is part of a guide's responsibility for the care of soul. Holding the space for a person means creating a physical space where they can be comfortable and secure; an emotional environment in which they can feel cared for and valued for who they are; an intellectual environment in which they can be heard and understood; a spiritual space in which they can thrive and expand their soul.

The care of soul

The role of a shamanic guide is to care for the souls of those who seek their aid. This means helping them to live more abundant lives, with more joy, love and fulfilment, and helping them expand their souls as they grow in self-worth and self-esteem, self-awareness and self-will, and as they make the soul-journey towards the realisation of who they truly are.

In the case of physical sickness, the shamanic guide can offer a healing presence through his or her relationship with the person who seeks their aid, and shamanic journeying can help them to relax and to find an inner serenity and composure to assist them in their journey to health.

Sometimes, a bereaved person suffers extreme distress, perhaps where they feel there is unfinished business, or a sudden death gave no time to say goodbye, or there are words not spoken. Here, a shamanic guide can use a shamanic journey to help the bereaved person to reconnect imaginatively with the departed soul, dialogue with them, say their goodbyes, and make peace.

Where the one seeking aid has psychological concerns, the shamanic guide can help them to explore these issues using soul retrieval.

Soul retrieval and depth psychology

With the shamanic guide holding the space for them, a soul retrieval ceremony allows a client who is seeking relief from the effects of trauma to access a deep part of their psyche and retrieve their lost soul energy as part of a healing process. I deliberately use the term "ceremony" rather than "technique" or "procedure"; rather than carrying out a procedure, the guide creates the ritual space for the journey and holds the space, whilst it is the client themselves who makes the journey.

However, a soul retrieval ceremony is only the beginning of this soul healing work, which the guide and their client undertake. In dialogue with their guide, the client needs time to process and integrate the images and insights that arise in the soul retrieval and space for the self-reflection, mourning, forgiveness and self-acceptance, which their soul requires.

The client will need further soul retrieval and soul healing work: to reveal the way trauma has affected their character and behaviour; to be empowered to make the psychological change necessary to choose a new way of being and acting in the world and in relation to others; to integrate their knowledge of the trauma, such as to be relieved of its distorting and limiting influence, and be free to continue their emotional, psychological and spiritual growth.

Thus, whilst inducing a trance state is simply a technique, soul retrieval is a transpersonal psychotherapeutic intervention; hence, my introduction of the term "client".

A soul retrieval

Matthew is highly intelligent and successful in business, yet he struggles with the dilemmas he faces in his personal life. Faced with a dilemma, he repetitively "argues the case" in his mind, almost to the point of exhaustion, then he splits off into a place of numbness. This is a familiar pattern for him, rooted in a childhood in which his controlling parents would not tolerate any attempt on his part to make choices for himself, his only choice then being to withdraw into himself. He undertook a soul retrieval with the intention of restoring his capacity to exercise choice:

> I brief Matthew about the shamanic journey he is going to make and invite him to choose a place in nature where he will begin his journey. He lies on a reclining chair with a blanket covering him and a scarf over his eyes. I invite him to focus on his breathing and I speak relaxing words, whilst playing slowly on the drum, to help him enter a shamanic trance. I play the medicine drum throughout the journey.
>
> Matthew begins his shamanic journey at his chosen place in nature, a small island off the Irish coast. He states his intention for the journey then finds a tunnel that leads him to the Lower World. The tunnel opens out into the landscape of the Lower World. There he meets a white horse. He greets the white horse and lets the horse lead him along a straight path between deep ditches.
>
> In our subsequent dialogue, Matthew comes to understand the straight path as representing a quality of clarity that he can bring to his dilemmas and thereby avoid the pitfalls at either extreme. He says that from now on he will walk the straight path alongside his white horse and find his way to making clear choices.

Myths and folktales: breakthrough of the sacred

Bruno Bettelheim (1976) summarises the difference between myths and fairy tales, or folktales, in terms of "the pervasive pessimism of myths and the essential optimism of fairy tales" (p. 41).

Mircea Eliade regarded a myth as a breakthrough of the sacred into this world, affording value, direction, and purpose. This section considers the meaning of this breakthrough and the relationship between folktales and shamanism, and introduces the book's Appendix, a reflection on a powerful Russian folktale, "The Bold Knight, the Apples of Youth, and the Water of Life".

Life divined from the inside

In considering dream images and symbols as expressions of the unconscious mind, Freud (1949) points out a common symbolism throughout the varied forms of human expression: "We derive our knowledge from widely different sources: from fairy tales and myths, jokes and witticisms, from folklore, i.e. from what we know of the manners and customs, sayings and songs, of different peoples, and from poetic and colloquial usage of language".

This points to the relationship between the inner world of individuals and what we know about that inner world from dreams, customs, myths, and stories. The relationship between the inner world and the outer world is at the heart of Bruno Bettelheim's enchanting work *The Uses of Enchantment* (1976), in which he shows "how fairy stories represent in imaginative form what the process of human development consists of (p. 12)" and why fairy tales make such a great and positive psychological contribution to a child's (and an adult's) inner growth.

The stories encapsulate a collective and profound wisdom in relation to the inner world and so "give meaning and value to life (p. 35)". Bettelheim says that fairy stories and myths embody the cumulative experience of a society, as we recall past wisdom for ourselves and transmit it to future generations. These tales are the purveyors of deep insights that have sustained humankind through the long vicissitudes of its existence, a heritage that is not revealed in any other form as simply and directly, or as accessibly, to children (and adults).

Whilst there are close similarities between the "fantastic events in fairy tales and those in adult dreams (pp. 35–36)", the fairy tale "is very much the result of common conscious and unconscious content having been shaped by the conscious mind, not of one particular person, but the consensus of many in regard to what they view as universal human problems, and what they accept as desirable solutions (p. 36)".

Bettelheim concludes that "myths and fairy tales speak to us in the language of symbols representing unconscious content. Their appeal is simultaneously to our conscious and unconscious mind ... and to our need for ego ideals as well. This makes it very effective; and in the tale's content, inner psychological phenomena are given body in symbolic form (p. 36)". This is "life divined from the inside (p. 23)".

Bettelheim garners support for his assertion that myths and folktales are life divined from the inside by quoting Mircea Eliade (p. 35):

> Mircea Eliade, for one, describes these stories as 'models for human behaviour [and] by that very fact, give meaning and value to life'. Drawing on anthropological parallels, he and others suggest that myths and fairy tales were derived from, or give

symbolic expression to, initiation rites or other rites of passage—such as a metaphoric death of an old, inadequate self in order to be reborn on a higher plane of existence. He feels that this is why these tales meet a strongly felt need and are carriers of such deep meaning.

Eliade writes, 'Initiatory scenarios—even camouflaged, as they are in fairy tales—are the expression of a psychodrama that answers a deep need in the human being. Every man wants to experience certain perilous situations, to confront exceptional ordeals, to make his way into the Other World—and he experiences all this, on the level of his imaginative life, by hearing or reading fairy tales'.

Russian folktales and shamanism

In 1998, I wrote my MA thesis on the relevance of folktales to the field of psychology, and ever since, as a psychotherapist and storyteller, I have seen the power of folktales to achieve breakthrough and transformation in people's lives. There are two groups of Russian folktales that are particularly compelling:

1. Feminine rite of passage stories about attaining personal power; for example, a young girl, Vasilisa, is sent by her wicked stepmother to beg for fire from the dreaded Baba Yaga.
2. Masculine rite of passage stories about attaining true manhood; for example, a young archer, aided by the horse of power, is forced to bring Princess Vasilisa, the bride of a wicked Tsar, from the edge of the world.

I have observed the close correspondence between the ethos and character of these two types of powerful Russian folktale and the ethos and character of Russian shamanism. It is as if they emerged from a common folk culture, so that to reflect upon one is to reflect upon the other. In the Appendix I illustrate the shamanic world by reflecting on a Russian folktale, "The Bold Knight, the Apples of Youth, and the Water of Life", from the collection of Aleksandr Afanas'ev (1945). This folktale both implicitly mirrors the shamanic landscape and has a powerful psychological resonance, and at the same time implicitly shows the interrelationship between the shamanic and psychological perspectives. The reflection also reveals how I relate personally to the material.

CHAPTER THREE

The Medicine Wheel: shamanic psychology

What we call the beginning is often the end
And to make an end is to make a beginning.
The end is where we start from ...
With the drawing of this Love and the voice of this Calling
We shall not cease from exploration
And the end of all our exploring
Will be to arrive where we started
And know the place for the first time.

—*T. S. Eliot*, from "Little Gidding", 1944

This chapter introduces the second of the two threads brought together in this book, shamanic psychology. The chapter is a contemporary restatement and interpretation of an historic shamanic psychology. The first original source of information conveyed in this chapter is the Native American Twisted Hairs Metis Medicine Societies Council of Elders, whose Original American forebears safeguarded the Medicine Wheel teaching within their culture and languages from ancient times. Harley SwiftDeer Reagan (1941–2013) tells how he was mandated by the Council of Elders to translate the teachings into

English, to make them far more widely available. His resulting book *Shamanic Wheels and Keys* (1980) is now in its fifth edition.

It is interesting that Mircea Eliade, in his comprehensive book *Shamanism: Archaic Techniques of Ecstasy* makes no mention of the Medicine Wheel. It seems, at the time this book was first published, in 1964, the Medicine Wheel teaching was still held in secret by the Native American community, lest it become besmirched and dishonoured, as had the rest of their ancient culture.

The second original source of information conveyed in this chapter is Hyemeyohsts Storm's (1994) autobiographical book *Lightningbolt*, in which he charts his spiritual journey, an adventure towards Self. Storm's book includes sections on the history and ancient teaching of the "Flower Soldiers" of Yucatan three thousand years ago. Storm tells us, the Flower Soldiers believed in democracy, gender equality, honouring the earth, opposition to slavery and human sacrifice, and a psychology of Self. Their psychology is expressed in the many aspects of the Medicine Wheel, the wheel of health and wholeness. To Hyemeyohsts Storm, the Medicine Wheel is an inheritance that belongs to all the people of the Earth.

I was introduced to the shamanic Medicine Wheel teaching by Nick Headley as part of my psychotherapy training at The Institute of Psychosynthesis in London, and from the beginning have incorporated aspects of the Medicine Wheel teaching into my work as a psychotherapist. In recent years I trained as a shamanic guide at Eagle's Wing College of Contemporary Shamanism under Dawn Russell, Lorraine Grayston, and its founder Leo Rutherford. Both Nick Headley and Leo Rutherford received the Medicine Wheel teaching from SwiftDeer.

Two books on the Medicine Wheel by Leo Rutherford have also been an important source: *Your Shamanic Path* (2001) and *The View Through the Medicine Wheel* (2008). These books set out Leo's perspective on the Medicine Wheel teaching, which he has developed over thirty years of shamanic practice. This chapter is my perspective, taken from a psychological point of view.

A view of human personality

The importance of the shamanic Medicine Wheel teaching for me, as a psychosynthesis psychotherapist and a shamanic guide, is that the teaching is profoundly psychological and psychospiritual:

1. The teaching provides a map of the various elements of the human personality—body, feelings, mind, spirit, and lifeforce—the vital energy that manifests as sexual and creative energy.
2. It shows how these elements interact and how they employ bodily energy in different ways.
3. It shows how the trauma of inadequate parenting with inauthentic mirroring distorts both these interactions and a person's uses of energy, and thereby prejudices emotional, psychological and spiritual development and physical health.
4. There are maps that portray the cycles of a human life both at the macro and micro level, including major turning points and spiritual crises and emergencies.
5. These maps spiral down towards a comprehensive map of personality, called the Circle of Mirrors, which depicts the vicious cycle, or maintaining cycle, that is familiar to psychotherapists and counsellors and within which clients become entrapped.
6. There are psychotherapeutic procedures based on these maps, including a psychotherapeutic procedure based on the Circle of Mirrors that lays bare for the client the impact of holding a false core belief, before helping the client to take a path towards an authentic core belief, and helping them escape the maintaining cycle.

I briefly touch on the psychotherapeutic procedures based on the Medicine Wheel teaching in this chapter; they are discussed in detail in subsequent chapters. I will also unfold the story of Peter. In brief, Peter is a neglected child, with his mother being preoccupied by her own life issues and therefore relatively inaccessible to him and unable to give him the love he needs to develop a healthy and balanced sense of self. Hence, with a core feeling of being unloved, Peter developed the core belief "I am unloveable".

Understanding the Medicine Wheel

We are accustomed in the Western world to view time as sequential. In gaining an understanding of the Medicine Wheel teaching, however, we need to get used to an alternative view of time; that time is circular and often spiral. The quotation from T. S. Eliot at the head of this chapter eloquently expresses the experience of time as a spiral.

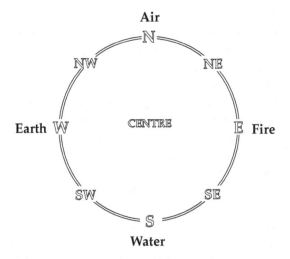

Figure 3.1. The Medicine Wheel: the four elements.

In its basic structure, the Medicine Wheel has the form of a compass, with eight directions and a centre. The four "cardinal directions"—South, West, North, East—relate to the four shamanic elements—Water, Earth, Air, Fire. The cardinal directions hold and stabilise the wheel. The four "non-cardinal directions"—South East, South West, North West, North East—provide the energy to animate the elements, serving to create the transitions that turn the wheel, as discussed in subsequent paragraphs.

In the shamanic context, the term "medicine" means wholeness and energy for life.

Elements of human personality

Figure 3.2 shows the various elements of human personality—Emotional, Physical, Mental, Spiritual and Lifeforce—in relation to the traditional shamanic five elements. However, the context around which the map revolves is soul. My definition of soul in this book is, "The principle of life, being alive, and our experience of being alive". When using this map, what is important is how a person experiences all the elements of human existence: emotional, physical, mental, spiritual, as well as sexual and creative.

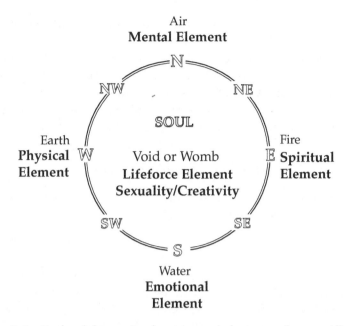

Figure 3.2. Cycle of shamanic elements and elements of personality.

The relationship between the shamanic elements and the elements of personality is explained by the resonance between them:

South   The flow of Emotions resonates with the fluidity of Water.
West   The physical Body resonates with the stability and endurance of Earth.
North   A lively Mind resonates with the free movement of Air.
East   The human Spirit resonates with the transforming power of Fire.
Centre   Lifeforce—manifested as Sexuality and Creativity—the vital energy that seemingly can create something wonderful out of nothing, "The force that through the green fuse drives the flower" (Dylan Thomas, 1937), resonates with the creative Void or Womb.

Lifeforce is the central element of personality, the womb from which sexuality and creativity unfold. It energises and profoundly affects all other elements. It causes us from the beginning to seek relationship with others. Sexuality inspires us to seek union with another, to desire and to enjoy the physical act of lovemaking. It has the power to carry us to heights of spiritual rapture. Sexuality inspires us to create children and holds us in the family relationship throughout the long period of nurturing children. Creativity inspires us to combine our emotional, physical, mental and spiritual energies and to express ourselves inventively in dance, music, poetry, song, whatever we give birth to.

The Choreography of Energy

"When people respect the Balance of the Self, they will learn to respect something as grand and powerful as Life"

—Hyemeyohsts Storm

Figure 3.3 enlarges on the above discussion about elements of personality. The map is used to discern a person's soul experience for each of the elements of their human existence. Our energy is in constant movement, a perpetual dance. Hence, the "Choreography of Energy" is how we organise and dispose our energy between the elements of our personality.

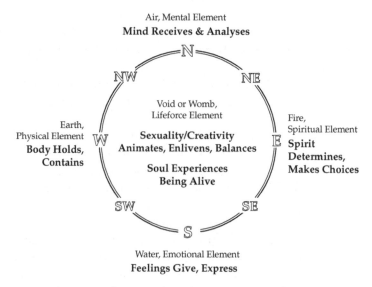

Figure 3.3. Elements of personality: the energetic cycle.

The emotional cycle

The optimal choreography of energy is when an energy balance is maintained between the elements of personality. In Figure 3.4 the emotional cycle (Boyesen, 1980) of the autonomic nervous system illustrates how the human being has evolved to maintain balance and self-regulation as part of the energetic cycle.

We are charged up energetically by the sympathetic nervous system to enable us to express ourselves in some way; to perform an action or to face a threat or challenge. Afterwards, the parasympathetic nervous system enables us to wind down and return to rest. Before a storytelling performance, my pupils dilate, and my heart rate increases. I feel nervous, anxious, and on edge, doubting my ability to deliver the performance. Yet I am fully charged as I step upon the stage. My anxiety is immediately superseded by feelings of exuberance and rapport with the audience. I am in the groove, with my energy, words and bodily expression simply flowing spontaneously. I am elated as I receive and acknowledge the audience's acclaim. Then I need to allow myself to wind down, which usually takes a couple of hours.

The emotional cycle has two stable states, rest and expression, and two transitional states, charging and winding down.

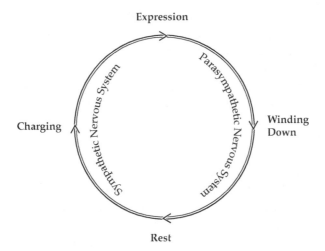

Figure 3.4. The emotional cycle.

How we are meant to be

Here is how the human being has evolved so as to choreograph their energy in an optimal way:

South: Feelings Give
> Feelings flow like water and express themselves spontaneously in our facial expression, stance, gesture.

West: Body Holds
> The skin, the largest organ of the body, sets our physical boundary and contains our whole physical being. Within this boundary, the body is a container for all the emotional energies existing within our being. We are grounded in the body.
>
> The body constantly monitors and reads our environment using our five senses, our visceral senses, and whatever other clues might be around. Hence, our intuition is seated in the body.

North: Mind Receives
> The mind receives information from our body and our feelings about what is going on, our external and internal environment, what people around us are saying and doing and what feelings this brings up in us, and what threats there might be and what opportunities.
>
> The mind sifts and analyses all this information, reflects upon it, sometimes in very quick time, drawing conclusions and setting out alternative ways forward.
>
> The mind has another capacity, which is to use air, the rhythm of the breath, to enter a deep meditative state where the soul can experience a profound connection with the inner being and receive a gift of wisdom not available to normal consciousness.

East: Spirit Determines and Exercises Will
> Informed by the mind's conclusions and options, at times the human spirit experiences an influx of determining energy, "One day you finally knew what you had to do ... you strode deeper and deeper into the world, determined to do the only thing you could do—determined to save the only life you could save" (Oliver,

1986). It may not always be so dramatic—though sometimes it truly is—but when the human spirit is fired up it has the insight, the conviction and the will to make choices about our life direction and self-concept, and the passion and vitality to make it happen. Spirit is filled with energy for life and free to make choices and to act with conviction and passion.

Centre: Lifeforce Animates
The central element of personality is the lifeforce, the vital creative force that drives the wheel of the human organism and maintains balance and harmony between its elements.

The energetic cycle has a further important feature. Each element provides both a particular perspective and contains the whole, just as every part of a hologram contains the whole image. Each of the cardinal directions participates in giving, holding, receiving, and determining, though to differing degrees and in different ways, as in the following example of an energetic cycle: the body gives its sensual and intuitive knowledge to the mind; the mind gives its judgements to the spirit; the spirit gives the passion of its determining will to the feelings to be its expression in the world.

How we are

The foregoing discussion of the use of energy forms an image of how the human being has evolved to use energy. However, the traumatic residue of inadequate parenting with inauthentic mirroring distorts the image.

Referring first to the emotional cycle, the effect of trauma on a person overwhelms their autonomic nervous system. As a result, the winding down part of the cycle fails to be completed, so that a residue of unresolved energy remains in the body, and the person is left perpetually in an energetically aroused and anxious state. This leaves them prone to anxiety attacks, depression, psychosomatic and behavioural problems, and physical ailments.

Referring now to the energetic cycle, the residue of unresolved energy remaining in the body disturbs the balance between the various elements of personality in their uses of energy: the way they give, hold, receive, and determine. The following example illustrates the distortions in the use of energy, beginning with Peter's story:

Peter is a neglected child. His *feelings* are repressed; he *holds* them down rather than expressing them, because his underlying *feelings* are the fear and terror arising from being inadequately nurtured. On the surface, he is remote from his *feelings*, yet ironically at times of stress he finds them intensely painful.

He suffers generalised anxiety in stressful social situations. In response to stress or perceived threats, with his *body* unable to contain the underlying terror, this is expressed as passive-aggression, paranoia, panic attacks, depression, or physical ailments.

As a neglected child, Peter builds his core beliefs, "I am unloveable", therefore, "there is something wrong with me", so it follows that, "I have no right to exist".

He compensates for his disconnection from *feelings* by developing strong rational and cognitive abilities. When his *mind* receives his core beliefs, its compensatory rationalisations produce the mental construct, "I am special. I am a very fine person".

Hence, Peter's *spirit*, determined to establish a place in an alien, uncaring world, adopts as a self-concept the spiritual fantasy, "I am a caring, loving person".

Peter shuns intimacy, sabotages potential *sexual* relationships, and where these do form they lack emotional depth. In this way, he limits his lifeforce.

In psychotherapy and counselling, it is necessary to help the client to build awareness before their spirit can summon the will to change. Working with the elements of a client's personality and the way they use energy serves to make explicit the way in which their energy is out of balance, thereby providing a focus for subsequent therapy work.

Examples of unbalanced energy include: a client's repressed feelings burst out as rage, which the body cannot contain; a client is so overwhelmed by feelings that the mind cannot think coherently; when a client who is cut off from emotions is asked about feelings they reply with thoughts.

The time cycle

Figure 3.5 shows how our various elements of personality relate to the different views of time—time past, time present, and time future.

South: Our emotional element relates to the past, reflecting the extent to which, as an infant, we received good parenting with authentic mirroring.

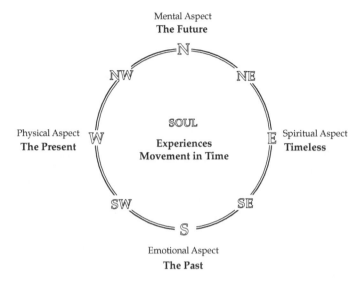

Figure 3.5. The time cycle.

North: Our mental element relates to the future, as we make plans
and set targets for ourselves.
West: In our physical element we are always present in the here and
now.
East: Our spiritual element relates to a timeless state, our limitless
potentiality, perpetually available to come into form.

The life cycle

Figure 3.6 shows the cycle of a person's life. The cardinal directions—
East, South, West, North—hold and stabilise the wheel. The non-cardinal
directions—South East, South West, North West, North East—are the
processes of transition and change that turn the wheel.

In the East, the spring of life, there is fecundity and potency, a latent
fruitfulness waiting to be engendered and given form.
In the South East is the process of conception, gestation and birth as
we are given life and form.
In the South is our long summer of childhood.
In the South West is where we suffer the upheaval of puberty.

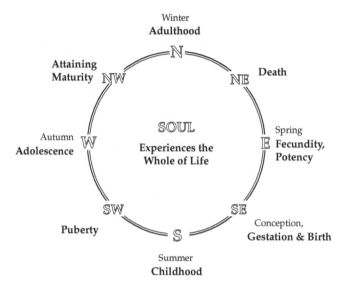

Figure 3.6. The cycle of the seasons: the cycle of life.

In the West is the autumn of our adolescence where we first taste the fruits of the tree of knowledge.
In the North West is our dangerous rite of passage into the cares and responsibilities of adulthood.
In the North is the long winter of our adulthood, where we can work to give our lives purpose and realise the reason for being here.
In the North East our life reaches its fulfilment and its end.

Dawna Markova's (2000) poem "I will not die an unlived life" passionately portrays the cycle of life when lived to the full with beauty, courage, fire, compassion, and love.

> I will not die an unlived life.
> I will not live in fear
> of falling or catching fire.
> I choose to inhabit my days,
> to allow my living to open me
> to make me less afraid,
> more accessible
> to loosen my heart,
> until it becomes a wing,

a torch, a promise.
I choose to risk my significance;
To live
so that which came to me as seed
goes to the next as blossom
and that which came to me as blossom
goes on as fruit.

The spiral of life

"When I was a child, I spoke like a child, thought like a child, reasoned like a child; but when I grew up I finished with childish things. At present we see only puzzling reflections in a mirror, but one day we shall see face to face. My knowledge now is partial; then it will be whole, like God's knowledge of me"

—Apostle Paul, 1 Corinthians 13:12

At various points on the cycle of life—latency, puberty, maturity, and so on—we have the opportunity to finish with the way we are accustomed

Figure 3.7. The spiritual spiral of life: "seven year" cycle.

to speak, think, reason and understand life, and to begin to speak, think, reason and understand life in a new way, a new paradigm. Our knowledge remains partial, but with each new paradigm we have the opportunity to move closer to seeing and understanding the whole.

Figure 3.7 is the cycle of life taken to a more detailed level, portraying life as a spiral. With each turn of the spiral there comes a new paradigm; we begin to speak, think, reason and understand life in a new way. Each turn of the spiral represents the exploring and unfolding of a paradigm through one phase of life: latency, adolescence, young adulthood, etc. Thus: "We shall not cease from exploration/And the end of all our exploring/Will be to arrive where we started/And know the place for the first time" (T. S. Eliot, 1944).

There is a school of thought, to which I tend to subscribe, that there is a seven year cycle in the life of a human being. However, the human soul doesn't work to a timetable, so the times in the following table are notional:

Phase of life	The shift to a new paradigm
Age 7—Latency	I become self-aware but not yet self-conscious, so I can express myself confidently, I can be trusted to travel and visit shops on my own, and I am able and willing to take responsibility for what I do.
Age 14—Adolescence	I experience myself as a sexual being, with all this entails. I shift my identification from parents to peers, though I may find this shift daunting and fear to make it. But I have no choice.
Age 21—Young Adulthood	This is a critical time for me, even a dangerous time, to be faced with such adult pressures and responsibilities before I have gained the wit and wisdom to handle them. It feels like a big hill to climb, from being a freewheeling teenager to accepting myself as a mature adult walking into an unknown future.
Age 28—"Saturn Return"	My early adult crisis—I had got used to being a young adult, there was plenty of partying, friends, and fun. Now I am assailed by doubts and I question: "What is my life about?" I become more serious about my life and career.

Age 35—Ego Completion	I feel at the height of my powers. The world is my oyster. I will make my mark upon the world.
Age 42—Crisis of Meaning	I feel disillusioned. My achievements turn to dust and ashes. They don't seem to mean anything to me any more. I have lost my oomph. I turn my focus from external achievement towards gaining an internal sense of achievement.
Age 49—Crisis of Spirit	My God! My death is on the horizon. There is more of my life behind me than before me. So, what is the meaning and purpose of my life? How can I attain a sense of fulfilment? I turn towards gaining a sense of purpose and meaning, and to giving my life significance.
And it doesn't stop!	

Figure 3.7 shows the spiritual cycle, spiralling about a person's life. As before, the cardinal directions hold and stabilise the wheel. The non-cardinal directions are the processes of transition and change that turn the wheel.

North East: "Death"

A new cycle may be triggered by an event such as a death, divorce, moving house, a child leaving home, or it may seem to arrive out of the blue.

In any event, the end of a cycle can feel to me like a death, as the old way I am accustomed to speak, think, reason and understand life comes to an end.

East: Spring
Potentiality

Whatever sets off the new cycle, there is always something waiting to happen, a latent opportunity for spiritual growth and renewal that is primed to respond.

South East: "Birth"

The response is my rebirth into a new paradigm, often in agony, as I am delivered from the comfortable womb of the old paradigm into the harsh light of a new day.

South: Summer
Realising Change

> I long for what I have lost and suffer the pain of realising now that change is irrevocable. I grieve for what is lost. I don't know who I am any more. My feelings are raw.

South West: "Puberty"

> Slowly I become aware of myself, and I discover who I am in this new paradigm. I find meaning in my new way of speaking, thinking, reasoning and understanding life.

West: Autumn
Realising Meaning

> As I live, I grow into my skin, filling out my sense of who I am and the meaning this life has for me.

North West: "Attaining Maturity"

> I grow to accept myself as I now am and to attain self-mastery.

North: Winter
Myself Realised

> I am a mature self-realising person in the present phase of my life, with a stable personality, a clear sense of meaning, and a purpose to fulfil.
>
> Note: I felt uncomfortable about the state of myself "realised in the mature paradigm" being designated "winter" on the map. Then I realised the aptness of the metaphor; in winter much is happening beneath the soil, a plant's rhizome and roots are growing and are storing starch and proteins to support the following spring shoots. Just so, in the maturity of one paradigm, the unconscious is preparing for the following cycle.

North East: "Death"

> Suddenly it seems that stability turns to instability, my life is in turmoil, everything I valued and everything of meaning and purpose is turned upside down. My soul suffers unspeakable anguish. This is spiritual emergence, an emergence in the soul of an opportunity for growth. The emergence of a new paradigm may not always be so dramatic, but can nevertheless create a profound change. It

is not uncommon, for example, at the peak of ego development, for a person to go into business for the first time or embark upon some new venture.

When powerful enough, spiritual emergence becomes spiritual emergency, looking and feeling like pathology, sometimes even like psychosis. James Hillman (1983) says about soul suffering, "Pathology keeps the person in the soul, that torment, that twist that you can't simply go along in a natural way, something broken, twisted, hurting, forcing reflection. There's a work going on all the time, a fire burning, something elemental happening, the soul's way of working on itself, the pathology necessary to that working of imagination (p. 23)."

It is clearly important for a psychotherapist or counsellor to differentiate between pathological symptoms of past trauma and the symptoms of spiritual emergency, and to recognise when a client is entering a period of life crisis and change. This is for the client an opportunity for spiritual growth, an expansion of their soul, a closer alignment with Self. Thus, it is important for the psychotherapist or counsellor to reassure the client by explaining about life crisis and change, making spiritual emergence the context of the psychotherapeutic work around the torment or chaos that the client may be suffering, and guiding the client as they enter a new paradigm and begin to speak, think, reason and understand life in a new way.

The Circle of Mirrors: a map of personality

The shamanic psychological model the "Circle of Mirrors" described in this section is all about mirroring. An infant gains a sense of themselves according to the quality of mirroring provided by the mother. Sustained empathic and authentic mirroring affords the infant a stable sense of their own being, existing and continuing in time. However, with inconsistent, unempathic and inauthentic mirroring, "the infant does not really come into existence, since there is no continuity of being" (Winnicott, 1987). Again, for the infant, "When I look I am seen, so I exist" (Winnicott, 1988). The corollary is, in the absence of authentic mirroring: When I look I am not seen, so I do not exist. To avoid the terror of annihilation, the infant identifies with those parts of him- or herself that reflect relative acceptance by the unempathic parent and around which a relatively stable "survival personality" can therefore cohere. (Note: this is dealt with in much more detail in Chapter Six.)

The Circle of Mirrors model reveals the influence of a core belief (whose origin is in the quality of mirroring) on the personality as a whole. As with the energetic cycle, the Circle of Mirrors is similar to a hologram; each of the eight directions offers a perspective on the personality, and all perspectives must be seen together to apprehend the whole. Moreover, each perspective highlights and strengthens the whole reflection. The Circle of Mirrors is portrayed in three diagrams:

> *Perspectives:* This depicts the eight perspectives around the wheel. At its centre is Soul.

> *The myth of the wounded child and the dark mirror:* This represents a person's reality. The reality that their soul experiences is the survival personality. The mirror is dark because it delivers a murky and inauthentic image of what ourselves and our life could be. The diagram's function is to reveal the impact of a false core belief on the entire personality. The dark mirror is a representation of the kind of maintaining cycle in which psychotherapy and counselling clients are often seen to be so tightly caught.

> The western side of the dark mirror from south to north is about how in childhood the core belief becomes entrenched throughout the personality. The eastern side of the dark mirror from north to south is about how in adulthood an entrenched core belief is maintained, affecting our entire adult life and shaping our sense of self.

> *The myth of the whole child and the light mirror:* This represents an ideal model whose function is to chart the way forward out of the dark mirror, breaking the grip of the maintaining cycle. The light mirror is light because it delivers a clear and authentic image of what ourselves and our life could be.

Perspectives

Figure 3.8 depicts the eight perspectives of the Circle of Mirrors:

Figure 3.8. The Circle of Mirrors: perspectives.

South: Myths and Core Beliefs
Water, Feelings Give

The quality of love, holding and mirroring, which a mother *gives* to her infant governs the "core *feeling* sense" the infant has of themselves. An infant enters the world in a state of innocence: trusting and free to be themselves. However, the trauma of unempathic mothering, holding and mirroring instils the opposite of innocence, which is fear; the fear of non-being.

So, the infant's core feeling sense, whether characterised primarily by love, freedom and trust or by fear, depends upon the quality of mothering and mirroring. "Core feeling sense" is also referred to in this chapter as "core belief", because in time it becomes articulated as a belief that is reflected throughout the personality.

South West: Process of Life Experience

The child's core feeling sense is reflected in their life as it unfolds. A negative core belief attracts related negative experiences and relationships, thereby curtailing their opportunity of living life fully.

West: Daydreams and Thoughts
Earth, Body Holds

The quality of mirroring that an infant receives affects whether their reflection in the mirror of life is primarily a clear or a distorted image. Where there is regret about how their life is, their core belief is reflected in the way they hold resentment in their body, blaming themselves and later maybe blaming others. They comfort themselves by daydreaming of a better life in which their core belief is countered.

North West: Life Patterns

The child's core belief is reflected in the way they fashion their life patterns as a reaction to their core belief, creating a holding pattern for their life in the form of rules and laws that they live by on a daily basis.

North: Beliefs
Air, Mind Receives

Across the circle from Myths and Core Beliefs, as their mind forms it provides words for the core feeling sense and rationalises this core belief into a set of beliefs about themselves.

North East: Choreography of Energy

Across the circle from Process of Life, their life experience governs their life choices and the extent to which they balance their energy (see The Choreography of Energy, above). They may begin to recognise what their core belief has manifested in their life and begin to take responsibility for their life choices.

East: Illusion or Vision
Fire, Spirit Determines

Across the circle from Daydreams and Thoughts, they face the payoff for the life they have chosen: either a clear vision of their life or unfulfilled dreams and illusions; either self-reflection or self-delusion.

South East: Concept of Self

Across the circle from Life Patterns, the crux of the whole circle is the relationship with Self. Their life's holding pattern, combined with what their spirit determines for their life, reflects a sense of who they are. This may be the limited image of the survival personality or they may see through to the Self. In the words of George Herbert ("The Elixir", 1633): A man that looks on glasse/ On it may stay his eye;/Or if he pleaseth, through it passe,/And then the heav'n espie.

The myth of the wounded child and the dark mirror

Figure 3.9, depicts how, with the trauma of inadequate parenting, inauthentic mirroring is reflected throughout the personality:

South: Myths and Core Beliefs
Water, Feelings Give

When an infant is not given its birthright of love and consistent, empathic holding and mirroring, they suffer the loss of innocence

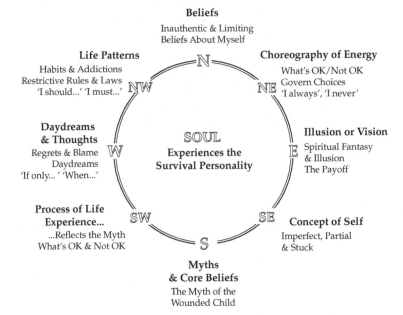

Figure 3.9. The Circle of Mirrors: the dark mirror.

and trust, and blame themselves for the core *feeling* sense of fear and distress that they endure. The resulting false core belief is the myth of the wounded child. Psychotherapists and counsellors are familiar with such myths, articulated as: "Nobody loves me," "I am unloveable," "I am unworthy," "I am worthless," "I am a failure," and so on.

South West: Process of Life Experience

The child's negative core belief, the myth of the wounded child, is reflected in what happens in their lives, attracting negative experiences and negative relationships that reinforce their core belief (what's OK), and shunning positive opportunities that challenge their core belief (what's not OK).

What this means is a rejection of themselves. They will mirror their early environment by rejecting in themselves what was rejected by others. They will try to hide that which has been rejected and they will work diligently to compensate for it. They will shun or be angered by those who display what they have rejected in themselves.

A child such as Peter (above), whose core feeling sense is that he is unloveable, learnt how unsafe it was to express his feelings, because to do so threatened his survival, whereas to be quietly detached—seen and not heard—kept him relatively safe. When this is reflected in Peter's life, expressing feelings or getting close to people will not be OK, and he will shun intimacy, whereas remaining quiet and withdrawn will be OK. It is likely he will avoid unstructured social occasions, in which he can quickly feel lost, and seek situations where he can exchange thoughts and ideas with others about subjects not too close to home.

West: Daydreams and Thoughts

Earth, Body Holds

The core belief that they are unloveable/unworthy/a failure is reflected in the way they hold regret and resentment in their *body*, blaming themselves for the negative experiences and negative relationships they suffer in life. Blaming themselves, or projecting blame onto their partners, only reinforces their false core belief and negative experience of life.

Thus, it is a sign of improving psychological health to be able to direct the blame and resentment where it belongs, most likely onto parents or caretakers. The way they try to comfort themselves is by daydreaming; little plays in which they are loved/worthy/successful …

They are disconnected from themselves, and their daydreams are grounded neither in their bodies nor in the here and now, but in the past, "If only such a thing had happened," or in the future, "When such a thing happens." When the trauma they have endured and their blame and resentment are held in the body, this may cause physical illness or a distortion of body shape and facial expression into adulthood.

North West: Life Patterns

As every action causes a reaction, so the child's myth of the wounded child is reflected in the way they fashion their life patterns, the habits they adopt, the addictions they form, how they fabricate a restrictive holding pattern of rules, "I should …," and laws, "I must," which govern all aspects of their daily life, limit their self-expression, and stifle their lifeforce.

Referring again to the example of Peter, his reaction to the core belief, "I am unloveable," is a repetitive pattern of avoiding intimacy, relating to others at a safe practical level, withdrawing into himself when feeling stressed, and by sabotaging potential sexual relationships restricting his lifeforce.

It is said (Davis, 1996), Jackie Kennedy's mother, Janet Lee, was a cold, domineering woman who was emotionally and even physically abusive to her daughters, especially to Jackie. While Jackie grew up surrounded by wealth and opulence, none of it was hers; she always felt like a poor relation—this seems very like a core belief that fuelled her later habitual, even addictive, acquisitiveness.

North: Beliefs
Air, Mind Receives

Across the circle from Myths and Core Beliefs, as the child's *mind* develops it provides words for the negative core belief and rationalises this myth into a set of limiting beliefs about themselves. For example, from the myth "I am unloveable," the mind may form inauthentic beliefs such as, "I am flawed," and "I have no right to exist."

At the same time, their mind may form compensating inauthentic beliefs; for example, the myth, "I am unloveable," may result in beliefs such as, "I am special," and "I am a very fine person."

North East: Choreography of Energy

Across the circle from Process of Life, their choices are governed by what feels OK or not OK. They are likely to choose jobs and careers that are essentially technical rather than relational, where they can relate to others at a safe practical level. They are unlikely to ask for feedback and feel threatened when it is offered. Referring to the "How we are" paragraph (above), their energy is out of balance, as in the example of Peter.

East: Illusion or Vision
Fire, Spirit Determines

Thus, across the circle from Daydreams and Thoughts, the payoff for the life they have allowed their core belief to choose is a *spirit* mired in illusion and spiritual fantasy. The spiritual cycle is stuck. There is no will. For Peter, the payoff is a safe but empty life, alone, with low energy, without intimacy.

South East: Concept of Self

Across the circle from Life Patterns, their restrictive life pattern and limited self-expression, combined with ungrounded daydreaming and spiritual fantasy, form an imperfect and partial self-concept that is stuck in the survival personality and unable to evolve.

Psychotherapeutic use of the Circle of Mirrors is discussed fully in subsequent chapters. Briefly, working round the west of the dark mirror from south to north reveals to a client how, as a child, their core belief became entrenched and was reflected in every area of their life. Then working round the east of the dark mirror, from north to south, challenges the client to recognise how, as an adult, they have chosen to allow their life to be configured and their sense of self shaped by the image they see in the distorting mirror of their core belief.

Arriving at the South East—Self-Concept—with these revelations, the client is invited to ask themselves the simple yet penetrating question, "What gift does my wounded child need from me?" The wounded child is the "Child of History", born to the pain and suffering of being in the world of experience. Careful reflection upon this question leads the client back to the beginning of the circle, to acknowledge and grieve their wounding and core feeling sense, to question the core belief that became entrenched—the myth of the wounded child—and to take responsibility for their lives.

This makes way for the client to find and afford themselves the gift of a new core myth, the myth of the whole child; the child, whole and unbroken, before the wounding began, is the "Child of Self". Finding their answer to the question "What gift does my wounded child need from me?" serves to open the client to the wisdom of Self. Then, working around the light mirror, the client can visualise a life and a sense of self that reflects their new myth. They can see the way to break the grip of the maintaining cycle of the dark mirror by aligning more and more with Self. However, it must be borne in mind that the myth of the whole child is still a myth! Because its realisation is the ongoing journey of a lifetime, which Figure 3.10 seeks to portray.

The myth of the whole child and the light mirror

South: Myths and Core Beliefs
Water, Feelings Give

> The core *feeling* sense the infant has of themselves is the love, consistent, empathic holding and mirroring the infant is *given* prior to any wounding. The myth of the whole child might be expressed as, "I am free to be wholly myself."

South West: Process of Life Experience

> Their myth affords them freedom to experience life to the full, to be willing to learn from their mistakes, to be willing to relate to others with an open heart. They develop values of freedom, wholeness, openness, participation, and the courage to be themselves and fully to express who they are.

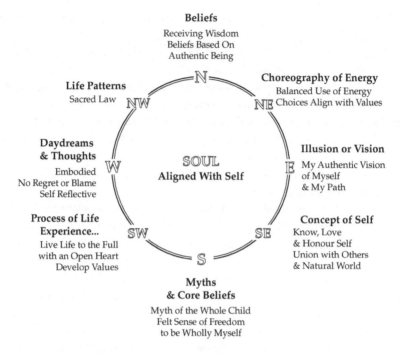

Figure 3.10. The Circle of Mirrors: the light mirror.

West: Daydreams and Thoughts
Earth, Body Holds

> They do not entertain regret or blame but take responsibility for their own actions. They show respect for their *body* and they are *embodied*, grounded in the here and now, self-aware and self-reflective.

North West: Life Patterns

> Their life pattern is founded on a transcendent Sacred Law. The Sacred Law that I learnt from Nick Headley reflects the ethos of the Medicine Wheel and the Circle of Mirrors:
>
>> All things are born of woman—for a man, of his feminine.
>> Nothing shall be done to harm the children or the child within.
>> Death brings life. Life brings rebirth. Rebirth is movement.
>> Movement is change. Change is death.
>> The Light Mirror is my birthright.

North: Beliefs
Air, Mind Receives

> Across the circle from Myths and Core Beliefs, their *mind* forms the belief that wholeness is a process of becoming, a growing into Selfhood by responding to the promptings of Self, with a mind open to receive wisdom from significant others, as well as the wisdom lying deep within.

North East: Choreography of Energy

> Across the circle from Process of Life, their values inform their choices, for which they take responsibility. Optimally disposing their energy means keeping their energy in balance (see The Choreography of Energy, above).

East: Illusion or Vision
Fire, Spirit Determines

> Across the circle from Daydreams and Thoughts, their capacity for self-reflection creates a context in which their *spirit* exercises will and *determines* their future path.

South East: Concept of Self

> Across the circle from Life Patterns, informed by the Sacred Law and aligned with Self, they know, love and honour themselves. They reflect this loving inner environment outwards, understanding their significance as part of a greater union, with other people and with the natural world.

Conclusion

This chapter has described an advanced understanding of psychology that has been held within Native American society from ancient times. The basis of this shamanic psychology is the Medicine Wheel, whose many aspects model the complexities, facets, phases and opportunities for spiritual development that make up a human life.

CHAPTER FOUR

Attachment theory and shamanic psychology

Introduction and scope

This chapter provides a digest of Colin Murray Parkes' (2006) book *Love and Loss* on the subject of attachment theory. The book includes an account of Parkes' review of existing research into infants' attachment to their mothers or "mother-figures", followed by an account of his own meticulous research into the way childhood attachment carries over into adult life. His overall conclusion was of a close correlation between a child's attachment pattern and the attachment pattern that they subsequently exhibit at adults. (Note: This chapter is concerned with Parkes' conclusions. Details of Parkes' research procedures and statistical analyses are outside its scope.)

One of the foundations upon which Soulfulness is based is an understanding of how an infant's experience of an unempathic maternal environment distorts his or her developing psyche, to form a restricted "survival personality" that he or she retains into adulthood. Thus, Parkes' review and research are directly relevant to the subject of this chapter, namely to offer an insight into the different patterns of attachment that children form with their mothers, the nature of attachment patterns and behaviours, the way these attachment patterns carry over into adult life, and how the problems that cause adults to seek psychotherapeutic help often make manifest the particular pattern of attachment they made to their mothers in childhood.

Applying Medicine Wheel teaching to attachment patterns

Alongside the description of Parkes' review of infant attachment and his research into adult attachment, this chapter shows how the Medicine Wheel maps provide a systematic, cognitive method of analysing a person's attachment pattern in order to build up a picture portraying the influence of their attachment pattern on their world view and personality:

> The Choreography of Energy map is used, for a person with a particular attachment pattern, to explore their use of energy and balance of energy in relation to the five elements of personality: feelings, body, mind, spirit, and lifeforce.
>
> The Circle of Mirrors map is similarly used to explore the core feeling sense at the root of the person's attachment pattern and how it influences the way they view the world and the way their personality develops through childhood into adulthood. The product of this exploration is a life narrative.

This chapter lays the ground for a description of how the Medicine Wheel maps are employed psychotherapeutically, which is provided in Chapter Ten.

Parkes' research story in brief

John Bowlby: Attachment theory

John Bowlby (Bowlby, 1953) undertook a review of empirical studies for the World Health Organization regarding the effects of maternal deprivation. This work established just how much harm could be inflicted on infants by a mother's absence or rejection. Rather than use the word "love", with its wide range of meanings and emotional connotations, when referring specifically to the love between a mother and child, Bowlby introduced the word "attachment" to denote a child's tie to its mother.

Mary Ainsworth: attachment categories

Mary Ainsworth (Ainsworth, 1978) applied Bowlby's attachment theory in her work with mother-child interactions. She made an important distinction between strength of attachment on the one hand and security of attachment on the other, addressing the question, "Is the child who clings to his mother, who is afraid of the world and the people in it, and who will not move off to explore other things or other people, more strongly attached or merely more insecure?"

Ainsworth developed a systematic method of observing and classifying the patterns of attachment between infants and mothers. This placed the study of the parent-infant bond on a firm scientific footing and showed how the way a mother behaves with her infant can have a profound effect on the ways they come to view themselves and their world. In Ainsworth's Strange Situation Test (SST), infants in the second year of life and their mothers were observed through a one-way mirror throughout a brief period of separation and then reunion in a strange playroom.

With her colleague Mary Main (Main & Goldwin, 1984), Mary Ainsworth established four categories of attachment that infants form with their mothers:

1. Secure
2. Insecure: Avoidant
3. Insecure: Anxious/Ambivalent
4. Insecure: Disorganised/Disoriented

In the secure category, the child of a mother who is sensitive towards them, and responsive to their need to explore their world from a secure base, can tolerate brief separations with little distress and respond rapidly and warmly to their mother's comforting behaviour when she returns.

With the avoidant category, the child of a mother who does not show her feelings or cannot tolerate closeness, or punishes attachment behaviour, learns to inhibit their natural impulse to cling and to cry. When mother leaves the room they appear indifferent and uncaring. When she returns they often continue playing, ignore her, or turn away from her.

In the anxious/ambivalent category, the child of a mother who is insensitive towards them, who is over anxious, and who is unresponsive to their need to explore their world from a secure base, shows great distress during the period of separation, then clings and cries angrily for a long time on her return.

In the disorganised/disoriented category, the child of a mother who is severely depressed behaves in a way that is unpredictable and inconsistent both during separation from mother and reunion with her. They may cry during separation but avoid mother when she returns, or oscillate between approaching and avoiding her, perhaps rocking backwards and forwards, or suddenly freeze in the middle of a movement, or repeatedly hit themselves. The child is left helpless in the face of a mother who is incapable of responding to any of their efforts at establishing a bond with her.

The depressed mother is likely to have suffered a grievous loss or trauma during the perinatal period. Physical or sexual abuse, neglect, alcoholism and drug dependency are factors that further undermine, in the infant, any sense of safety or security.

Limitations of Ainsworth's method

Parkes considers a deficiency of the SST is its failure to measure the strength of the attachment patterns it describes, suggesting a spectrum of secure and insecure attachment. The inference here is that Ainsworth's attachment categories should be seen as a very valuable model, with the caveat that in reality category boundaries are not so clear-cut.

Mary Main: adult attachment

Mary Main (Main and Goldwin, 1984) proceeded to work on adult attachment. Her Adult Attachment Interview (AAI) is considered the most reliable measure of the lasting influence in adult life of childhood attachments. Main's attachment categories in adults approximately correspond to the four infant attachment categories above.

The AAI is not a retrospective measure of the parenting received in infancy, nor is it a measure of current attachments. Its value is its ability to predict the patterns of attachment (as measured by the SST) that many mothers have with their own infants. Followed over three generations, it was found that: the AAI categories of grandmothers correctly predicted 75 per cent of the AAI categories of mothers; these, in turn, predicted 77 per cent of the SST categories of the infants. These findings indicate that the AAI is a reasonably good indicator of a mother's predisposition to make a particular attachment bond with their infant.

Parkes' research project

For Parkes, Main's work did not go far enough, because AAI was not a retrospective measure. He therefore commenced his own research project to test the prediction that attachment patterns adopted as children carry over into adult life. The main instrument of research that he developed was the Retrospective Attachment Questionnaire (RAQ).

In the Introduction to his book, Parkes makes it clear that, of the many major life-changing losses, bereavement, being one of the most severe, makes it a suitable topic for clinical research. At the same time, types of problems suffered after bereavement are not unique to bereavement, and the lessons to be learnt from studying them reach into the roots of human psychology. Hence, Parkes' research volunteers included bereaved and non-bereaved psychiatric patients and a comparison group of bereaved and non-bereaved young women who were not psychiatric patients. In fact, the research showed that patterns of attachment across all four groups were much the same.

The findings from Parkes' research project are discussed later in the chapter. His overall conclusion was of a close correlation between a child's attachment pattern and the attachment pattern that they subsequently exhibit as adults. He points out, however, that whilst this close correlation supports the theory that childhood attachment patterns continue to influence the lives of adults, it will require a longitudinal study, which follows people from infancy to adult life, to establish a causal link.

Internal models of the world

"We do not see things as they are. We see them as we are"

—Anaïs Nin

This section describes the concept, reported by Bowlby and described by Parkes, that the pattern of attachment expressed by each infant reflects assumptions about themselves and their mother that comprise the child's individual perception of the environment into which they have been born, a unique internal model of their world. I also discuss how the shamanic map of the personality, the Circle of Mirrors, provides a systematic method of elucidating a person's unique internal model of their world.

Bowlby's greylag geese

Reviewing the attachments of infants and mothers of animal species, Bowlby was fascinated by the concept of "imprinting", from a study of greylag geese. When hatching from the egg, the greylag chick becomes "attached" to the first large moving object that it espies.

Bowlby went on to describe the sequence of behaviours by which an infant's "attachment" to the mother is formed and expressed during the first two years of its life. These "attachment behaviours" include sucking, crying, smiling, clinging, and following. Attachment behaviours are modified from birth in response to the mother's handling and mirroring of the infant, so that by the end of the second year large differences are already evident between the patterns of attachment expressed by different infants, reflecting each child's individual perception of the environment into which they have been born, which is their internal model of the world.

The formation of an internal model of the world is illustrated by a party game in which guests are invited to guess what pictures are depicted, like in Figure 4.1 (Evans & Russell, 1990). This is not easy while we lack any internal reference to guide us. However, once we have seen or been shown what the picture is, we can always see it. It becomes part of our internal reference system, our internal model of the world. If you still can't see it, go to the end of the chapter.

Figure 4.1. Party game (a): Who is this?.

The attachment that an infant makes to their mother enables them to build up assumptions about themselves, their mother, and the world at large, constituting templates against which a later event, such as a subsequent sight of the picture, is compared and through which it can be comprehended.

Whilst a child's internal model of their world contains assumptions about everyday objects, which enable them to recognise these things when they encounter them and plan their behaviour accordingly, it also contains all they take for granted, everything that is part of their internal model of the world, which Bowlby called their "assumptive world". This includes assumptions about themselves and their mother, their ability to cope with threats, and the countless perceptions that make up the complex structures on which their sense of meaning depends.

A person's assumptive world is their most valuable piece of mental equipment; without it they are literally lost. However, it is not fixed, but is constantly being influenced by the arrival of new data, which may modify particular assumptions or enlarge and enrich the model. This means that a person's view of the world is essentially subjective; their view of reality is unique, not "reality" but an abstraction from reality. There is no objective truth to be known, but any knowledge or truth that a person holds is created within their own internal model. Every person's view of the world is unique to them, even when it is the product of a shared environment, even between twins.

To go back to the beginning, the primary function of an infant's internal model of their world is to protect them from threats to their survival within their environment. Ainsworth's and Main's attachment patterns are created by the child in a process of trial and error as the infant learns ways of coping with their less than optimal maternal environment, and thereby they create their internal model of the world:

> An infant with an *avoidant* attachment has learnt to survive in a world where their mother discourages emotional demands, which most likely gives rise to an attachment pattern such as controlling their emotions, turning away, and seeking approval through the exercise of their cognitive abilities.
>
> An infant with an *anxious/ambivalent* attachment has learnt to survive in a world where their mother attends to and rewards emotional demands, which most likely gives rise to an emotion-focused attachment pattern, such as clinging and crying.

An infant with a *disorganised* attachment has learnt to struggle in a world where their mother is inconsistent, blowing hot and cold, most likely giving rise to an attachment pattern of disorientation, helplessness, and a high level of anxiety.

The Circle of Mirrors

The section on the Circle of Mirrors in Chapter Three discusses the influence of a "core feeling sense" on an individual's personality as a whole as it is formed in childhood.

An infant enters the world in a state of innocence: trusting and free to be themselves. However, the infant's core feeling sense, their perception of unempathic holding and mirroring, instils the opposite of innocence, which is fear, the fear of not existing. This triggers the infant's survival instinct, impelling them to persist in seeking an attachment to the mother, albeit an insecure one. Thus, the infant's core feeling sense, being so primary an experience, is at the root of their survival personality, with its particular model of the world, as their core feeling sense becomes articulated as a core belief.

Figure 4.2. The Circle of Mirrors: the dark mirror.

Moving clockwise around the Circle of Mirrors from the south (Figure 4.2), a picture is built up step by step of a person's survival personality as it took shape in childhood: in the south, their core belief, the myth of the wounded child; moving to the south west, the life experience that unfolded; moving to the west, the thoughts and feelings about their life situation that were formulated; moving to the north west, the pattern of thought and behaviour that became established; moving to the north, the beliefs and mindsets that became crystallised.

Moving clockwise around the Circle of Mirrors from the north, a picture is built up step by step of a person's survival personality, with its particular model of the world in adulthood, exposing the payoff for the life they have allowed their core belief to determine: in the north, rigid, self-limiting mindsets; moving to the north east, unbalanced energy, a self-limiting life pattern, and life choices governed by the past; moving to the east, illusions entertained about themselves compensating for narrowly limited self-will and self-expression; moving to the south east, a restrictive life pattern and limited self-expression, combined with ungrounded daydreaming and illusion, forming a distorted, partial and seemingly immutable self-concept.

The picture that is built up of a person's survival personality, in childhood and in adulthood, takes the form of a life narrative. This is illustrated in subsequent paragraphs. The kind of dialogue between guide and client employed to formulate such a life narrative is discussed in Chapter Ten.

Though people do not fit neatly into categories, some core beliefs are in general accord with attachment patterns:

Avoidant: "I'm unloveable," "There's something wrong with me." "I'm flawed."
Anxious/ambivalent: "I'm lost without him/her." "I don't need anyone, I can do it all myself."
Disorganised/disoriented: "I'm worthless." "I'm a failure." "I can't do anything right."

Thus, the Circle of Mirrors provides a vehicle for exploring and mapping an individual's survival personality, with its particular model of the world, as it was shaped in childhood and has unfolded throughout their life. The resulting life narrative is a description of the person's survival personality.

Attachment as infants: Parkes' review of attachment research

It is a misconception to think of the insecure attachment patterns as dysfunctional. Each attachment pattern is a strategy learnt by infants to secure their survival in, to a greater or lesser extent, a threatening world. Each attachment pattern therefore has a function as a strategy for survival:

> The *avoidant* infant is forced to stand on their own feet from an early age and to learn to inhibit attachment behaviour (cuddling, crying, etc.). This strategy, being successful within the context of the relationship in which it arose, is likely to be perpetuated.
>
> The *anxious/ambivalent* child learns to cope by clinging, staying close to the mother, and protesting vigorously when she departs. This strategy persists because it enables this child to relate to the mother.
>
> The strategies of coping for the *disorganised/disoriented* infant are less obvious, but they may learn to avoid potential conflicts, to keep as low a profile as they can, and to adopt the human equivalent of "freezing" in their response to a threat (see Chapter Six).

Secure attachment

A child with a secure attachment can tolerate brief separations from mother without great distress and will respond readily and warmly to their mother's comforting behaviour when she returns. Followed up to the age of ten, the significant differences between secure and insecure children are sustained, with secure children showing more self-assurance and competence. Parkes concluded that those who recall being securely attached made more secure relationships in adult life and were less distressed by losses than the insecurely attached.

Avoidant attachment

The child of a mother who cannot tolerate closeness and punishes attachment behaviour learns that expressing affection is dangerous. They may distrust others, and as they grow older and meet their peers they may both keep their distance and learn to control others by means of dominance, assertion, and aggression.

The infant typically responds to reunion with mother by alternately approaching and veering away from her, and without looking into her face will move away until he or she reaches a certain distance from her, usually about three feet, just out of her reach. The child needs to stay close to mother and at the same time learns what is a safe enough proximity to her. Thus, they learn to be distrustful of others and to stand on their own feet.

However uncaring a child with an avoidant attachment may appear to be, they are in fact energetically charged, as reflected in a rapid heart rate, during the period of separation and for a long time afterwards; their indifference is more apparent than real.

Avoidant children show low levels of both understanding and sensitivity towards others.

Anxious/ambivalent attachment

The child of a mother who is anxious and controlling, who is concerned for her child's safety and yet is insensitive to their need for autonomy and who discourages their need to explore their world will react to separation with distress and when their mother returns will cling to her and continue to cry in an angry manner.

Thus, they learn that the world is a dangerous place in which they will not survive unless they stay close to mother and put their trust in her. When they reach school age, they will typically lack the assertiveness, confidence and trust in themselves needed to engage effectively with their peers, and will be prone to anxiety.

Disorganised/disoriented attachment

The child of a mother who is depressed will typically exhibit both anxious and avoidant attachment, at times clinging and crying, at other times curbing their impulse to show affection.

When the infant's mother is unresponsive to any of these efforts to make a relationship with her, when all the child's ploys at engaging her are exhausted, with no way to turn, the child is left in a traumatic state of helplessness, fear, and high anxiety, facing a crisis of life and death. Moreover, the child's plight is likely to be compounded by neglect, physical or sexual abuse, and parental alcoholism and drug dependency.

Caught between the threat of non-being and their survival instinct, the child's only recourse is to lose their life in order to save it. This means adopting a strategy of being as unobtrusive and near invisible as possible, passive, compliant, freezing in the face of danger, and being a carer for their mother whenever opportunity presents.

Infant insecure attachment and the lifeforce

The central element of personality described in Chapter Three is the *lifeforce*, the energy for life, the determination to go on living, and therefore from the beginning of life an infant seeks a relationship with the one who carried them in her womb, who bore them, and/or upon whom they must rely to stay alive. However,

> When the mother of an *avoidant* child does not show feelings, cannot tolerate closeness, and rejects the infant's attachment behaviour—sucking, crying, smiling, clinging, and following, or
> When the mother of an *anxious/avoidant* child is insensitive and unresponsive to their infant's needs for security and a safe base from which to explore their world, or
> When the mother of a *disorganised/disoriented* child is over-anxious and fearful, or is overcome by some trauma, grief or depression,

then the infant's *lifeforce*, their energy for life, is skewed by being forced into an unnatural course. Their *lifeforce* is diminished and the energy for life, which from the beginning seeks relationship with another, is thereafter distorted, which may result in conflicted relationships throughout life, as well as poor self-care and scant regard for personal safety.

Formation of survival personality in childhood

The Circle of Mirrors provides a vehicle for portraying a person's survival personality, with its particular model of the world, as it was formed in childhood. The western side of the dark mirror (Figure 4.3) from south to north is about how in childhood a core belief becomes entrenched throughout the personality to form a survival personality. This is illustrated using the life narrative of Peter.

> Peter's mother wants the baby, but the demands on her time, energy and emotions breed resentment of him. Her handling of him, changing his

Figure 4.3. The Circle of Mirrors: the dark mirror—West.

nappy, dressing him, even feeding him, becomes brusque. She spends little time cuddling him or mirroring him. She leaves him to cry in his cot. In his infantile way, Peter's core feeling sense is of being unloved, which in time becomes articulated as the *Myth*, "I am unloveable."

As the *Process of Life* unfolds for Peter, it is a matter of life and death to stay as close to his mother as feels possible, so he curbs his impulse to show her his love. He takes it into his head, this is how he should be, not showing his love too openly, keeping a safe emotional distance. This is how it was to be for all his later relationships. He can never trust that his love will be received, so he holds back. He can always trust himself, and this gives him some sense of control, even some confidence in himself on a social plane.

In his *Daydreams*, before going to sleep each night, Peter receives the love that life denies him. His constant *Thought* is, "If only someone were to love me, then I could be happy." But he isn't happy. He feels deep envy towards those children he sees as having it all. Feeling unloveable, he resents them, even hates them, blaming them for receiving what should have been his birthright. Sometimes in his blame and rage he can be aggressive towards other children, though usually he is as good-natured as he has learnt to be.

As time goes by, Peter's *Life Patterns* take shape. He learns to read early and to develop his mind. In the books he enjoys, confident, outgoing, sporty schoolboys enter his daydreams, so different from himself yet with whom he can identify. Whilst feeling distant and different from other children, he relates to them by becoming an entertainer, an inventor of imaginative games. Later, as an adult, he sometimes has a sense of how his life pattern lacks flexibility and spontaneity; that he is running on rails.

He applies *Rules and Laws* to himself, perhaps at first simple rules like, "I should not tread on the cracks in the pavement," and, "If I shake my right hand I should shake my left hand as well, so as to be fair," and then stricter laws: "I must not cross or upset people," "I must always be fair to people," "I must not rely on others but trust in myself alone," "I must use my mind so as to be competent in anything I want to achieve," "I must always be good-natured, and hide my feelings (even from myself, especially from myself)."

Peter thinks of himself as fair-minded and good-natured. His mind cleverly compensates for the core belief that he is unloveable and his sense of being different by developing the *Beliefs*, "I am special," and "I am a very fine person,"—and even, "I am likeable," which of course he is, because he has worked hard to make himself so.

Attachment as adults: Parkes' adult attachment research

This section relates Parkes' research findings regarding infant attachment patterns carrying over into adult attachment patterns to the shamanic psychology maps, "The Choreography of Energy" and "The Circle of Mirrors", described in Chapter Three.

The main focus of this section is insecure attachments, taking into account:

The Choreography of Energy: The ways in which adults in the different categories of insecure attachment are likely to suffer an imbalance in their use of energy.
The Circle of Mirrors: An illustration of the way an adult is likely to maintain an entrenched core belief and a survival personality with its particular model of the world.

Parkes' research concerned the ways in which patterns of childhood attachment can influence the subsequent security, self-confidence and trust of the adult, and perpetuate their model of the world. This in turn influences their relationships with others (be they friends, family, or partners) and the way they react when these relationships are impacted by events that invoke insecurity, stress, and loss.

Parkes pointed out that every person with an insecure attachment in adulthood remains bound by a life situation and assumptions about themselves and others that reflect a view of the world that is now obsolete.

An adult's attachment pattern is reflected in the balance between the five energetic elements of personality (Figure 4.4). These include feelings, body, mind, spirit, and lifeforce or energy for life. With the caveat observed by Parkes that Ashworth's categories are too clear-cut and people often do not comply with categories or fit neatly into maps and models, a typical balance of energies is considered in relation to each type of attachment.

Parkes examined the influence of people's recollection of secure attachments in childhood on the security of their attachments in adult life and their subsequent reaction to insecurity, stress, and loss. He concluded that those who recall being securely attached made more secure relationships in adult life and were less distressed by catastrophic events than the insecurely attached.

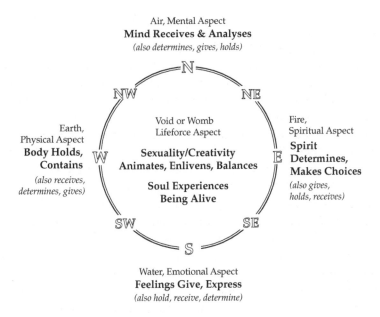

Figure 4.4. Elements of personality: the energetic cycle.

The subsection "How we are meant to be" in Chapter Three describes how a person would be if their five energetic elements were in perfect balance. This description is in accord with the description of adult secure attachment in the present chapter. A person with a secure attachment is full of vitality, open, adaptable, and exudes an *energy for life*.

Avoidant attachments and the Choreography of Energy

Parkes showed how an infant will develop an avoidant strategy to enable them to cope with a mother who cannot tolerate the child's natural impulse to cuddle, to cling, and to cry. A person might be expected to find it difficult to unlearn such a strategy as they grow up and to let go of the belief that they deserve punishment if they should take the risk of getting closer to the object of their love.

Parkes' research did in fact indicate that the attitudes and assumptions formed in childhood are reflected in a corresponding strategy in adult life, complicating love relationships and giving rise to guilt and deep regrets. At times of insecurity, stress and loss in adult life, the person will reassert the habits of thought ingrained in childhood because they enabled them to survive.

Parkes concluded that a person who reports avoidant attachments in childhood typically perceives as threatening attachments in adulthood that are too close, fostering distrust of others, compulsive self-reliance, and relationship problems. The avoidant person will either inhibit their emotions and thus have difficulty showing affection for their partner, expressing their feelings, and communicating at an intimate level, or else will be aggressive and assertive towards them, resulting in marital discord in either case.

Parkes related avoidant attachment to the diagnostic category of "schizoid personality", corresponding to Stephen Johnson's (1994) descriptive category of "the hated child". In the example of Peter, discussed in Chapter Three, Peter is a "hated child".

A person in the avoidant group, with their attachment pattern of emotional control, will have suppressed their *feelings*, though their underlying anger may be expressed through the *body* in the form of aggression or physical bullying. Suppressing *feelings* will have meant that the person has inhibited their natural impulses to show affection to the mother. The effect on the *body* of inhibiting their natural impulses is to contract their musculature. In adulthood, the resulting distortion of posture and sculpting of the body becomes a chronic condition with possible health repercussions.

Alongside their suppression of *feelings*, they will have developed their *mind's* cognitive capacities, such as assertiveness or continually analysing, assessing and adjusting emotional closeness to/distance from a partner, as witnessed by the familiar push-pull dynamics. Having dissociated their *feelings* from their *mind*, they use their mental abilities to gain achievement in life. This affords them some self-confidence, but, with limited powers of self-reflection, self-confidence easily tips over into arrogance.

Thus, they exhibit an assertive and aggressive *spirit*, which they seek to employ to exert control over their world by dominating other people, but with limited sensibility in relation to others or capacity to change their view of the world. The avoidant person protects their life by curbing their *lifeforce*—their natural expression of bodily and emotional processes—by dissociating from *feelings* and contracting their *body* against the expression of natural impulses.

Anxious/ambivalent attachments and the Choreography of Energy

Parkes showed how an infant will develop an anxious/ambivalent strategy to enable them to cope with a mother who is insensitive towards them, over-anxious, and unresponsive to their need to explore their world. The child learns that it is not safe to wander or explore, and the mother learns that the child will punish her with extreme anger and anguish if she does not stay close. Both are caught in a trap from which they see no escape.

Parkes demonstrated how a person who recollected an anxious/ambivalent attachment in childhood will typically be predisposed to be clingy, and to react with severe and lasting grief to losses in adult life. They will form clinging but ambivalent relationships with partners who are seen as more powerful than they, and will lack confidence in their ability to cope alone.

A person's anxious/avoidant attachment pattern persists into adulthood out of a deep-rooted assumption that their survival depends on maintaining the pattern of clinging behaviour that enabled them to survive as infants. This pattern can manifest in a variety of ways:

Some will remain permanently attached to one or both parents, with their attachments to spouses and children taking second place.
Some find a partner who is willing to take the role of protective parent and thus is the pattern perpetuated.

Some find themselves repeatedly at odds with partners who, whilst resenting the needy and clinging behaviour, are willing to suffer it, either because they cannot bear the anger that their bids for freedom evoke, or for the sake of children, or for the enticement of a healthy sex life.

Some move from relationship to relationship as successive partners back away. Eventually they may learn to mitigate their clinging but at the cost of persistent anxiety.

Parkes related anxious/ambivalent attachment to the diagnostic category of "dependent personality", corresponding to Johnson's descriptive category of "the abandoned child (p. 100ff)". A person in the anxious/ambivalent group, with their emotion-focused attachment pattern, is dominated by their *feelings*, their anxiety covering suppressed rage for abandonment and perpetual fear of re-abandonment.

Their anxiety is expressed in their *body* as a perpetually charged sympathetic nervous system. In order to try and contain their anxiety, their breathing is shallow, with their shoulders pulled forward and rounded and their chest sunken. In a section on the energetic expression of a person in this category, Stephen Johnson (1994) succinctly describes this *body* sculpting from the perspective of body-oriented therapy (p. 120):

> To inhibit the crying and despair, the person will tense the lower abdominal muscles to restrain the sobbing and tighten the muscles at the base of the neck and up to the jaw. These energetic changes also serve to suppress aggressive impulses and fear. The tension in the shoulder girdle, upper back, and pectorals inhibit striking out, as well as reaching out, as the constriction around the base of the neck and in the jaw inhibit the direct expression of aggression. The inhibition of breathing inhibits the experience of fear itself, as does the clamping of the jaw.

Their anxiety floods their *mind* so that they are constantly preoccupied by their condition and alert to whatsoever and whomsoever fuels their anxiety. With a history, as it seems to them, of repeated abandonment, the fear of re-abandonment colours every relationship, even one with a guide. With a *mind* preoccupied, unreceptive to anything but fear and anxiety, and thus lacking a capacity for self-reflection, they are low in *spirit*, unenthusiastic, and downhearted. By tensing the body, inhibiting their breathing, and suppressing their rage, the person stifles their *energy for life*.

Disorganised/disoriented attachments and the Choreography of Energy

Parkes showed how an infant will develop a disorganised/disoriented pattern when they are unable to form a bond with a mother who is depressed and beyond their powers to influence. Thus, the assumption of helplessness lies at the root of the disorganised attachment pattern.

Whilst a person with an anxious/ambivalent attachment as an infant grows up lacking trust and confidence in themselves, and a person with an avoidant attachment grows up lacking trust in others, Parkes showed how a person who reports a disorganised attachment in childhood grows up lacking trust both in themselves and others. They remain trapped by self-defeating assumptions about themselves and others. Faced with disasters in adult life, they tend towards helplessness, turning in on themselves, and reacting with high levels of anxiety, panic, and depression.

A person with a disorganised attachment may use alcohol or other drugs to help them cope or to escape their suffering, and are more in danger of self-harm or suicide than those with other attachment patterns. It may be, having faced the threat of non-being when they were infants, their survival instinct goes into reverse, offering them what seems like the only way out of a hopeless dilemma.

Parkes suggested that, while a child with a disorganised attachment is not able to resolve their dilemma, they may learn to cope to some extent by being passive, compliant, inconspicuous, freezing, and caring for mother. However, if they fail to do this, in adult life their lack of trust in themselves and others leaves them anxious and helpless in the face of adversity and inclined to give up too easily when obstacles and dangers are put in their path. Parkes related disorganised/disoriented attachment to the diagnostic category of "borderline personality", corresponding to Johnson's descriptive category of "the owned child".

A person in the disorganised group, with an attachment pattern of disorientation, mistrust of themselves, fear and mistrust of others, helplessness, and high anxiety, is deeply split between the avoidant and anxious aspects of their personality.

In their avoidant mode they are overwhelmed by *feelings* of blame, fear and rage at perceived abandonment or rejection—especially when fuelled by alcohol. The *feelings* of blame, fear and rage flood their *mind*, so that they are constantly preoccupied by their condition and vigilant to whatsoever and whomsoever fuels their emotions and reactions. They are driven to express these *feelings* through the *body* in the form of uncontained and uncontrollable verbal and possibly physical aggression towards others, particularly their partner. As infants, because their natural aggressive impulses were heavily discouraged or actively punished they have never developed a well-modulated assertiveness.

In their anxious mode they are overwhelmed by *feelings* of helpless frustration, neediness and of remorse for earlier aggression. *Feelings* of fear, neediness, remorse and despair flood their *mind*, driving them with desperate "never again" promises, to appeal to their partner for sympathy and forgiveness and not to abandon them. In both their avoidant and anxious modes their *body's* sympathetic nervous system is in a state of perpetual charge.

Something Parkes seems not to have observed in the disorganised group—at least in regard to men—is that they can be disarming, charming, and manipulative. A child who loved his mother, and was totally dependent upon her for his survival, soon learnt to hone his manipulative skills, *thinking* and *thinking* all the time about ways to charm and manipulate his mother so as to get close to her or to get a response from her. As an adult, he is still *thinking* and *thinking* all the time about ways to charm and manipulate a partner whom he is unable to trust to be close to him and respond to his demands. This is often mixed in with at least verbal aggression, which for his partner can be confusing and confounding.

The *spirit* the disorganised person expresses, whether they are being disarming and charming, or demanding, or remorseful, is one of untrustworthiness, unreliability, even danger, because they lack a capacity for self-reflection and, in whatever mode, their fear and rage make them prey to unconscious impulses and sudden outbursts.

The Circle of Mirrors: the survival personality in adulthood

The Circle of Mirrors provides a vehicle for portraying a person's survival personality, with its particular model of the world, as it exists in adulthood. The eastern side of the dark mirror (Figure 4.5) from north

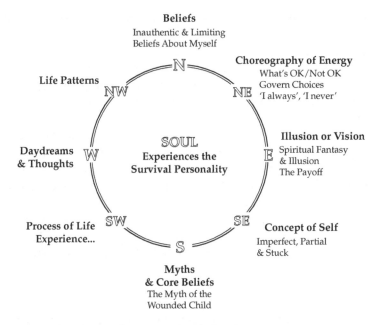

Beliefs
Inauthentic & Limiting
Beliefs About Myself

Life Patterns

Choreography of Energy
What's OK/Not OK
Govern Choices
'I always', 'I never'

**Daydreams
& Thoughts**

SOUL
Experiences the
Survival Personality

Illusion or Vision
Spiritual Fantasy
& Illusion
The Payoff

**Process of Life
Experience...**

Concept of Self
Imperfect, Partial
& Stuck

**Myths
& Core Beliefs**
The Myth of the
Wounded Child

Figure 4.5. The Circle of Mirrors: the dark mirror—East.

to south is about how in adulthood an entrenched core belief serves to maintain their survival personality, affecting a person's entire adult life up to the present and shaping their sense of self. This is illustrated using the life narrative of Peter:

> As an adult, Peter's *choreography of energy* is out of balance. He is cut off at the neck, not aware of his feelings and disregarding of his body, which he abuses by an unhealthy diet, smoking, and too much alcohol, though he is not actually alcoholic. Although on the surface he is remote from his *feelings*, ironically at times of stress he finds them intensely painful. He uses his mind to good effect as a professional engineer, so that in the technical sphere he is creative, articulate, and in argument is powerful, even at times aggressive, and in this sphere his spirit is strong. Not so at a personal level!
>
> He never asks a woman he likes to go out with him; showing his feelings so openly raises too much fear and mistrust in him. He has a repeated pattern of sabotaging promising *sexual* relationships, and those relationships which do form are always when the woman takes the lead. In relationships, he is OK with sex but not OK with intimacy, keeping a safe

emotional distance from his partner, and in discussing intimate matters or communicating his feelings he is almost completely inarticulate and weak-spirited.

At a social level he is OK in a small group discussing general subjects, but in a large social group he quickly feels lost, and compensates by adopting the role of entertainer, telling jokes, playing the fool, inventing imaginative games.

The *payoff* for Peter, in the life he has chosen, is a life of unfulfilled dreams, his spirit mired in the poignant *illusion* that he is special, a fine person who will somehow come to be loved, to discover real intimacy with a woman, to know that his life has some meaning, some significance, and to gain a sense of freedom. Instead, his life is unfulfilled, except in the narrow sphere of engineering. His relationships exist at a practical, day-to-day level, and lack emotional content, leaving him empty, isolated, and alone. In his relationships with others he is mistrustful and often hides behind the mask of entertainer. He seethes with envy of men who seem to have it all and has sustained resentment of those who offend him.

If he could but know it, Peter is profoundly depressed. Where he had seen the pattern of his life as running on rails, his perspective now is of rails narrowing down into a distant point of nothing. His *Concept of Self* is a despairing, "I am flawed."

The spiral of life: attachment patterns are not immutable

The section on the spiral of life in Chapter Three discusses the various crisis points on a person's life cycle— including "Young Adulthood" around age twenty-one, "Saturn Return" around age twenty-eight, the "Crisis of Meaning" around age forty-two, and the "Crisis of Spirit" around age forty-nine—when they have the opportunity to change, to begin to speak, think, reason, and understand life in a different way, to discover a new paradigm. Moreover, life crises are often brought about by a major life-changing loss, such as bereavement, or the ending of a relationship, or the termination of an employment.

Whilst it may appear from the previous discussion that attachment patterns are immutable, this is not so. An attachment pattern may not produce a pleasurable life, but at least it is a well-known, long-standing way of being and thereby represents a person's comfort zone.

Life crises, however, have a way of destabilising the status quo and inflicting upon the person unfamiliar and disturbing symptoms. This

Figure 4.6. The spiritual spiral of life: "seven year" cycle.

is a point when the person may decide to seek the help of a guide. Of course, the person may think they want to regain their comfort zone, but the soul has other ideas; soul suffering, "that twist that you can't simply go along in a natural way, something broken, twisted, hurting, forcing reflection" (Hillman, 1983, p. 23), is in the service of evoking change, and "forcing reflection" is key.

When a person in life crisis embarks upon the self-reflective journey of therapy, this involves addressing both unresolved issues from their past—issues of attachment, in fact—and the issue of what is seeking to emerge in their experience of living. The emergence of a new paradigm means a radical shift in the person's model of the world as they embrace the new paradigm and thereby expand their soul.

Conclusion

Colin Murray Parkes reviewed attachment theory and researched the possibility of a link between infant and adult attachment patterns, including the persistence into adulthood of a model of the world formed in childhood. His overall conclusion was of a close correlation between a child's attachment pattern and world view and the attachment pattern and world view that the child subsequently exhibits when they grow up.

The Medicine Wheel maps of shamanic psychology provide a cognitive approach to helping a person analyse the influence of a core belief on their attachment pattern and their survival personality, with their particular model of the world, to produce a narrative of the life they have chosen.

Finally, attachment patterns are not immutable. On the spiral of life, the opportunity is offered, at key points in a person's life, for them to revise radically their model of the world and to expand their souls as the outcome of a life crisis.

Figure 4.7. Party game (b): It is this.

CHAPTER FIVE

Shamanic journey and soul retrieval ceremonies

Introduction and scope

This chapter is a practical description of shamanic journey and soul retrieval ceremonies. Detailed explanations and examples of these ceremonies are left to subsequent chapters. I choose to use the term "ceremony" rather than "technique" or "procedure", because these terms infer a practitioner performing an action; in a shamanic journey or soul retrieval the guide's role is to create the ritual space and to hold the space for the journey, whilst it is the client themselves who makes the journey.

Following on from the discussion of contemporary shamanism in Chapter Two this chapter covers:

- The role and qualities of a shamanic guide.
- Types of shamanic journey, including a script for a simple guided reflection journey.
- A description of how to lead a Soulfulness group, which has at its heart a shamanic journey ceremony.

- A description of how to conduct an individual shamanic journey ceremony.
- A discussion of the Soul Retrieval Ceremony, including a description of how the ceremony is conducted.

Drums and rattles

Drums and rattles appear throughout the world in societies both ancient and modern. They have been seen as sacred instruments for thousands of years. They are used as part of the ritual in the shamanic ceremonies discussed in this chapter, in order to help focus, intensify and deepen the experience of the ceremonies for participants.

The Soulfulness shamanic guide

Chapter Two describes the shamanic guide's role and character. The guide's role is the care of soul and to hold the space for shamanic journey and soul retrieval ceremonies, including helping participants to set their intention before the journey and to ground and integrate their experience afterwards.

The need for a guide to have been trained to lead these ceremonies, and to have a respectful and empathic attitude towards participants in the ceremonies, be they individuals or a group, cannot be overstated. Mircea Eliade (1964) offers a compelling model (see Chapter Two) for the kind of character that a guide might strive to emulate.

Types of shamanic journey

When teaching people to journey it is as well to begin with simple journeys, to provide experience of the process, before moving on to more searching journeys.

Examples of the various types of journey that may be undertaken are shown below. A guide needs to have experienced each of these or similar types of journey, and have been trained how to conduct them, as part of their training. The simplest journeys may be in the form of a guided reflection:

- A visit to a quiet place in nature.
- A visit to the inner world of a tree, flower, or animal (illustrated below).

- A visit to a familiar place to see it with inner eyes and experience it with all the inner senses.

The following are two important foundation journeys. They put us in touch with some of our allies in our inner world:

- A journey to the Lower World to meet an animal ally (illustrated below).
- A journey to the Upper World to meet a wise person.

Having met animal allies and wise persons, they are available to be a helpful presence on subsequent shamanic journey and soul retrieval ceremonies, which may be deeper and more emotional.

- A journey with the intention of meeting the ancestors along the female line.
- A journey with the intention of meeting the ancestors along the male line.
- A journey into a folktale that has a powerful psychological resonance. For example, the story of Vasilisa and Baba Yaga (England, 1998) is used to illustrate how a journey into a folktale can reveal to a person something about where they are in their personal development.
- A journey with the intention of gaining insight into a day-to-day problem.

A simple journey

Here is a simple, guided reflection that I have used several times in a group setting. The guide introduces the journey:

> This is a journey about our connection with the living world, plants, animals, birds, and insects.
>
> The intention of the journey is to help you to gain a deeper empathy with these living beings, so that you connect not simply with your mind but with your whole being, your human spirit, your bodily senses and instincts, your feelings and intuitions, as well as your thoughts.
>
> We invite you, in the journey, to focus on one living being by reflecting on it with your inner senses (if you like, through the imagination): what the living being looks like, feels like, sounds like,

smells like. Let it tell you something of its yearly cycle and of its life cycle, so you can gain an encompassing sense of your subject, of its essence.

To empathise with your subject means gliding with your feelings into its dynamic structure and, as it were, tracing it from within. We suggest you choose, as your subject for reflection, a living being that you feel drawn to in the natural world, perhaps a favourite tree, a wild animal, a favourite bird. Please, give some thought about what to choose as your subject.

In ancient times, people tacitly acknowledged that every living being, every tree, every creature, had its animating spirit. This journey aims to convey, through the power of reflection and imagination, the same sense of empathic connection with the spirit of a tree or creature as those ancient peoples experienced.

The key words for this journey are intention and trust. We don't expect you to have a particular feeling or experience in the course of the reflection. We simply invite you to have the intention of a deep connection between your spirit and that of your subject, and to trust that whatever emerges is right for you.

Choose a partner with whom you will work later, and sit beside them for the journey. Make yourself comfortable. Think of a living being you would like to focus on in this journey, a plant, a wild animal, or a bird.

The guide needs to lead the guided reflection slowly, with significant pauses between sections of the script, to allow people to enter deeply into their inner world of imagination with minimal interruption:

I invite you to close your eyes, or leave them just partly open. Turn your attention to your breathing. Observe your breathing in and your breathing out, your living breath sustaining your vital energy, your lifeforce.

Begin to lengthen your out breath; imagine breathing out right down your body and out through your feet, like a sigh, allowing any unnecessary tension or tightness, in any part of your body, to melt away as you relax more and more.

Breathing in, after a moment, breathing out—right down your body and out through your feet—like a sigh. Notice that moment of stillness just before your in breath. Stay focused on your breathing,

breathing in, breathing out like a sigh, a moment of stillness, breathing in again, relaxing more and more.

Now, bring your attention to the living being, the subject you chose to focus on. Greet your subject. Reach out to it with your inner senses: what it looks like, what it feels like, what it smells like, what sound it makes, gain an overall sense of your subject. Glide with your feelings into its dynamic structure, trace it from within.

Draw back a little and get a sense of your subject's yearly cycles. Now get a sense of your subject's whole life cycle, its incarnation in the womb or egg or womb of the earth, its cycles of growth, its world, its life as it unfolds, its life as it departs. Allow this imaginative journey to unfold.

Focus on your subject as it is now—its looks, its feel, its sound, its smell, your overall encompassing sense of this living being. Stay with your overall encompassing sense of your subject. If words come in, gently put them aside, say, "I'll listen later."

As you stay with your overall encompassing sense of your subject, allow your sense to go deeper, and deeper, gaining a closer and closer empathy with this living being.

Now, allow an image or a feeling or a word to enter your thoughts that sums up for you your encompassing sense of your subject: don't censor it, accept whatever is there. If nothing comes, quietly wait for what might emerge. Keep this image or feeling or word in mind; it can help you later to empathise with other living beings.

Now, thank the living being, say goodbye, and let it go. Bring your attention back to your breathing. As you breathe in, feel energy, muscle tone and vitality coming into your arms and legs. As you breathe in, feel energy, muscle tone and vitality coming into your whole body. Wiggle your fingers and toes. And when you are ready, open your eyes and come back into the room. Have a stretch.

[Grounding.]

We shall have a short time of silence for you to make notes. I invite you now to turn to your partner and discuss your experience of the journey, as far as you are willing to do so.

[Participants come together again in the circle.]

There is a space now for you so talk about anything you may wish with regards to your journey to the whole group.

Finally, the guide ends the session with a "one word round", where each member is invited to say one word that sums up what they are feeling.

A Soulfulness group, including a shamanic journey

This section describes the conduct of a typical Soulfulness group, including a shamanic journey ceremony. This ceremony follows the principle explained in Chapter Two that participants are taught to make the journey for themselves.

Programme

A typical programme and approximate timings for a Soulfulness group are set out below. I have found that two and a half hours is the minimum time that needs to be allowed. There is a break following each journey—one way then the other—to allow time for those who have journeyed to return fully to normal consciousness.

Activity	Minutes
Welcome	6
Opening the circle	6
Check-in	6
Chanting and readings	6
Introduction to shamanic journeying	6
Introducing today's shamanic journey	6
Shamanic journey in pairs—One way	24
Grounding and making notes in pairs—One way	6
Break	12
Shamanic journey in pairs—The other way	24
Grounding and making notes in pairs—The other way	6
Break	6
Grounding in the group	24
Check-out and closing the circle	6
Finish	6
Total time	**150**
	(2 hours 30 minutes)

Creating the space

Before the Soulfulness group assembles, the guide creates the space as follows: the eight directions of the Medicine Wheel, around which the group will assemble, are set out at the centre of the room using stones and crystals. The centre of the Medicine Wheel is left empty, as this is the creative void. If possible, there should be dim lighting with candles, or electrical candles, illuminating the space, to provide a pleasant atmosphere for the group. Blankets and cushions, and scarves to cover the eyes, will be available for members of the group to use if required during the shamanic journey.

The guide will have available a talking stick or stone. Whoever is speaking will hold the talking stick and is thereby entitled to be heard. The guide will symbolically "clear the space", and the space around his or her own person, of any residual negative energies. Traditionally, this is done by smudging with burning dried sage, though I prefer to use Tibetan cymbals or a Nepalese singing bowl for their clarity and purity of tone.

Welcome and opening the circle

The guide welcomes the assembled members of the group. Then, moving clockwise around the Medicine Wheel, each member "clears the space" around their partner. The guide opens the circle, calling on the "spirits" to be present. For me, these "spirits" are the healthy instinctive and intuitive allies who dwell within the deep psyche of everyone. The guide may use a rattle, as part of the ritual of the ceremony, to invoke the presence of the spirits. In the following typical script we also identify with all the creatures who share this planet with us. I vary the script according to the season and the proximity of annual festivals, such as the solstices and equinoxes.

As we open this circle, we call on the Spirits of the South, the West, the North, the East, to be present with us. I invite you to stand and to turn towards each direction as I call it. The first direction is South.

Spirits of the South, which exist in all the creatures of the rivers and seas, the water that refreshes us, the feelings we express, we bless you and ask for your wisdom and blessing to be with us in this circle. [rattle] Spirits of the South: hail and welcome. I invite you to respond: *hail and welcome.*

Spirits of the West, all the creatures that dwell within and upon the earth, the earth that bears us, our bodies that hold us [A spring variation might be: and Mother Earth herself, who nourishes life in secret until it blossoms forth] we bless you and ask for your wisdom and blessing to be with us in this circle. [rattle] Spirits of the West: hail and welcome. [Response: *hail and welcome.*]

Spirits of the North, which exist in all the creatures of the air, our living breath, the insights our minds receive, we bless you and ask for your wisdom and blessing to be with us in this circle. [rattle] Spirits of the North: hail and welcome. [Response: *hail and welcome.*]

Spirits of the East, which exist in fire, passion, creative inspiration, in new beginnings and new horizons, in spiritual illumination [A summer variation might be: and Father Sun himself, who gives us warmth and light] we bless you and ask for your wisdom and blessing to be with us in this circle. [rattle] Spirits of the East: hail and welcome. [Response: *hail and welcome.*]

We turn to the Creative Centre, the lifeforce, where the four directions are gathered together in union and harmony:

South, West, North, East;

Feelings, Body, Mind, Spirit.

May this circle be a place of union, love and reverence. [Rattle.]

The guide invites the group in turn, clockwise around the circle, with the talking stick, to include themselves, by giving their names and saying something about themselves and what they want to gain from the group. The response to acknowledge the inclusion of each participant is: *Ho!*

Chanting and readings

Chanting serves to bring the group together, intensifying the experience of community, and creating a sense of the sanctity of the space. (Note: Chant CDs and Books are available on the Eagle's Wing website.) Relevant poems or other readings may be used before the chanting, either selected by the guide or brought and read by group members.

Introduction to shamanic journeying

The guide introduces the concept of a shamanic journey. A typical script is as follows:

In traditional shamanism, the shaman journeys into the spirit world on behalf of someone seeking their aid. In my training at Eagle's

Wing College of Contemporary Shamanism, people are shown how to journey for themselves, whilst a shamanic guide holds the space for them. This is how we journey in the Soulfulness group, and this is why we work in pairs, one holding the space for the other.

We don't have to believe literally that the "spirit world" exists—we can and many do, and that's fine—but we don't have to. Whether we believe literally or in a metaphorical way, the "spirit world" is a place outside of everyday reality. I regard the "spirit world" as our inner world of limitless imagination.

In a Russian folktale there appear the words, "Sleep now. Morning is wiser than evening". Maybe you have said, "I'll sleep on it," when struggling with some seemingly intractable problem. Maybe you have woken in the night or in the morning knowing the answer to a puzzling dilemma. When we can turn away from a problem and relax, a part of our mind is able to discover answers that our conscious mind seems unable to find.

A shamanic journey helps us to do this, by relaxing to a drumbeat and allowing the imagination to focus on some issue with which we are struggling. A drumbeat of about 240 beats per minute is said to correspond to the frequency of electrical waves in the brain associated with deep meditation, the threshold of the subconscious, and dreaming. [Demonstrate the drum beat.] During a shamanic journey, this drumbeat helps us to enter this "state of inspiration", where creativity, exceptional insight and vivid visualisations can arise. [Note: medicine drums can be obtained by contacting drum maker Jonathan Weekes at his Heron Drums website.]

In this way, bringing the wisdom of the ancient healing practice of the shamanic journey into contemporary life can help us to know ourselves more deeply and to enjoy more fulfilled and abundant lives, especially when we meet and journey together, sharing our experiences, witnessing one another's journeying, and supporting one another in our personal growth, creativity, relationships, and spirituality.

Introducing today's shamanic journey: to meet and get to know an animal ally

The guide introduces the shamanic journey that the group members are about to make, in this case a journey to the Lower World to meet an animal ally. My choice is to confine group sessions to Lower World journeys. A typical script for introducing the journey is as follows:

> For those who have not journeyed before, I invite you now to make a shamanic journey into your inner world of imagination, to a place of instinctual wisdom, which in shamanism is called the Lower World. The three key words for your journey are: *intention, connection,* and *attention.*
>
> The *intention* for the journey is to meet and get to know an animal ally, a wise creature who will help you in later journeys as you build a relationship with them. It is important to have this *connection* with your own instinctual wisdom, this aspect of yourself that the animal ally represents.
>
> For those who have met their animal ally in an earlier group, you can make the intention for the journey to meet your animal ally and ask them a question.
>
> You might imagine there is a tunnel, or a ladder, or whatever you choose, as your portal to the Lower World. Some like to fly down to the Lower World. Before you begin your journey, you must stand at the portal and state your intention three times.
>
> When you emerge from the tunnel, or whatever you choose, into the Lower World you will find and enter a different landscape. This is where you will meet your animal ally. Accept whatever they are and allow them to journey with you and guide you; they are part of your inner wisdom.
>
> Always keep some part of your *attention* on the drumbeat. Give your *attention* to whatever emerges on the journey, most likely an image, and allow the journey to unfold like a dream.

Guiding the group into the journey

The guide leads the group into the journey, a typical script being as follows:

> Take a few moments to think about your intention for your journey, and make a note. You will lie down for the journey, which is what the cushions and blankets are for. You will work in pairs, one holding the space for the other and supporting them. I suggest you tell your partner what your intention is for your journey.
>
> I use gentle words and a slow drumbeat to help you achieve a state of awareness that is both relaxed and focused. I maintain a

regular drumbeat [demonstrate the drumbeat] to help maintain this state of awareness.

You will begin by imagining yourself in a lovely place in nature of your choosing. You then stand at the portal to the Lower World and state your intention quietly to yourself three times. Then you begin your journey.

If nothing seems to happen, just focus on the drum and give your attention to whatever emerges. It may be an image, a sound, a physical sensation. Whatever sense it is, give it your attention and see what unfolds. Look out for your animal ally.

The journey time is 20 minutes. The change in the drumbeat [demonstrate a slow drumbeat] is the call-back from your journey to your place in nature. I will then invite you to return to the room and open your eyes. Now, please, select a place in nature where you would like to start your journey. Are there any questions?

The guide answers any questions and makes sure everyone is clear about their journey.

The shamanic journey

The guide invites the group to form pairs then invites them to find a place in the room where one person can lie down and make him- or herself comfortable whilst the other person sits beside them. This person will make the journey first; the other will help them and hold the space for them. Then, after a break, the second person journeys, with the other helping and holding the space.

Working in pairs has two advantages:

- If a member of the group who is journeying encounters difficulties and needs to finish early, there is someone immediately on hand to support them, without the guide having to leave off from drumming.
- A member of the group who is holding the space gains the experience of actively supporting their partner.

Shamanic induction

When the group is ready, the guide begins the induction to help those journeying achieve a relaxed and focused state of mind. A typical induction is as follows. (Note: don't speak the words that are in upper case letters or the words in brackets, and allow a period of silence where it is indicated by ellipsis (…).)

EYE CLOSURE … Make yourself physically comfortable … and gently close your eyes …

PERSONAL PREPARATION … take a few moments to get comfortable and prepare yourself for this journey in a way that is helpful to you …

BREATH … now become aware of your breathing … there's no need to change it … just allow it to ebb and flow as it finds its own steady rhythm … knowing that with every out breath … you relax more and more … imagine that you're breathing out right down through your body and out through your feet … letting any unnecessary tension flow away…

GROUNDING … and as you breathe out imagine your grounding roots like the roots of a wise, old tree … spreading out and down connecting with the safety and security of the earth …

CENTRING … and as you breathe out notice that moment of stillness right at the end of your out breath … and allow that moment of stillness … to take you even deeper … into that inner place of peace and calm … safety and security …

STAR … now imagine a star above the crown of your head, a source of pure, healing light flowing right through your body to the tips of your toes and the tips of your fingers … gently and lovingly filling you as it bathes every part of you … on every level … physically … intellectually … emotionally … intuitively … spiritually … and imagine this pure light all around you … enveloping you in pure, protective radiance.

ESTABLISHING A SAFE PLACE … Now imagine your beautiful place in nature … where you feel comfortable and safe … notice all the colours … and textures … observe how you are sensing it … with your inner senses, what you are seeing, hearing, feeling, tasting, smelling, or just inwardly knowing.

PORTAL … Now, move to the place where you begin your journey, the opening of a well or tunnel to the Lower World, or whatever is right for you … State your intention for your journey quietly to yourself, three times [my intention is to journey to the Lower World to meet an animal ally] … Now let your journey unfold.

RETURN … [The guide maintains a drumbeat of 240 beats per minute throughout the journey.]

At the end of the journey time the guide plays the slow call-back rhythm on the drum and gently invites those journeying to come back from their place in nature to the room, a typical script being as follows:

Bring your attention back to your breathing. As you breathe in, feel energy, muscle tone and vitality coming into your arms and legs. As you breathe in, feel energy, muscle tone and vitality coming into your whole body. Wiggle your fingers and toes. And when you are ready, open your eyes and come back into the room. Have a stretch.

Check-out and closing the circle

The guide invites those who have made a journey to share their experiences with their partner, then to make notes for themselves. Using the talking stick, group members are invited by the guide to bring to the whole group, when they feel ready, what they choose of their experiences during their journey. The guide acknowledges what each member brings and may choose to make a response where they feel this will further help to ground the experience.

The guide then invites the members of the group, in turn clockwise around the circle, to take the Talking Stick and say what each would like to say to the group in closing. The guide closes the circle. A typical script is as follows:

I invite you to stand for the closing of the circle. As we close this circle, we thank you: Spirits of the South for giving us refreshment, Spirits of the West for holding us and giving us life, Spirits of the North for giving us insights, Spirits of the East for giving us illumination. Spirits of the South, West, North, East, hail and farewell. [Response: *hail and farewell*.] [Rattle.]

Individual shamanic journey ceremony

The Lower World relates to our past and to our instinctive wisdom. We make a Lower World Journey when we want to explore some aspect of our past. In the Lower World we meet out animal allies, who represent parts of our instinctive wisdom. We typically travel to the Lower World by going down a tunnel or a well, though there are some who are averse to dark places and may choose other ways to travel, such as flying down.

The Upper World relates to our future and our intuitive wisdom. We make an Upper World Journey when we want to explore something about our future, such as the path our life might take. In the Upper World we meet our wise persons, allies representing parts of our intuitive wisdom. Common ways of travelling to the Upper World include climbing a ladder, riding a white horse, sometimes a winged horse, and whirling up in a vortex. My way is to wait and see what means of travel to the Upper World emerges.

When a guide is conducting an individual shamanic journey ceremony with a client, whether it is a Lower World or Upper World Journey, the ceremony is basically similar to a group session, but with some variations:

- The guide creates the space as described above. If space is limited, a smaller Medicine Wheel is set out on a table.
- The guide welcomes the client, then "clears the space" around them.
- The guide briefly opens the circle. The script may be based on the above, or better still the guide will write their own.

If this is the client's first journey, the idea of a shamanic journey is discussed along the lines of the introductions above. For subsequent journeys, the client is simply reminded of the main points about the journey, in particular the key words *intention, connection,* and *attention.* The guide helps the client to decide what their intention is going to be.

The journey itself is conducted as discussed above, beginning with a shamanic induction. To start with, the journey time should be twenty minutes, which may be increased for an experienced client. At the end the guide briefly closes the circle, before beginning the grounding work.

Working with an individual client, the grounding will be much longer and deeper than is possible in a group setting. Whatever arose in the journey, the client and guide reflect together on the meaning that it has for the client and the significance it may have for their life. The client may be encouraged to make notes about their journey, either in the session as part of the grounding or later at home.

Soulfulness as a spiritual practice

In Chapter One, "spirituality" is seen as a movement towards Self and the transmitting of the potentiality throughout our lives from spirit into matter, bringing expansion to our soul. And Soulfulness is seen as a spiritual practice that enhances our experience of living and enables us to live more abundant and fulfilled lives.

Soulfulness is able to make a significant contribution to a person's regular spiritual practice and hence their spiritual growth: The Medicine Wheel, in its many aspects (illustrated in Chapter Three), provides boundless scope as a subject of focused meditation, not least the elements of water, earth, air, spirit, and void or womb as metaphors for the elements of personality, feelings, body, mind, spirit, and lifeforce or sexuality and creativity.

Reflecting on their choreography of energy with the aid of the Elements of Personality map may help a person to gauge their progress in consciously seeking to change the balance of energy in their life. As Hyemeyohsts Storm (1994) so powerfully expresses, "When people respect the Balance of the Self, they will learn to respect something as grand and powerful as Life".

Once a person is familiar with shamanic journeying, they can make a journey at home to explore some day-to-day issue of concern, which can be helped along by using a drum CD. As a simple, personal example, when in my writing work I feel blocked, a twenty minute shamanic journey into my current subject matter helps me to unravel and understand what it is that I am seeking to express. It happened many times during the writing of this book!

In terms of a person's life as a whole, reflecting on the cycle of life and the spiritual spiral of life maps helps the person locate themselves on their path of life and clarify the particular challenges faced and opportunities offered in that place. After completing a Circle of Mirrors ceremony with their guide or a shamanic friend, the outcome provides a person with endless scope for contemplation.

As a movement towards Self, spirituality necessarily involves questions about how we live our lives, practical questions about the challenges we face, the dilemmas that confront us, the obstacles we encounter, and our values, meaning, purpose, our call to service, and our relationship with the wider world.

For my part, I cannot work through these issues without the enormous help that others afford me; therapists, close friends, and in particular in recent years the friends in my shamanic group. We hold a sacred space for each other, sharing our concerns using the talking stick, chanting together, journeying together, assisting group members by means of soul retrieval and Circle of Mirrors ceremonies, and altogether sustaining and affirming one another along our individual spiritual paths. I view this as a model of how a Soulfulness group might evolve as the group relationship deepens.

Soul retrieval

There is a sense in which all shamanic journeys are psychotherapeutic. Taking Robert Johnson's (1986) suggestion that "anything in the imagination is an authentic representation of something in the unconscious", the act of delving into one's inner imaginative world may, as he observes, "draw up ... material from the unconscious, clothe it in images, and transmit it to the conscious mind (p. 8)" where it needs be dealt with.

Having said that, I regard it as essential to the health and safety of the subject that any journey that goes further than intending insight into day-to-day problems should be regarded as explicitly psychotherapeutic and needs to be facilitated by a trained shamanic guide who is also a qualified psychotherapist or counsellor.

Such journeys include: a shamanic journey whose intention is to gain insight into some troubling aspect of a person's history, experience, or behaviour; or a soul retrieval (once a loss of soul energy, such as the loss of self-esteem, has been recognised), whose intention is to retrieve the lost soul energy and restore the person's soul. Journeys such as these may prove to be deeply moving experiences for the person, involving extensive mourning, grounding, and integration work. Hence the importance of the psychotherapeutic space being strongly and sensitively held by a shamanic guide who is also a psychotherapist or counsellor.

A soul retrieval, having the intention of retrieving soul energy that the client has lost in the past, is a journey to the Lower World. Meeting an animal ally to support the client and lead them to where they need to go to retrieve their lost soul energy is an essential aspect of the journey.

Individual soul retrieval ceremony

Following on from the introduction to soul retrieval in the Chapter Two section "Soul retrieval and depth psychology", I offer a description of how a soul retrieval ceremony is conducted one-to-one by a guide with a client.

The client needs already to be familiar with shamanic journeying, the shamanic universe, their allies in the inner world, and the key concepts of intention, connection, and attention. The term "soul retrieval" needs to be explained. The loss of soul energy needs previously to have been identified, such as loss of self-worth or loss of innocence, and the intention of the soul retrieval journey needs to be discussed.

The guide creates the space as described earlier and welcomes the client. The guide then "clears the space" around them before briefly opening the circle with a script that accords with the intention of the soul retrieval ceremony. The guide briefly reminds the client about what the ceremony involves, including the support of an animal ally. The guide briefs the client to find some symbolic token of the lost soul energy that is to be retrieved and to return with it from their journey.

The client and guide discuss the soul retrieval journey that the client is going to make and the client confirms what their intention is going to be. The length of the journey is agreed, which needs to be at least twenty minutes from the time the client crosses the portal. This journey is conducted as any other shamanic journey, beginning with a shamanic induction, the guide drumming throughout the journey, and ending with the call-back on the drum for the client to return to their place in nature.

Upon the client's return the guide uses their rattle—they rattle the symbolic token of the lost soul energy into the client's heart. As the conclusion to the ceremony, the use of the rattle has a ritual significance for the client; it affirms and reinforces the restoration of the client's soul; and it shakes off any lingering traces of the original trauma, like an antelope shaking off the lingering effects of a threat to its life.

Then the guide gently invites the client to come back from their place in nature into the room, a typical script being as follows:

Bring your attention back to your breathing. As you breathe in, feel energy, muscle tone and vitality coming into your arms and legs. As you breathe in, feel energy, muscle tone and vitality coming into your whole body. Wiggle your fingers and toes. And when you are ready, open your eyes and come back into the room. Have a stretch.

The guide briefly closes the circle, before beginning the grounding work, which may involve one or more sessions of work by the client and guide as they reflect together on the meaning of whatever arose in the journey; in particular, the nature of their animal ally, where the client travelled to retrieve their lost soul energy, how this was achieved, and what the symbolic token of the lost soul energy was. They discuss what significance the soul retrieval has for the client's life.

Here is an example of grounding work:

Jamie has an uneasy feeling that there is something missing in his life. I hold the space for him to journey, his intention being to explore what might be missing. In the journey, Jamie's animal ally is a crow, who directs him towards a house on a hill. Jamie keeps trying to go in different directions, along paths and through woods, but they all turn out to be dead ends, and the crow keeps directing him back to the house, which at last he enters. The house is sound but unfurnished, and is empty except for a confusion of thoughts and children's voices. In the house he realises that he doesn't need to visit other places, the answer is in the house.

In the grounding work, Jamie comes to understand that the house represents his psyche. When we come to unravel the image of the unfurnished house, Jamie realises that what is missing in his life is within the house, within the psyche, not in some external aspect of his life. He is puzzled about the children's voices. I ask, "What do children do?" He replies without hesitation, understanding dawning on his face, "They grow up." During the following week, Jamie comes to realise that his perception of other people has shifted, has become clearer. In the next session, I articulate his change of perception as a paradigm shift, which he immediately relates to, describing the changes that he sees in himself. He has more energy, a stronger focus, and a willingness to undertake creative work writing stories and poems, which he has been putting off for a long time. I give him my interpretation of the crow, "Crow is the bringer of knowledge."

CHAPTER SIX

Trauma and the wounded soul: perspectives

Introduction and scope

This chapter considers four books that address issues of trauma and its impact upon psychic development from different theoretical perspectives: Donald Kalsched's (1996) deeply insightful work, *The Inner World of Trauma*; Peter Levine's (1997) groundbreaking and popular book, *Waking the Tiger: Healing Trauma*; from the founder of psychosynthesis, Roberto Assagioli (1965): *Psychosynthesis: A Manual of Principles and Techniques*; and from the foremost exponents of psychosynthesis theory after Assagioli, John Firman and Ann Gila (1997), *The Primal Wound: A Transpersonal View of Trauma, Addiction and Growth*. The following chapter then discusses the Soulfulness theoretical perspective on developmental trauma.

Trauma in analytical psychology: possession

Synopsis

When an infant is traumatised, dissociative defences protect the infant's personal spirit from suffering trauma and ensure its survival by splitting the psyche: the inviolable personal spirit is frozen in time and secured within a protective self-care system. However, the self-care system proves overprotective, the protector becoming also a persecutor, isolating the personal spirit from interaction with the world and preventing creative expression and the normal unfolding of awareness and personality.

Without access to the personal spirit, the residual psyche forms an impaired, neurosis-prone personality lacking the potential of the personal spirit for psychological growth, expanding awareness, creative expression, and a capacity for spontaneous action in the world.

The traumatised psyche is self-traumatising, the original trauma being played out by the traumatised psyche through the neurosis-prone personality in a cycle of repeated traumatic events. It is as if the person were possessed.

Clinical studies of dream imagery reveal the inner drama enacted by split fragments of the traumatised psyche: the isolated personal spirit is typically depicted as an animal or a vulnerable child; the protector/persecutor in its protector aspect is typically depicted as an angel or wild horse; the persecutor aspect as a demon.

Possession

From his careful, clinical study of dream imagery related to developmental trauma, Donald Kalsched has drawn his main hypothesis: "the archaic defences associated with trauma are personified as archetypal daimonic images", such dream imagery representing "the psyche's self-portrait of its own archaic defensive operations (p. 2)".

Kalsched describes developmental trauma in these terms: trauma is any experience that causes the child's psyche such intolerable pain or anxiety as to overwhelm the psyche's natural defences, its protection against stimuli, and so threatens the personality and the personal spirit. This threat is counteracted by a "second line of defences", the dissociative defences or the "archetypal self-care system (p. 4)", which serves to protect the child's psyche from trauma: archetypal in the sense both of being archaic and typical of the psyche's defensive operations.

The effect of trauma is a fragmentation or splitting of the psyche. One side of the split—the "true self" (Winnicott, 1996)—remains at the infantile level, securing in secret the child's inviolable personal spirit. The other side of the split—the "false self"—engages with the outside world and becomes caretaker to the "true self", protector of the personal spirit against further trauma. Alas, protection of the personal spirit turns out to be overprotection in the service of survival at all costs. The protector becomes a persecutor, isolating the personal spirit from relationship with the outside world and preventing any spontaneous creative expression of Self in the world.

Kalsched depicts this protector/persecutor as "duplex", a figure with two faces, one benevolent, the other malevolent. For us to comprehend the protector/persecutor, we need always to keep in mind, however persecutory it may appear to be, that its sole motivation is the protection of the personal spirit.

Survival at all costs has consequences for a person's personality and behaviour, which persist into adult life. Without access to the potential of the personal spirit for psychological growth, expanding awareness, creative expression, and a capacity for spontaneous action in the world, the residual psyche forms an impaired, neurosis-prone personality, for example: the person may be withdrawn and unfeeling; they may be prone to addictions; they may have a poor sense of identity, weak boundaries, and live a chaotic emotional life. Such a high price is paid, in terms of the person's limited lifeforce and crushed creativity, for the sake of simple survival.

Kalsched highlights the central problem—not only for the stricken person but also for a therapist trying to help them—as being that the protector/persecutor is "not educable", its primitive level of awareness ossifying at the very time the trauma was happening. From its primal perspective, every opportunity to engage with life is seen as a threat of further trauma that it must resist at all costs. Thus, Kalsched sees the original trauma perpetually played out in the person's inner world, and concludes "the traumatised psyche is self-traumatising (p. 5)"; the persecutory inner world is reflected in the outer world, with the person experiencing a cycle of repeated traumatic events—"almost as if the individual were possessed by some diabolical power or pursued by a malignant fate".

Whilst a person's personality and behavioural traits may infer the presence of trauma, the protector/persecutor and the personal spirit remain unconscious. Nevertheless, the inner drama between the protector/persecutor and the personal spirit is at times revealed to consciousness in dreams. Kalsched expresses this with brilliant succinctness, "The idea that dreams should be capable of representing the psyche's dissociative activities and holding the fragmented pieces together in one dramatic story is a kind of miracle of psychological life (pp. 2–3)".

Kalsched describes the personal spirit as appearing typically as a vulnerable child self or animal self. He describes the protector/persecutor typically appearing in its protector aspect as an angel, wild horse, or dolphin, and in its persecutor aspect as a diabolical and terrifying figure.

So, the drama that is thus revealed in dreams is of a self-care system whose genesis was in trauma, whose function was essentially defensive, but which has become personified not only as a protector but also as a brutal and ineducable persecutor within the psyche that repeatedly prevents any spontaneous expression of Self in the world. It is as if the person were possessed.

Afterthoughts

This is an all too brief précis of Donald Kalsched's highly recommended book, drawn mainly from his introductory discussion of the impact of trauma and the archetypal self-care system. As both a professional storyteller and psychotherapist, I particularly appreciate in his book the psychological interpretation of fairy tales and myths as reflecting the drama playing out in the inner world of trauma.

I struggled with the idea of the duplex protector/persecutor. It seemed to me this represented a further split between the benign figure and the malign figure. Moreover, I was struck by the resemblance between the dream imagery of an animal-self and a shamanic, Lower World animal ally, both representing an aspect of the deep psyche. Yet, it troubled me that an angel and wild horse, which I could readily relate to as a shamanic Upper world wise person and a shaman's transport respectively, should be lumped in with a malevolent figure.

As I read the part of the book about fairy tales and myths, I realised how often a duplex figure appears in fairy stories, with both malign and benign aspects helping to move on both the story and the hero/heroine. Here are my reflections on the Grimms' fairy tale *Hansel and Gretel*:

> In the Hansel and Gretel story, the old witch in benign mode rescues the children from starvation in the forest, takes them in, feeds them, puts them to bed between clean sheets, and so gives them a taste of what life might be for them: they thought they were in heaven. But, the following morning the old witch in malign mode makes Gretel

start fattening up Hansel for the pot, giving her naught to eat but crayfish shells.

It is generally the case in fairy tales that the malign figure is either killed or simply fades from the story. For Gretel, a turning point comes when she reaches the depths of despair and self-negation—if only the wild beasts had eaten us in the forest—then acts to take responsibility for herself and shoves the old witch into the oven, an act we might call de-bewitchment.

On a similar theme, Kalsched writes of the "gradual deconstruction of the self-care system in the transference ... a constant movement back and forth between unconscious bewitchment, on the one hand, and reality on the other (p. 154)", a process in which a combination of hard work, deep suffering, despair and self-negation seems to be a necessary component.

Trauma in human physiology: rape of the soul

In his book *Waking the Tiger: Healing Trauma*, Peter Levine discusses how for many millennia shamanic healers have known not only how the mind affects the body but also how each organ of the body has an analogue in the mind. In seeking to heal trauma, therefore, it is essential to consider the impact of trauma on the body as well as on the mind.

Levine explains how the response of an animal to an overwhelming threat is the familiar fight or flight, but if neither is possible the animal will enter an altered state of consciousness—the freeze response—and await a chance to escape. Once free from danger, the animal literally shakes off any lingering effects of the freeze response to resume normal control over its body.

As human animals, the experience of shaking off the effects of at least minor trauma is quite familiar. After a visit to the dentist, I will shiver and shake off the effects of the shock to my system. Sometimes, when I hold a qigong stance for a lengthy period, my body will spontaneously shake as stuck energies are released.

As discussed in the emotional cycle section of Chapter Three, when a human's life is threatened, their sympathetic nervous system charges them up energetically to enable them to face the threat. Afterwards, the parasympathetic nervous system enables them to wind down and return to rest. This is the normal operation of the autonomic nervous system.

Whilst an animal can shake off the freeze response, the effect of trauma on a human is to overwhelm their autonomic nervous system. As a result, the winding down part of the cycle fails to be completed, so that a residue of unresolved energy remains frozen in the nervous system, and the person is left perpetually in an energetically aroused and anxious state. In other words, as Levine points out, the person remains in a chronically frozen state, leaving them prone to depression, psychosomatic and behavioural problems, and physical ailments. These are the human body's means of containing the residual undischarged energy.

On this subject, Kathrin A. Stauffer writes of

> autonomic space ... a matrix consisting of a multiplicity of possible states of activation of the [sympathetic and parasympathetic nervous systems]. The system ... moves mostly on the trajectory between high sympathetic/low parasympathetic and low sympathetic/high parasympathetic activity, but a state of high arousal of both branches is possible in this model. Such a state has been called 'freeze' or 'tonic immobility' and represents shock or trauma. ... It is thus particularly important for psychotherapy. (2010, pp. 51–52)

"Trauma is so arresting", says Levine, "that traumatised people will focus on it compulsively. ... The situation that defeated them once will defeat them again, and again (p. 66)".

Quoting Mircea Eliade (1964, p. 215), Levine writes that "rape of the soul"—otherwise called soul loss—is claimed by shamanic healers to be the most damaging and the most widespread cause of illness; illness is a consequence of soul loss, leaving a person stuck in "spiritual limbo". The healing work of a shaman is a ceremony to restore the "lost soul" to the sick person. Just as an animal shakes off any lingering effects of the freeze response, so the person might shake off the energetic residue in the nervous system towards the completion of the ceremony.

Levine's main principle for overcoming the freeze response is to initiate and encourage our body's inherent drive to discharge the energy trapped in the nervous system. He argues that it is not necessary for a person to relive their emotional pain in order to heal trauma, and to do so may be re-traumatising. His alternative is to arouse and utilise our deep physiological resources by focusing on our physical sensations, allowing them to lead us to where in the body we experience trauma, and thence guide us to our instinctual resources.

It should be noted, however, that the stated focus of Levine's book is on "shock trauma". As he points out, whilst "developmental trauma" produces similar symptoms, the support of a therapist is needed "to help them work through the issues that have become intertwined with their traumatic reactions". I would add that the working through of emotional pain is often part of this therapeutic process.

The approach offered by Levine for accessing these instinctual resources is the "felt-sense", coined by Eugene T. Gendlin (1982), described at length on pages 67–83 of Levine's book, which I recommend the reader to study. Also, Gendlin's book *Focusing* (1978) is an essential text for practising the felt-sense. Gendlin says that the practice of the felt-sense is to gain a "bodily awareness of a situation or person or event (p. 32)". It is a process of self-reflection upon the ever-changing flow of our bodily and emotional sensations.

Levine writes about how advances in neuroscience have provided evidence of the mutual interaction and interdependence of mind and body. Writing on a similar theme, body psychotherapist Kathrin A. Stauffer provides a useful description of the felt sense that is worth quoting in full:

> We know from the work of neuroscientists … that two kinds of information contribute [to our picture of what is happening right now]. One is sensory information about the environment: This is information that reaches the central nervous system through the senses of sight, hearing, smell, touch, and taste. The other is information about what is happening inside our bodies: This is information that reaches the central nervous system through the senses of interoception [the process of perceiving sensations that tell us what is happening inside the body] and proprioception [the perception of posture and movement through stimuli in the receptors embedded in the joints, tendons, and muscles], including our perception of what emotions we are feeling. The brain has the capacity to synthesize these two kinds of information into a coherent picture that we could call the 'felt sense' of here and now. By doing this, we constantly create not only a meaning of what's going on and what we might need to do, but also our sense of Self as a relatively constant feeling. (2010, pp. 51–52)

Assagioli's model of the psyche: the Egg Diagram

This section provides a fuller description of Assagioli's Egg Diagram model, introduced in Chapter Two, which Roberto Assagioli describes in his groundbreaking book *Psychosynthesis: A Manual of Principles and Techniques*. There are close parallels between the Egg Diagram and the shamanic universe with its Lower, Middle and Upper Worlds. (Note: my references to the shamanic universe in the following text are supplementary to Assagioli's conception of the Egg Diagram.)

The *Lower Unconscious* represents an individual's psychological past. It includes those inherent, instinctive and unconscious psychological activities that direct the life of the body and coordinate bodily functions. The Lower Unconscious is also the place where we repress the woundings with which our conscious mind is unable to cope. When, for example, the child says, "Mummy, look at my picture of myself," and she repeatedly replies, "Not now, I'm busy," the child's feelings of rejection, hurt and disappointment are repressed into the Lower Unconscious.

With the psychic energy necessary to maintain repression, these complexes are charged with intense emotion. (Note: Assagioli's definition

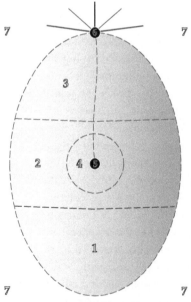

The components of the model are:
1. The Lower Unconscious (Lower World)
2. The Middle Unconscious (Middle World)
3. The Higher Unconscious (Upper World)
4. The field of consciousness
5. The personal self or "I"
6. The Higher Self
7. The collective unconscious

Figure 6.1. Assagioli's Egg Diagram: model of the psyche.

of a "complex" is a conglomeration of psychological elements that have developed a strong emotional charge.) So, the Lower Unconscious contains, in Lower World terms, both the instinctive energies, which are personified as helpful supporters and guides, and the repressed complexes, which are personified as wicked and destructive figures.

The *Middle Unconscious* represents an individual's psychological present. It includes everything that is accessible to consciousness—our ordinary mental and imaginative activities—whilst the *field of consciousness* represents everything we are aware of moment by moment: the flow of sensations, images, thoughts, feelings, desires and impulses that we can observe—the shifting contents of our consciousness.

At the centre of the field of consciousness is the *personal self or "I"*, our experience of being alive, the point of pure self-awareness, which is distinct from the shifting contents of our consciousness. "I" is like the conductor of the orchestra, whose focus is wholly outwards and who directs every section of the orchestra while at the same time is fully aware of their playing. And the *Higher Self* is like the composer, who channels his or her creative energy and vitality to the conductor through the musical score. Without the composer, there would be no music, no conductor, no orchestra.

The differentiation of "I" from the shifting contents of consciousness is attained by self-reflection as we increasingly expand the scope of our self-awareness and expand our experience of being alive. By attaining self-knowledge, we gain the freedom to make choices and attain a sense of self-mastery and personal will.

The *Middle Unconscious*, corresponding to the Middle World, abounds with tales of a derided youngest son who, through many trials, emerges triumphant, wins the hand of the princess, attains the crown of kingship, and rules the kingdom with wisdom and power. These stories offer a powerful and succinct metaphor for the emergence and attainment of "I".

The *Higher Unconscious* represents an individual's psychological future. It is the source of intuition and insight, of creative potentiality, of moral imperative and call to service, and of wisdom and understanding. The Higher Unconscious is also the place where we repress the wounding to our sense of Self. When, for example, the child says, "Mummy, look at my picture of myself," and she repeatedly replies, "Not now, I'm busy," the child experiences these aspects of its self-expression and creativity as unacceptable to the mother and so they are repressed in the Higher Unconscious. (Note: this is called repression of the sublime.)

So, the Higher Unconscious contains, in Upper World terms, both the creative energies and intuitive insights that are personified as wise persons and spirit guides, and the repressed complexes that are personified as spiritually perfectionist, idealised and inflated personalities. Thus, in a workshop that I attended led by John Firman and Ann Gila, they referred to repression in the Lower and Higher Unconscious respectively as opposite sides of the same traumatic wound. The negative aspect of the wounding, the rejection and hurt, are repressed in the Lower Unconscious; the positive aspect, the unacknowledged self-expression, is repressed in the Higher Unconscious. Thus, the long process of personal growth is about reclaiming our wholeness by pushing back the boundaries of the Higher and Lower Unconscious.

Firman and Gila describe the Higher Self (which they also refer to as Transpersonal Self or just Self) as "a deeper source of being beyond the conscious personality". The personal self or "I"—our experience of being alive—is a projection of this deeper source of being onto the screen of our conscious personality. Self, the unseen projector, is the enduring source of all we are, our experience of living, our sense of being who we are.

In his poem "We are transmitters", D. H. Lawrence (1950) wrote, "As we live, we are transmitters of life/And when we fail to transmit life, life fails to flow through us". To be a transmitter of life, to "ripple with life through the days", we also need to be a receptor of life, and the source of life energy is Self, an abiding presence in our life conveying invitations for us to follow a particular life path or to realise an aspect of our self-expression and creativity hidden away in our Higher Unconscious.

Though the projector is unseen, we may receive such promptings of Self as a call or a sense of vocation or a sudden insight. With our personal will we have freedom to respond or not respond to the promptings of Self. So, we need to extend the projection metaphor: we are more than flashing images on a screen; we are not puppets; we have choice. Yet, the Transpersonal Will, it will go on prompting.

Hence, we have a dialogue going on between Self and personal self, which is why Firman and Gila assert that Self is not an "It" but a "Thou". This is a really important statement that warrants sustained reflection by the reader. Self is a Thou. Self is not some theoretical concept; it has real existence, real being, a real presence in our lives.

Here is my personal testimony to the interplay between "I" and Self, an illustration of Transpersonal Will before consciousness:

> Some years ago, I was feeling increasingly discontented with my work in IT, when a friend whom I had not seen for some time asked me, "What do you really want to do?" I replied without hesitation, and completely out of the blue, out of nowhere, "I want to be a psychologist," which surprised us both. "Well, that's interesting," she said, "Because I'm doing this course in psychosynthesis." It was the first time I had heard the word. This brief exchange changed the direction of my life.

"I" is a projection of Self. Hence, the personal self and the Higher Self are connected in the diagram to reflect this I–Self relationship, this I–Self axis. The journey of life, the path of Self-realisation, is towards an ever closer alignment of "I" with Self and of the personal will with the Transpersonal Will.

Although shown at the top of the diagram, the Higher Self infuses the whole being, operating throughout to facilitate personal growth and spiritual development, from incarnation of the human soul, through building a mature ego, and attaining "I", to realising Self. Self is ever-present throughout life's unfolding journey. (Psalm 139:1–15 can be read as an appreciation of the ubiquitous Self.)

All the lines in the Egg Diagram are dotted to signify they are porous; there can be an interchange of energy between the different components of the diagram. This is particularly the case with the *collective unconscious*, which Assagioli describes thus (p. 19):

> Human beings are not isolated. … They may at times feel subjectively isolated, but the extreme existentialistic conception is not true, either psychologically or spiritually. The outer line of the oval of the diagram should be regarded as 'delimiting' but not as 'dividing'. It should be regarded as analogous to the membrane delimiting a cell, which permits a constant and active interchange with the whole body to which the cell belongs. Processes of 'psychological osmosis' are going on all the time, both with other human beings and with the general psychic environment.

It is significant, therefore, that Assagioli places the Higher Self on the outer line of the oval, the boundary between the individual and collective, where individuals can encounter one another at their deepest level.

Psychospiritual psychology

One of the defining characteristics of psychosynthesis is as a "psycho-spiritual psychology". This section is a reflection on the meaning of this significant term "psychospiritual". Stephen Johnson (1994) describes life as "a race between maturity and senility (p. 92)". Life offers us the opportunity to run life's race towards Self-realisation, as we increasingly experience the reality and vitality of mature Selfhood, affording us bodily energy, emotional groundedness and fluidity, intellectual clarity, intuitive insight, and a sense of spiritual purpose and fulfilment. This is what psychosynthesis means by "psychospiritual", the lived experience of spirituality throughout life, at every stage of life's unfolding journey.

The effect of trauma, however, particularly childhood trauma, is to arrest this natural progress towards Self-realisation. Life continues, physical growth continues, but psychologically and psychospiritually the person is frozen at the point of arrest. Life goes on, but "rape of the soul" (Levine) leaves a vital part of the person in the past, leaving them on a path that leads to increasing stuckness, sterility, and ultimate senility.

Yet, arrest of the natural progress towards Self-realisation is not the whole story; the persistence of the human spirit, in its repeated, albeit self-defeating, re-enactments of an original trauma, could be seen as bearing witness to the human spirit's determination to resume the race towards Self-realisation. It is as if the human spirit struggles to escape the vicious cycle of hope and disappointment with, it often seems, a limited strategic resource. But what strategic resource? What source of determination drives the vicious maintaining cycle so familiar to psychotherapists and counsellors?

Kalsched provides the clue, it is "almost as if the individual were possessed by some diabolical power (p. 5)", just as in fairy tales both malign and benign aspects of a duplex figure serve to move the story on. The duplex figure of the protector/persecutor, in its benign aspect, protects the "real self" from further trauma, whilst in its malign aspect, by perpetually playing out the original trauma, manifested as a vicious cycle, maintains the prospect of restoring the "true self". And, it needs to be remembered, the protector/persecutor is no more than an image in dreams that represents the inner working of the psyche. This means the psyche is perpetually working towards the redeeming and realising of Self. Self-realisation is built into the workings of the psyche.

Trauma in psychosynthesis: the primal wound

Synopsis

As human beings we are relational and our deepest relationship is within the *I–Self*, which is a crucial empathic relationship through which we experience *continuity of being*, the sense of remaining the same person whatever life brings.

In the way a mother holds her infant, and in her eyes and face mirrors the child, the infant comes to know himself or herself; through *authentic mirroring*, the mother acts as an *external unifying centre*, mediating Self to the child, together with the sense of their continuity of being.

Where the mother fails to be an authentic mirror, as an inadequate external unifying centre, she mediates neither Self nor the sense of a continuity of being, and instead the infant faces the threat of *non-being*. This disruption of the I–Self is the *primal wound* of non-being.

The mother's role as an external unifying centre is gradually internalised, an analogue of the mother's quality of holding and mirroring, world view, beliefs and values being formed permanently within the psyche.

Where the mother is an inadequate external unifying centre, the infant faces the threat of non-being. The psyche's defence against primal wounding is the *primal split*. The psyche is split into fragments: *positive and negative unifying centres*, analogues respectively of when the mother seems loving and accepting and when she seems hating and rejecting; and *positive and negative personalities*, analogues respectively of when the child feels good, accepted, and loved, and when the child feels bad, rejected, and hated.

In the absence of the I–Self relationship: the unifying centre fragments provide a substitute for Self; the personality fragments provide a substitute for "I". Splitting the psyche means that internal mirroring is through a cracked mirror: on one side, the positive unifying centre reflects love and acceptance to the positive personality; on the other side, the negative unifying centre reflects hatred and rejection to the negative personality. Each of these four fragments is a result of primal wounding, a distorted substitute for "I" or Self, "negative" and "positive" simply referring to opposite sides of the same traumatic primal wound.

The primal split spreads throughout the psyche, forming *subpersonalities*, each one derived from one of the positive or negative personalities or unifying centres. Subpersonalities are semi-autonomous parts of the personality, each capable of acting as a person, like many people living in the same house. "I" is always *identified* with one subpersonality or another. The oxygen line of being from Self to "I" provides the energy to acquire the ability to *disidentify* and thus the freedom to choose where to identify next.

Without the oxygen line to Self, "I" acquires no such freedom of choice, and "I" becomes increasingly identified with those subpersonalities that reflect relative acceptance by the unempathic mother and around which a relatively stable *survival personality* can therefore cohere. The positive and negative unifying centres from which the survival personality is derived is a controlling and constricting *survival unifying centre*.

When a person is controlled by a survival unifying centre and identified with the constricted role dictated by that centre, they enter the *survival trance*, and may remain in the trance throughout their lives.

The primal wound produces a psychic organisation adverse to change, lest this creates instability and threatens non-being; a rigid and immutable survival personality in the clutches of an intractable psychic organisation; and a person denied the opportunity for natural psychological growth into mature Selfhood.

Psychic organisation is the determinant of personality and behaviour. So, therapy work on the integration of subpersonality pairs, with an eye to the underlying psychic organisation, can gradually serve the reintegration and healing of psychic splits and thus create opportunity for psychological growth.

The primal wound

In their book *The Primal Wound: A Transpersonal View of Trauma, Addiction and Growth*, John Firman and Ann Gila explain the "primal wound" and its effect on the formation of personality. I recommend the reader to study this key text.

This section discusses the formation of subpersonalities and the survival personality as a product of primal wounding. (Note: unless otherwise stated, all quotations in this section are from *The Primal Wound*.)

The human being is relational (Note: or in object relations terms, quoting Fairbairn (1994), "Libido is primarily object seeking".), and at the deepest level this relationship is between "I" and Self, personal self and Higher Self. The "I–Self" is the crucial empathic relationship through which "we experience a continuity of being in our lives (p. 72)". The primal wound is a disruption of this fundamental, empathic relationship between "I" and Self.

For an infant, the I–Self relationship is mediated by the mother as an authentic mirror for the child (Figure 6.2). However, if the mother's quality of holding and mirroring is not good enough, "then the infant does not really come into existence, since there is no *continuity of being*" (Winnicott, my emphasis).

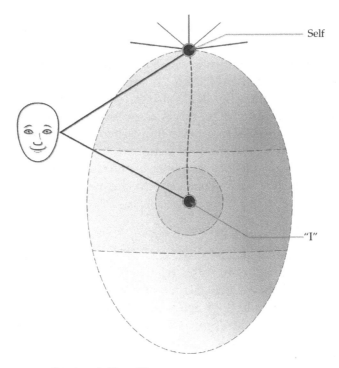

Figure 6.2. Reflecting Self to "I".

Again, for the infant, "When I look I am seen, so I exist" (Winnicott, 1988). Lack of authentic mirroring, however, leads to the opposite of Winnicott's statement: not to be seen is not to exist. As Self is the enduring source of being, disruption of the I–Self relationship creates the experience of non-being, of annihilation, an experience that the psyche must avoid at all costs.

Writing about the real self in action, James Masterson (1990, p. 49) describes the experience of continuity of being in terms of a core that persists through space and time; that remains the same whether we are up or down, accepting failure or living with success; that remains the same even as we grow. The "real self", he writes, "does not insulate us from the shocks of external reality nor from the negative feelings and frustrations which are an intrinsic part of our inner reality". On the contrary, "the real self has a sense of continuity through success and adversity, is able to use our sense of vulnerability as a source of wisdom, is able both to honour our multiplicity and to integrate our many moods and roles".

External unifying centre

Throughout life, each authentic, empathic relationship that we experience reflects the mediation of Self to "I" (see Figure 6.2 above), strengthening the I–Self relationship and realising more of our essential essence. The authentic, empathic other serves as an "external unifying centre", mediating the transmission of being from Self to "I" and sustaining our experience of having continuity of being.

In particular, an authentic, empathic relationship with the mother is essential for the healthy psychological development of the child.

The primal wound of non-being

Where the mother is an inadequate external unifying centre, by failing to sustain an authentic, empathic relationship with her child she will thus fail to mediate the transmission of being from Self to "I", resulting in the disruption of the I–Self relationship. Such disruption of the I–Self relationship is the "primal wound of non-being". Firman and Gila attribute most psychological disorders to the primal wound. (Note: compare Fairbairn (1994), "It is to disturbances in the object relationships of the developing ego that we must look for the ultimate origin of all psychopathological conditions".) For the wounded psyche, the experience of non-being, of annihilation, must be avoided at all costs.

Internal unifying centre

The mother, as her child's external unifying centre, is gradually internalised by the psychological process of "introjection", whereby an analogue of the mother's quality of holding and mirroring, world view, beliefs and values is formed within the psyche. This acquired permanent psychological structure continues, within the psyche, the functions that the mother had previously fulfilled; her holding and mirroring environment is superseded by the person's internal holding and mirroring environment, affording them a personal sense of self and of meaning in their lives, and an internal point of connection for the transmission of being from Self to "I", maintaining their experience of having continuity of being.

Splitting: positive and negative unifying centres

When the mother, as her child's external unifying centre, fails to mediate the transmission of being from Self to "I", there is disruption of the I–Self relationship, "a seeming rejection by the Source of Being itself (p. 101)", turning into a threat of non-being that must be prevented.

In order to defend against the primal wound, the psyche's experience of the inadequate external centre is split into parts (p. 101):

- A "positive unifying centre", located in the Higher Unconscious, an analogue of the acceptance and love the child feels from the "pure, good" positive part of the mother.
- A "negative unifying centre", located in the Lower Unconscious, an analogue of the rejection and hate the child feels from the unempathic, wounding negative part of the mother.

At the same time, a person's sense of self is also split, so that they have differing experiences of who they are:

- A "positive personality", bonded with the positive unifying centre. When evoked, the positive personality feels good, accepted, and loved.

- A "negative personality", bonded with the negative unifying centre. When evoked, the negative personality feels bad, rejected, and hated.

Splitting of the internal unifying centre and personality into positive and negative aspects forms a kind of "holographic break" in the I–Self relationship: the unifying centre aspects provide a split substitute for Self; the personality aspects provide a split substitute for "I". The powerful bonding between the positive parts on the one hand and the negative parts on the other means that these pairings operate separately from each other whilst coexisting within the psyche, thus comprising opposite sides of the primal wound, the "primal split".

Instead of an internal holding and mirroring environment affording a personal sense of self and a point of connection for the transmission of being from Self to "I", the person—the child and later the adult—is shown a cracked mirror. On one side of the crack, the positive centre transmits acceptance and love to the positive personality; in their relationships and behaviour, the person expresses the "good side" of their personality. On the other side of the crack, the negative centre transmits rejection and hate to the negative personality; in their relationships and behaviour, the person expresses the "bad, wounded side" of their personality.

Use of the words negative and positive is deceptive, suggesting the negative parts align more with the primal wound whilst the positive parts align more with the true I–Self relationship. Rather, as Firman and Gila said at the workshop I attended, the negative and positive parts are opposite sides of the same traumatic wound, both a consequence of the primal wound and a distorted substitute for the I–Self relationship. So, in the present context, the words negative and positive are regarded as neutral.

Personality and subpersonalities

The positive and negative unifying centres and positive and negative personalities are actually energetic structures within the psyche resulting from fragmentation. The discussion now turns to the way these psychic structures determine a person's personality and behaviour.

By identifying with these psychic structures, a person circumvents the threat of non-being. By identifying with the positive personality, bonded with the positive unifying centre, the person believes, for example, "I am loved unconditionally," because they feel good, accepted,

Figure 6.3. Many living in the same house.

and loved. By identifying with the negative personality, bonded with the negative unifying centre, the person believes, for example, "I am worthless," because they feel bad, rejected, and hated.

Either way, whether the identification is positive or negative, whether they can state, "I am loved" or "I am worthless", the statement provides the person with a spurious sense of being and identity that serves to stave off the experience of non-being.

Once the primal split has occurred, "this split continues to spread throughout the personality (p. 151)". This creates "subpersonalities" (also referred to simply as "parts") based on the positive or negative personalities and unifying centres. John Rowan's (1990, p. 8) "working definition" of a subpersonality is "a semi-permanent and semi-auton-omous region of the personality capable of acting as a person". Sub-personalities are like many people living in the same house. It is often useful in therapy for descriptive names to be given to subpersonalities;

examples are shown in Figure 6.3. Jeni Couzyn's (1978) poem "House of Changes" is a graphic depiction of many people living in the same house.

Although expressions like, "Part of me feels …", have appeared in common language, we are generally unconscious of our subpersonalities. Until some eagle-eyed therapist points them out! Subpersonalities exist wholly or partly in the Lower or Upper Unconscious.

The simplest example of recognising our subpersonalities is when we say, "I'm just not myself today," or "I don't know what got into me." This is a tangible experience of being in a different place within ourselves than we normally are. We can see our subpersonalities in the roles we play, our traits, our moods, our reactions to people and situations, perhaps most of all in our behaviour. Here is an example of a person's subpersonalities:

> Martin is highly depressed and deeply withdrawn. This is his habitually depressed subpersonality. He is also a little rotund. Talking about his office party, he recognises his partygoer subpersonality, rounder and jollier than Martin's habitual self, more outgoing, spontaneous, flirtatious. He says—and I'm very moved by this insight—"It's like it's another person. It's me but it's not me."
>
> Then there is his tennis subpersonality, the doubles player. He is taller and more athletic than Martin's habitual self. He experiences stronger focus and intensity and an intuitive resonance with his partner. Martin is surprised to observe that neither his partygoer nor his doubles player is withdrawn or depressed.

Notice how Martin recognises the different parts: "It's like it's another person. It's me but it's not me." The parts have a differing body image, one rounder, one taller and more athletic; his subpersonalities have different feelings, one withdrawn and depressed while the others are more outgoing and able to engage with other people and are not depressed. The main elements that characterise a subpersonality—behaviour, body image, feelings, thoughts, and ideas—can differ widely between the same person's subpersonalities.

In Martin's depressed subpersonality is revealed the bond between the negative personality and negative unifying centre. In his partygoer subpersonality and his doubles player subpersonality is revealed the bond between the positive personality and positive unifying centre.

Identification and disidentification

In his book *Psychosynthesis*, Assagioli makes a key statement about psychosynthesis theory: "We are dominated by everything with which our Self becomes *identified*. We can dominate, direct and utilise everything from which we *disidentify* ourselves (p. 22)". The personal self or "I" is always identified with one subpersonality or another. As discussed in the section above on the Egg Diagram, when we attain the ability to disidentify then we have the freedom to choose where we direct our identification. Lacking the oxygen line from Self, the asphyxiating "I" has no power to disidentify or to exercise choice.

In the above example, Martin is habitually identified with his depressed subpersonality. Then, at times his identification shifts to his partygoer subpersonality or his doubles player subpersonality. In either case, his I–Self relationship being disrupted, he has no ability to disidentify and no power to choose where his identification is directed. So, when he remains identified with Depressed at a party he has no fun, and when he remains identified with Depressed during a tennis match his performance is poor.

Survival personality and survival trance

As in Martin's case, "I" can identify with several different subpersonalities. Referring to the above diagram, a person may identify with her compliant Good Girl, later identify with her exacting Bossy Boots, later still identify with her vulnerable Lonely Child, each of these subpersonalities having their own particular body image, feelings, and thoughts.

In the presence of multiple, sometimes conflicting, subpersonalities, some will rise to prominence, others fade into the background. When the mother fails to sustain an authentic, empathic relationship with her child, "I" becomes increasingly identified with those subpersonalities that reflect "relative acceptance" by the unempathic mother and around which a relatively stable "survival personality" can therefore cohere.

Taking Martin's three subpersonalities as comprising his survival personality, we may hypothesise about their origins—how Martin made the best of a poor situation in the way he sustained his connection with an unempathic mother, thereby maintaining some sense of self against the threat of non-being:

> Martin's mother could not tolerate closeness and punished any expression of feelings, so Martin learnt to hide his feelings and withdraw to a safe distance from her in order to maintain his connection with her. Martin's mother could at times be fun-loving and enjoy boisterous play, in which young Martin was only too happy to participate and take pleasure in these times of closeness to her.

It follows from this hypothesis that the predominant part of Martin's survival personality is based on his depressed subpersonality, which draws a sense of being from a negative unifying centre. His partygoer subpersonality, or his doubles player subpersonality, also has some purchase on his survival personality, which draws a sense of being from a positive unifying centre. These negative and positive centres comprise the "survival unifying centre".

The powerful attachment between a survival personality and an oppressive survival unifying centre blocks the unfolding of an authentic personality, severely constraining a person's vitality and capacity to be open to all life has to offer. Firman and Gila make this telling statement, "Whenever we are bonded to such a constricting unifying centre and identified with the constricted role dictated by that centre, a very curious thing happens: we enter a trance. ... We can be conceived, born, and mature, all within this fundamental and pervasive trance (p. 169)". This is the "survival trance".

I suggested in the foreword that developmental trauma can affect us all, and for Firman and Gila "primal wounding and splitting are commonplace (p. 165)"—so also survival personality and survival trance. Regardless of how well we function in the world, we retain a potential to live more abundant and fulfilled lives.

The survival personality and the primal wound

A person's underlying psychic organisation determines a person's personality and behaviour. When we work psychotherapeutically with subpersonalities, we need to keep in mind that they represent the tip of the iceberg, the one eleventh that appears above the surface. It is the ten elevenths below the surface that really need to change for the person to change.

It is common in therapy for a client to reject praise and deny their achievements and to refuse any efforts to persuade them otherwise. Looking at this psychically, there is most likely a self-effacing subpersonality derived from a negative unifying centre/personality pairing, which affords the person their sense of being and identity. If the person were to accept praise and achievements, this would prejudice the negative structure, thus undermining the basis of the person's sense of being and identity and creating the threat of non-being. This leaves the person no choice but to remain self-effacing, being in the grip of the negative structure.

It also happens in therapy that a client is ultra-sensitive to the slightest hint of criticism. On a similar analysis of the psychic organisation, an ultra-sensitive subpersonality would be derived from a positive unifying centre/personality, and for the person to accept criticism would prejudice this positive structure, undermining the basis of the person's sense of being and identity and creating the threat of non-being. Again, the person has no choice but to allow nothing to challenge their positive self-image, being in the grip of the positive structure.

Thus, below the surface, the primal wound creates: a psychic organisation adverse to change, lest this endanger the stability of the organisation and threaten non-being; a rigid and immutable survival personality in the clutches of an intractable psychic organisation; and a person who is denied the opportunity for natural psychological growth into mature Selfhood. At the same time, studying what is above the surface can throw light on what is beneath, as this section illustrates; exploring a subpersonality in therapy can provide insight into the underlying psychic organisation.

Afterthoughts

For me, Firman and Gila have brought clarity to the difficult task of unravelling the subtleties and complexities of the traumatised human mind and of presenting a helpful and serviceable model of the traumatised psyche. When on their first page they write, "The primal wound is the result of a violation we all suffer in various ways", I infer from this that a model of the workings and structure of the psyche needs to be represented in overly black and white terms for the sake of clarity; I agree that we all suffer the primal wound, yet we cannot all be completely cut off from our source of being.

We must all be on a spectrum that runs from thick-skinned narcissism at one end to Self-realisation at the other. At the left hand pole, the I–Self relationship is completely severed. A person may be highly effective in the world and build a mighty empire and yet be ossified psychologically and spiritually— "What shall it profit a man, if he shall gain the whole world, and lose his own soul?" (Gospel of St. Mark 8:36). At the right hand pole, the I–Self relationship is as natural as the air we breathe.

As adults, the overwhelming majority of us are somewhere on the line between the poles. This line is the spiritual path of wholeness and Self-realisation, along which we can progressively attain self-reflection, differentiate "I" from the shifting contents of consciousness, strengthen the I–Self relationship, increase our sense of being, extend the scope of our self-awareness, expand and enrich our experience of being alive, and recognise how much we are one with the interdependence of all beings.

It follows that for most of us the I–Self relationship is impaired but not completely severed. To some degree, there is transmission of being from Self to "I" and some experience of knowing continuity of being. These increase as we move along the line: by natural personal growth; under the influence of those who give us authentic mirroring; with the help of a guide.

The positive and negative unifying centres comprise a substitute for Self, creating a psychic organisation adverse to change, lest this threaten instability and non-being. The positive and negative personalities comprise a substitute for "I", which is in the grip of the intractable psychic organisation. As we sit somewhere on the line, there must be rival systems coexisting:

- The *I–Self* system providing being energy and allowing freedom to move along the line.
- The *substitute I–substitute Self* system staving off non-being and enforcing slavery and immobility.

Along the spiritual path there is an inherent, ongoing conflict between freedom and slavery of the soul. Writing about the vicissitudes of the spiritual journey, Assagioli says, "Spiritual development is a long and arduous journey, an adventure through strange lands full of surprises, joy and beauty, difficulties and even dangers (p. 39)".

CHAPTER SEVEN

Trauma and the wounded soul:
a soulfulness perspective

This chapter provides a perspective on developmental trauma from a Soulfulness shamanic perspective, taking account of the ideas expressed in the previous chapter. First, the relationship between these two models of the psyche is considered:

Shamanic Psychology The Medicine Wheel: Elements of Personality map (Figure 7.1), which was discussed in Chapter Three. This model can be used to map a person's choreography of energy.
Contemporary Psychology Assagioli's Egg Diagram model (Figure 7.2), which was discussed in the previous chapter.

At first sight these appear to be quite different models, yet closer scrutiny reveals much common ground, even though they were conceived thousands of years apart. The union of these models is greater and more illuminating than the sum of its parts.

The "womb" is a potent metaphor for creativity. A womb is empty, until out of this emptiness, this void, vibrant life is created. An empty womb is full of unbounded potentiality. The metaphor of the womb is readily applicable to Self, as witnessed in my unequivocal statement, recorded in the previous chapter, and arriving completely out

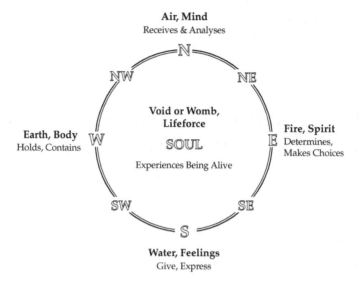

Figure 7.1. Medicine Wheel: elements of personality.

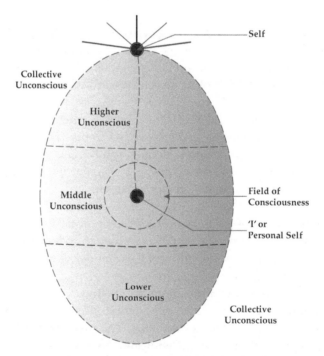

Figure 7.2. Assagioli's Egg Diagram: model of the psyche.

of nowhere, "I want to be a psychologist." Self is a womb of boundless creativity, insight, and inspiration:

> I was booked to give a talk one Friday morning to the Business Women's Luncheon Club in the French Dining Room of the Cliveden Hotel, the first man ever to do so, a few days before Christmas. On Tuesday, in the middle of the night, I half woke to find myself telling myself the seasonal story of Sir Gawain and the Green Knight. On Wednesday morning I read my favourite version of this enormously long tale. Then I wrote the version I had received in the night, timed to be told in twenty minutes. Well, it took thirty minutes to tell, but no one complained and no one walked out. Afterwards, one of the business women was telling me how much she had enjoyed the story, and I told her how I had received it in the middle of the night. "So," she said gravely, "The story was channelled."

She couldn't have put it better. The story arrived in the middle of the night, out of the blue, out of nowhere. It was channelled from the creative womb of Self to the personal self along the I–Self channel. I offer this account as an example, to emphasise that the I–Self relationship can bring creativity, insight, and inspiration at a mundane, day-to-day level, and isn't just there for life-changing moments.

It is clear from this discussion that I see no essential difference between womb or void in one diagram and Self in the other, and in fact Hyemeyohsts Storm's (1994) version of the basic Medicine Wheel has "Self" at the centre. Each is the source of the life energy or being energy, which is channelled to the personality.

Though "I" is not represented explicitly on the Elements of Personality map, it is nevertheless present by implication. The paragraph "How we are meant to be" in Chapter Three describes the human soul when there is an open lifeline to the source of life energy—our feelings flow like water; our body contains all our emotional energies; our mind receives and analyses information from our body, our feelings, and our surrounding environment; our spirit makes choices and exercises our personal will, so that our whole being is balanced and harmonious. This description is tantamount to a portrayal of the personal self when there is an open lifeline to Self.

The union of the above models of the psyche reveals an interesting symmetry of opposites, the creative life-affirming void of being and the uncreative life-denying void of non-being. An infant enters the world in a state of innocence: trusting and free to be themselves. When their core feeling sense is of their mother's warm embrace and loving face, then they have a lifeline to the source of being and know they exist.

The moment the infant's core feeling sense is of a mother who is distracted and whose holding is perfunctory, the lifeline to the source of being is traumatically broken and trust gives way to the primal fear of not existing, of the void of non-being. It is as if, in that moment of disillusionment at a seeming rejection by the source of being, in the twinkling of an eye—in the failure of the mother's eyes to twinkle—the void of being itself, so traumatically and tragically cut off, becomes for the infant the void of non-being.

Fragmentation and personification

Again, for the sake of clarity, I am here modelling the workings of the psyche in overly black and white terms; we are not totally severed from our source of being, but sit on a spectrum running from thick-skinned narcissism to Self-realisation. The shifts that happen in that primal moment are a diminution in the flow of life energy from "I" to Self and the shutters of the Higher and Lower Unconscious begin to close. These shifts cannot but be reinforced by subsequent, ongoing empathic failures, leaving each of us where we sit today on that spectrum.

In the moment of disillusionment, faced with the void of non-being, the infant psyche must seek a safe haven in order to survive, and the only safe haven they know is the womb. But, that avenue being no longer open to them, their recourse is to split off their experience of being prior to the trauma and retreat into that secure womb-like place. There they both save their life and lose it, for they exist only as a bee preserved in aspic, denied access to life-giving energy from Self and protected from the sorrows and the joys of life in the real world.

The four main authors featured in the previous chapter concur on the effect of trauma, which is to split the psyche, but envisage the structure of the psyche after the split in different ways: Kalsched, the archetypal self-care system and the protector/persecutor; Levine, the shamanic concept of soul loss or rape of the soul; Assagioli, the division into the Lower, Middle and Higher Unconscious; Firman and Gila, the positive and negative unifying centres and personalities, subpersonalities, and the survival personality. Taken together, these differing perspectives provide a rounded picture of the dissociative defences.

For Kalsched, underlying psychic structures are personified in dreams. For Firman and Gila, underlying psychic structures become personified in the form of subpersonalities. These complementary ideas both contribute to the present discussion; psychic structures are personified in dreams, and psychic structures have a formative effect on personality.

Exploring the personality

As mentioned in the previous chapter, studying what is above the surface of the iceberg can throw light on what is beneath. Exploring a client's personality in therapy can provide insight into the underlying psychic organisation when the guide maintains "twofold vision", keeping in sight not only the nature of the personality but also the underlying psychic drama. This does not mean trying to figure out intellectually the particulars of the underlying psychic drama. It means keeping in mind that, for the client to change and heal, the ten elevenths of the iceberg below the surface need to change, and that the context of therapy is not just about addressing the client's existential issues but is about healing their primal wound.

The Elements of Personality map can be used in therapy to illustrate, for the client, the way they choreograph the energy that is channelled from womb/Self to the four elements of personality: feelings, body, mind, and spirit.

In his helpful and highly recommended book *Character Styles*, Stephen Johnson (1994) illustrates the character styles that typify particular diagnostic categories, to which he applies descriptive names. The following table shows three relevant diagnostic categories, Mary Ainsworth's corresponding attachment categories (Ainsworth, 1978; Main & Goldwin, 1984), and Johnson's descriptive names:

Category	Attachment	Descriptive name
Schizoid	Avoidant	"The hated child"
Oral/dependent	Anxious/ambivalent	"The abandoned child"
Symbiotic/borderline	Disorganised/ disoriented	"The owned child"
(Note: the other character styles, outside the scope of this book, are: narcissistic, "the used child"; masochistic/self-defeating, "the defeated child"; oedipal/histrionic, "the exploited child"; oedipal/obsessive-compulsive, "the disciplined child".)		

The typical choreography of energy for each of the above three categories is provided in the "Attachment as adults" section of Chapter Four. Taking my cue from Levine (1997), it is as relevant for a guide to consider the impact of trauma on a client's posture and body sculpting as on their feelings and thoughts. The quote from Johnson (1994) in the "Attachment as adults" section is particularly telling.

As Johnson is careful to point out, however, rather than fitting only one of the above character styles, a person will exhibit a spectrum of the seven styles, with peaks and troughs displaying their individual character style. Moreover, a person will exhibit their peak styles at one of three levels: personality disorder, character neurosis, or character style.

Mapping a client's choreography of energy using the Elements of Personality map serves the client by increasing their awareness of the way their use of energy is out of balance, this being a necessary prelude to their choice to change. At the same time, mapping a client's choreography of energy provides the guide with insight into the nature and depth of their client's primal wounding.

Pairs of opposites: harmonisation and synthesis

Pairing of opposites is a feature of the post-trauma psychic organisation. Firman and Gila have pairs of subpersonalities emerging from the positive and negative unifying centres and personalities. Kalsched has the duplex figure of the protector/persecutor, both aspects of which are part of a person's neurosis-prone personality and behaviour. In both cases, the words used—protector and persecutor, positive and negative—are to be regarded as neutral terms representing polarised aspects of the psyche and of the personality.

Working in therapy with two opposing subpersonalities, one positive and one negative, such as the Good Girl and the Harsh Critic, can be particularly powerful when working towards drawing them into mutual acknowledgement, dialogue, and integration. By maintaining twofold vision—the pair of subpersonalities and the underlying psychic organisation—the work of integrating subpersonalities can also serve the gradual reintegration and synthesis of the psychic splits and with it restoration of the I–Self relationship, creating the opportunity for natural psychological growth.

The elements that characterise a subpersonality—feelings, body, mind, and spirit—can differ widely between the same person's subpersonalities. So, work with polarised subpersonalities means adding a further dimension to the Elements map, a subpersonality dimension; the Elements map can be used to explore each of the subpersonalities prior to any dialogue between them. It is prerequisite that the client be willing to acknowledge that both subpersonalities exist and to own the behaviour and qualities of both as being part of their personality.

Before introducing a dialogue between polarised subpersonalities, the context needs to be explained to the client; namely that however their energy is respectively choreographed, they owe their being to the one Self. Then the client can be invited to begin conducting an imaginative dialogue between the two subpersonalities, with the client identifying with each subpersonality in turn and speaking their words. Mostly, I do cushion work for the dialogue. Sometimes, I set up two chairs and invite the client to move physically from one chair to the other as they shift their identification from one subpersonality to the other.

At first the dialogue may be fractious, but over time, often quite a long time, with other work intervening, the polarised subpersonalities begin to cooperate in the dialogue, and it may be possible to invite them to embark on some joint project, each one bringing their particular gifts and qualities. Work between a pair of subpersonalities has their harmonisation and integration as its goal, as they learn to recognise each other's gifts and qualities. The Elements of Personality map continues to serve as a gauge to show the changes in the subpersonalities in terms of their choreography of energy, and the gradual unifying of the subpersonalities' use of energy. This work at the level of personality is about the synthesis of subpersonalities towards greater wholeness. And, with an eye to twofold vision, the work is towards synthesising the psychic splits and healing the primal wound.

The shamanic journey and soul retrieval

"Dreams and the contents of our inner world give us ample evidence of the importance of listening to the intelligence lying in the psyche, aligning ourselves to this wisdom, and connecting to its healing, transformative powers" (2012 p. xxi).

—Alan Mulhern

There are several complementary approaches towards synthesising the psychic splits and healing the primal wound. This section is particularly concerned with the soul retrieval approach, namely a shamanic journey by a client that is made with the specific intention of retrieving their lost soul energy. The discussion includes consideration of dream states and trance states, both of which feature in shamanic journeys.

The dream-like state of the shamanic journey

Alan Mulhern (2012) writes, "The inner world, experienced in ... visionary states, consists of images, symbols, stories, and metaphors which are identical to the dream world. ... However, the vital difference is that visionary, inner states allow the activation of inner awareness which is a direct participation of a part of consciousness in the drama (p. 109)."

The simulated dream state of a shamanic journey is just such a visionary state, and unlike a dream, the person making the journey, being conscious, can more reliably participate in the drama and remember what happens afterwards.

Discussing the personification of psychic structures in dreams, Kalsched makes the remarkable statement, "The idea that dreams should be capable of representing the psyche's dissociative activities and holding the fragmented pieces together in one dramatic story is a kind of miracle of psychological life (pp. 2–3)". I feel thrilled by this statement—by what it conveys about the inventiveness of the human psyche, even in adversity, perhaps especially so. And yet, the statement doesn't say that *only* fragmented pieces are personified in dreams. The psyche *must* consist of more than just fragmented pieces otherwise that "miracle of psychological life" might never happen. What this "more than" might comprise is suggested by Assagioli (1965) as part of his description of the Egg Diagram (pp. 17–18):

> *Lower Unconscious* "The elementary psychological activities which direct the life of the body; the intelligent coordination of bodily functions; the fundamental drives and primitive urges". As well as these instinctive elements, Assagioli also mentions (helpfully to my argument but I feel rather disparagingly) "Dreams and imaginations of an inferior kind".
> *Middle Unconscious* "This is formed of psychological elements similar to those of our waking consciousness and easily accessible to it".

Higher Unconscious "From this region we receive our higher intuitions and inspirations—artistic, philosophical or scientific, ethical 'imperatives' and urges to humanitarian and heroic action. It is the source of the higher feelings, such as altruistic love; of genius and of the states of contemplation, illumination and ecstasy. In this realm are latent the higher functions and spiritual energies".

So, the psyche has wounded parts and normally functioning healthy parts, which include instinctive and intuitive elements. It is these healthy elements that are personified in the dream-like state of a shamanic journey in the form of animal allies and wise beings.

The shamanic trance

Turning to the question of trance states, Kalsched (1996) writes of the traumatised psyche being self-traumatising, the original trauma being repeatedly played out "as if the person were possessed". Levine (1997) writes of rape of the soul leaving a person stuck in "spiritual limbo". Firman and Gila (1997) write of the "survival trance"; the effect of a traumatic splitting of the psyche enduringly alters a person's state of consciousness, for which the term "survival trance" is particularly apt.

Being possessed, spiritual limbo, survival trance! An aftermath of developmental trauma is an impaired state of consciousness, an involuntary and sustained survival trance. Unlike the involuntary survival trance, a shamanic journey takes place in a voluntary trance state. This is a relaxed and focused dream-like state of consciousness, which, bypassing the ego, enables a person to explore some aspect of their deep psyche.

In a soul retrieval, a client enters a trance state voluntarily with a specific intention of alleviating their suffering by retrieving a lost part of their soul energy and restoring their vital essence. In soul retrieval, we set a trance to catch a trance.

Kalsched envisages the characters appearing in dreams as being personifications of fragmented pieces of the split psyche. I envisage the characters appearing in a soul retrieval as including: personified fragments of the split psyche; instinctive elements of the psyche personified as animal allies; intuitive elements of the psyche personified as wise beings; alien energies personified as monstrous beings that have "attached" to the psyche as a by-product of trauma.

Again, by maintaining twofold vision—the client's suffering and the underlying psychic organisation—soul retrieval can also serve the gradual reintegration and synthesis of the psychic splits and healing of the primal wound.

Soul retrieval

Patrick suffered an avoidant attachment; his soldier father was absent for long periods, and his mother was sad and lonely and resentful that she couldn't travel with him. His avoidant behaviour betrayed a wound to his sexuality. His intention for the soul retrieval was to restore his lost male power. This is his account of his soul retrieval:

"I begin at a favourite place on Dartmoor where yellow gorse and purple heather grow together. I look around for a portal to start my journey and find what seems like the entrance to a burrow. I state my intention three times, to retrieve my lost male power, and begin my journey. I am immediately met by a rabbit, who says he will guide me to where I need to go. He leads me into the burrow and down its narrow labyrinthine tunnels until we emerge at the edge of a deep forest. The rabbit directs me to go to the heart of the forest and leaves me.

I walk into the forest, and at its heart I find a circle of stones within which a group of women are gathered around a fire. I ask to enter the circle, but the women will not permit me. They scoff at me and say that as women wise in the lore of the land they are unwilling to share their wisdom with the likes of me. They say they are dissatisfied with men, 'Men are weak,' they say. They tell me to move on, but I won't, 'There is something you have to give me,' I say. I somehow know this is something about fire, that they have fire to give to me.

Then they let me enter the circle. I ask for a gift. They pluck a brand from the fire and hand it to me. Then, the women huddle closer to the fire, including me in their circle. As we stare into the fire, a male figure appears in the flames, tall, bearded, strong, somehow embodying masculine and feminine qualities. I recognise that this is me, a brand from the burning, someone who I could be. I stand and step into the fire. There is exultation. Finally, I transform into a firebird. As the firebird, I rise from the flames, just as the drum is calling me to return, and fly back to my place on Dartmoor."

In our grounding work, Patrick recognised that in the journey he needed to assert himself with the women in order to get what he wanted; the gift of fire was to enliven his spirit and invoke his will and power; true male power is a union of masculine and feminine qualities; his ongoing psychological work was to embody the fire man. This example illustrates a number of important points about soul retrieval:

• Patrick was able to surrender to the process. This enabled the ego to be bypassed, allowing him to go deeply into his inner world.
• Patrick didn't know what would happen in the journey, beyond stating his intention. The soul retrieval journey simply unfolded. At the same time, he was not simply an observer, but was part of the unfolding drama.
• The rabbit, the women, the fire man, and even the firebird, were personifications of helpful healthy parts of the psyche—though the firebird was also a charming little piece of psychic humour.
• At the same time, the women were not pushovers, their wisdom had to be earned, and this itself was an aspect of their gift of wisdom, serving to embolden Patrick to work towards embodying the fire man.
• At another level, soul retrieval involves a collaboration between the conscious and the unconscious, which enables the unconscious to work upon itself towards the healing of the primal wound.

In Patrick's case, restoring his lost male power meant receiving a gift of wisdom from his unconscious, a quality of maleness poised to pass from spirit into matter, a potential energy moving to enliven his spirit and invoke his will and power. In other cases, a soul retrieval will take a client explicitly back to a wounding incident or a traumatically sustained failure of care. The outcome may not only be one of liberating the client's lost soul energy but also of freeing the client from the energetic consequences of the wounding, which is energy in the wrong place, witnessed for example as low self-worth, low self-esteem, depression, anxiety, addictions, and behavioural problems. This leads directly to another aspect of soul retrieval, which is soul deliverance.

Soul deliverance

I can't get away with slipping in "alien energies personified as monstrous beings attached to the psyche" without adequate explanation. In psychological terms, such alien energy is energy in the wrong place, typically from the impact of a projective identification being ingested into the psyche. The phenomenon of energy being in the wrong place and needing to be removed is illustrated by the following case example:

> Gerald speaks in therapy of his frequent feelings of rage, which sometimes overwhelm him. Gerald cannot understand why the rage can suddenly come upon him. Having made sure he is at present feeling relaxed, I invite him to put his rage onto a cushion. I ask him what he sees on the cushion. A little, crouching black goblin with a fierce face and flaming red eyes. I begin to question the goblin via Gerald. What is the goblin's name? Just Goblin. How long has Goblin been inside Gerald? Always. What does Goblin get out of it? Making life difficult for Gerald, making him angry. How did he come to be in Gerald? I jumped in when Gerald's father got angry with him in the workshop.
>
> Later, Gerald recounts the traumatic incident: six-year-old Gerald was doing jobs for his father in the farm workshop. Gerald wanted to go to the toilet, but his father insisted he carry on with his jobs. When Gerald wet himself, his father went into one of his frequent flaming rages, held Gerald up by his ankles and beat him, then threw him on the dung heap.
>
> Is Goblin willing to leave Gerald? No—laughing scornfully—why should he, he is part of Gerald, he is Gerald. At this point, Gerald speaks for himself, vehemently denying that Goblin is any part of him. I silently accept Gerald's denial and decide to undertake a soul deliverance. Doesn't Goblin need to be somewhere else, where he would be happier and receive healing? No, he doesn't need healing. I pause, wondering how I shall persuade Goblin to go, then Gerald tells me Goblin has changed colour, from black to grey, and seems less fierce. Perhaps Goblin needs to be somewhere else? Yes, he needs to be with his own kind, other goblins. Would Goblin like some of his own kind to come and take him to be with them? Yes. I say, they are coming now, taking you by the hand, lovingly carrying you away to be with them.
>
> When Goblin has left, I tell Gerald there is a source of healing light above the crown of his head, shining into the space in him where Goblin resided and filling it with pure light, so that Goblin can never return.

Gerald was glad to be working with his father, in his father's workshop. It made him feel wanted and valued. His father's violent behaviour towards him took away Gerald's sense of self-worth and put rage in its place, energy in the wrong place. Just as Patrick needed ongoing psychological work to embody the fire man, so Gerald needed ongoing psychological work to strengthen his psyche against the renewal of overwhelming rage and to reinforce his restored sense of self-worth.

With an eye to twofold vision, the soul deliverance both served to deliver Gerald's soul from the power of the misplaced rage and to remove the alien energy from the psyche.

Soul retrieval and soul deliverance

This example illustrates an important point, namely that soul retrieval and soul deliverance are complementary, working from opposite ends:

Soul retrieval is focused on retrieving lost soul energy, which may also result in removing energy that is in the wrong place. In Patrick's case, the soul retrieval served not only to restore his male power but also to remove his crippling sexual diffidence.

Soul deliverance is focused on removing energy that is in the wrong place, which may also result is restoring lost soul energy. In Gerald's case, the soul deliverance served not only to remove his overwhelming feelings of rage but also to restore his lost self-worth.

A final point about soul deliverance: in some cases an alien energy, energy in the wrong place, will manifest itself in a person's life in the tangible form of a monstrous presence. In such cases, the alien presence is referred to as an "attachment", because it seems like an alien being has attached itself to a person in a way that intrudes upon the person's life and affects their behaviour. As an example, a psychotherapy client felt there was something behind her. She could not see it but she felt its hot breath on the back of her neck, which was very frightening for her. We used soul deliverance to remove the attachment.

The maintaining cycle and the Circle of Mirrors

Kalsched (1996) writes, "The victim of psychological trauma continually finds himself or herself in life situations where he or she is re-traumatised (p. 5)". Levine (1997) writes, "Trauma is so arresting that traumatised people will focus on it compulsively. ... The situation that defeated them once will defeat them again, and again (p. 66)".

This is the maintaining cycle, familiar to psychotherapists and counsellors. Trauma produces a rigid, immutable, impaired and neurosis-prone survival personality in the clutches of an intractable psychic organisation. "It is as though the persecutory inner world somehow finds its outer mirror in repeated self-defeating re-enactments" (Kalsched, 1996, p. 5). Put another way, it is as if by repeated re-enactments the human spirit exhibits a determination not to be defeated, but to find a way out of the maintaining cycle.

The only way out of a maintaining cycle is through an act of will, and the exercise of will is not possible without a thorough awareness of the self-sustaining nature of the maintaining cycle. Such awareness can be achieved when client and guide work together around the Circle of Mirrors maps (Figure 7.3 and Figure 7.4). This map is explained in some detail in Chapter Four, where it is described as a cognitive approach. Whilst this is true, the self-revealing nature of the dark mirror can take a client so deeply and movingly into themselves that the will to step out of the dark mirror is invoked.

Work around the light mirror serves to reinforce the shift out of the maintaining cycle and to affirm the act of will involved. Subsequent work with the light mirror is the ongoing journey of a lifetime. By maintaining twofold vision—work on the dark mirror and its underlying

Figure 7.3. The Circle of Mirrors: the dark mirror.

Figure 7.4. The Circle of Mirrors: the light mirror.

psychic organisation, and subsequent work on the light mirror—the Circle of Mirrors is an approach that serves the gradual reintegration and synthesis of the psychic splits and healing of the primal wound.

Harley SwiftDeer Reagan (1980) has a different name for the Circle of Mirrors. He calls it the "Star Maidens Circle (p. 56)". Here is part of his portrayal of the Star Maidens Circle. (Note: SwiftDeer's terminology differs somewhat from that used in this book, but the meaning is still clear.)

> The Star Maidens Circle is a very powerful tool for gaining insight into our psyche—our actions, reactions, desires, beliefs, goals. Each position on the circle has both a Dark Mirror and a Light Mirror. For example, in the South—the place of mythology and entertainment—the dark mirror is how we entertain ourselves with stories that keep us closed down, in pain and at the effect of circumstances rather than free and in power. The Light Mirror, on the other hand, is mythologies which inspire us to move through life in balance and control. Once understood, we can master our choreography.

The "I–Self" or "Lower Self-Higher Self" relationship

In the description of the Egg Diagram in Chapter Six, the assertion is made that Self is not an "It" but a "Thou". The I–Self relationship is a two-way connection, a dialogue between personal self and Higher Self. Harley SwiftDeer Reagan has a remarkably similar conception of the relationship between "Lower Self" and "Higher Self", continuing his portrayal of the Star Maidens Circle (p. 56):

> As we heal and balance the dark mirrors by shifting all of our mythologies, symbols, daydreams, rules and laws, philosophies, designs of energy, fantasies and concepts of self into the light mirror, we move from being at the effect and stuck in the lower self [he or she who cannot see] to coming into the full power of our higher self [he or she who is learning or has learned to see]. Thus, in many ways, the Star Maidens Circle is a bridge to the Higher Self.

Referring to the flow of energy in the Star Maidens Circle, he writes, "All energy in motion moves on to the edge even as it returns to the centre".

The inner child

"In every human being there is a special heaven, whole and unbroken"

—Paracelsus

Completing these two theoretical chapters is this discussion of the inner child, beginning with the following true and moving story about the power and importance of connection with one's inner child:

> My friend Henry spent his whole life searching for some spiritual truth that would give his life meaning, filling two rooms of his family home with a wide assortment of books. He had read them all. Finally, he discovered Home Coming by John Bradshaw (1990), and spent the last three months of his life working through it, with the help and support of his wife Pauline, a committed Christian.
> After Henry's funeral, Pauline led me away from their family gathering into one of Henry's libraries and gave me the privilege of looking through

Henry's journal. I have a vivid and moving memory of reading letters from "Big Henry" to "Little Henry" and from "Little Henry" to "Big Henry". Through the relationship with his inner child, Henry had discovered his truth. He called this "Big W".

As he was dying, Henry said, "I can see them." Pauline asked him, "Who can you see?" In the midst of her grief, Henry's last words brought her joy, "The Father, the Son, and the Holy Spirit."

The Child of Self

Here is another true story. About six days after conception, the early embryo embeds itself into the inner wall of the mother's womb. I may have to begin the story this far back, because primal wounding can happen in the womb, such as when the mother is addicted to drugs or alcohol.

With that proviso, physically an embryonic infant dwells in the mother's womb unspoilt. Psychologically they dwell in the womb of Self whole and unbroken; the embryonic infant is all spirit, limitless potential. The shutters of the Higher and Lower Unconscious do not exist. In the womb of Self, the embryonic infant is wholly Self, primed to spend a lifetime giving birth to herself or himself. This is the Child of Self.

The Child of History

Then, the infant is born, to suffer the attendant woundings of being in the world of experience, squirming to feel loved, adapting to the quality of holding and mirroring they receive to secure their survival. They create the closing shutters of the Higher and Lower Unconscious, curbing their spirit, limiting their potential. They sacrifice the life they might have had to save what life they can. This is the Child of History.

Self-realisation

Yes, it is a self-betrayal, albeit an involuntary and inevitable one, even though its purpose is survival. Yet, this self-betrayal is not only to secure the survival of the Child of History, but also to protect in secret the infant's inviolable essential nature, the Child of Self, who remains ever-present throughout their life's unfolding journey.

Writing about the inner child, Joan Evans (2005) says, "The unseen mystery-laden essential Self can never be fully known as it is always unfolding in the process of becoming more itself", and further, "Self, immanent throughout, aims towards the realisation of its own specific and unique 'goals'. This is known ... as Self-realisation".

Yes, an infant sacrificing the life they might have had is both self-betrayal and alienation from their source of being, Self, who yet remains at once unseen and immanent. Self-realisation affords a process of redemption for this betrayal and a way back to Self. Self-realisation is a lifetime return journey of the Child of History to the Child of Self.

The inner child in therapy

The inner child is a familiar presence in therapy, when a client touches their vulnerability, often finding the experience uncomfortable, even intolerable. Often, the client is hostile towards this aspect of themselves and wants to be rid of it.

> In the One Thousand and One Nights tale, "The Fisherman and the Jinnee", the fisherman nets a yellow copper bottle, from which he releases a massive jinnee, who threatens to kill him. For the first 100 years in the bottle, the jinnee had said to himself, "I will bestow eternal riches on he who sets me free," and for the next 100 years, "I will open up the buried treasures of the earth for he who sets me free," then he threw himself into a rage, swearing, "I will kill the man who sets me free."

It sometimes seems to me that this reflects the experience of the inner child, isolated, alienated and massively angry to be left so alone for so long. There have been times, in cushion work with an inner child, when a client has visualised their inner child as being in a cell or a cage. I have often done a guided visualisation in which a client journeys as an adult to see their inner child playing on a beach or in a playground. Beforehand, I brief the client to wait and to allow the child to come to them. In many cases, the child appears hostile towards their adult self, ignoring them or being reluctant to engage with them.

It can take time and patience to overcome anger and mutual hostility between a client and their inner child, and to help them form a relationship. Such a relationship, once established, is invariably rewarding in terms of self-compassion, self-knowledge, and the integration of personality, as the client comes to value the time they spend with their inner child.

It is likely that a young child—say up to the age of seven—still lives in the environment of their primal wounding, a wound reinforced by subsequent, ongoing empathic failures. Thus, when a client makes a deep connection with their inner child, they are close to the trauma of primal wounding, the genesis of their ensuing survival personality. In inner child work, we are in the presence of the Child of History, and might even snatch glimpses of the Child of Self.

Thinking about the inner child uncovers a further facet of the Circle of Mirrors. The deep self-revealing nature of work around the dark mirror (Figure 7.3), especially its western side, serves to create empathy with the client's Child of History. Working around the light mirror (Figure 7.4) serves to illuminate for the client the next stretch of their return journey to the Child of Self.

CHAPTER EIGHT

Approaches to the deep psyche: active imagination and dreams

Introduction and scope

In his book *Healing Intelligence*, Alan Mulhern (2012) indicates the methods available to a psychotherapist practising with a spiritual dimension. He includes: active imagination, dream work, experiential focusing, and the practice of meditation. This chapter considers active imagination and dream work.

Mulhern further includes, "light trance states, which bypass the ego and lie between wakefulness and sleep (p. 5)". This is essentially what a shamanic journey is. In fact, Mulhern makes reference to shamanic practices (pp. 47–48):

> In the second half of the [twentieth] century it became possible to access an extensive literature on the world's religions and healing traditions such as shamanism, Eastern philosophies, and spiritual practices, which became better known in the West.
>
> We have become aware, for example, that shamanistic techniques, still in use in some parts of the world, are among the most ancient healing and spiritual practices we know of. As practitioners

become aware of the long healing traditions they may learn more from them.

However, beyond these tantalising statements, Mulhern makes no further reference to the psychotherapeutic application of these long healing shamanic traditions. It is my aim in subsequent chapters, respectfully, to make these ancient, shamanic healing and spiritual practices available to a psychotherapist or counsellor practising with a spiritual dimension.

This chapter and Chapter Nine look at four ways of approaching the unconscious or "deep psyche" in psychotherapeutic work with a spiritual dimension: active imagination, work with dreams, the shamanic journey, and soul retrieval. These approaches are all about the use of imagination. These two chapters consider what else these approaches have in common as well as what distinguishes each approach. The use of imagination—including not only inner sight, but also inner hearing, taste, smell, touch, together with visceral and kinaesthetic senses—is one of the foundation stones of Soulfulness.

Active imagination: an overview

This chapter, about the psychotherapeutic use of the extended active imagination technique, is a digest of "*Guided imagery: A psychosynthesis approach: History and manual for practitioners*" by Martha Crampton (1974 and second revised edition 2005, plus two articles 1969 and 1975), plus my explicit commentary and illustrations. In preparing her manual on the use of active imagination in psychosynthesis psychotherapy, Martha Crampton drew on the experience of other workers in the field of mental imagery practice, principally Andre Virel (1965) and Roger Frétigny.

Crampton begins her book by pointing out how humankind has long sought contact with the deeper and higher realms of the psyche through activities involving mental imagery, citing the Native American vision quest, through which, in a place of isolation, by "fasting, flagellation and other austerities", a young man seeks a vision of his totem animal. Thankfully, such privations are not a requirement of the imagery work described in the present chapter.

Quoting Karl Jung (1921), she describes active imagination as "one of the highest forms of psychic activity. For here the conscious and unconscious personality of the subject flow together into a common product in which both are united". It is this flowing together of conscious with unconscious that characterises the practice of active imagination and that she elucidates in her writing.

The client–guide relationship

Balancing a subjective and objective stance

Crampton emphasises the importance of the guide maintaining a subjective, non-verbal relation with the client during an extended imagery activity. It helps the client to relax and to feel secure when they sense a positive and attentive attitude on the part of the guide.

At the same time, it is important for the guide, whilst remaining caring and empathic, to keep a certain attitude of detachment, neutrality and objectivity, and to be accepting of whatever emerges, "without getting flustered by unusual happenings or by experiences that may be frightening" to the client. Calm and confidence on the part of the guide will be transmitted to the client and support them in facing their challenge with courage.

A non-directive approach

An extended active imagination procedure needs to be as non-directive as possible, with little intervention from the guide. This allows scope for the spontaneous unfoldment of images, and other sensual experiences, from the client's deep psyche into their consciousness. It seems evident from reading Crampton's book, however, that she expects a client to vocalise their experiences during the imagery procedure rather than encountering the flow of images and feelings in silence.

The guide can employ interventions that help to unfold the process without directing it; for example, by asking the client to describe the figures appearing in the imagery and what these figures are feeling, thinking, or doing. When the client seems to be stuck, the guide might use such non-directive interventions as, "Watch your mind screen and tell me what is happening," or "Just stay with this image until you sense some change," or "What seems to want to happen now?"

Level of directivity

From the work of Virel and Frétigny, Crampton distinguishes four levels of directivity on the part of the guide:

1. The non-directed approach, in which the imagery is allowed to unfold freely without intervention from the guide.
2. Supported imagery, in which the role of the guide is confined to supporting and reassuring the subject when they become anxious, suggesting means of psychic protection.
3. Non-directive questioning, aimed at helping the client remain in touch with important elements of their imagery, such as asking them to describe something that has emerged in more detail, or explore the place where it emerged, or follow up dramatic possibilities.
4. Directed imagery, such as a guided visualisation, in which the guide channels the client's flow of imagery. For me, the guidance needs to be sufficiently light to allow the client's own images to flow through.

Principles of active imagination

This section sets out the principles underlying the use of extended active imagination in a psychotherapeutic context. In particular, it indicates how these principles align with those of psychosynthesis psychology and practice.

The wisdom of the creative unconscious

A hallmark of the psychosynthesis approach to the application of active imagination is its profound respect for the wisdom of the creative unconscious. This is reflected in allowing the spontaneous unfoldment of the client's imagery and in the relatively non-directive attitude of the guide, and follows from the psychosynthesis concept of a spiritual essence, Self, which serves to direct the integration of the personality over time (Assagioli, 1965). The guide places trust in the wisdom of Self to allow unconscious material to emerge at a pace and time that is fitted to the client's developmental needs. It is the work of the guide to support this unfolding process with the care, gentleness and patience that respect for the psyche requires.

Every image is part of the psyche

A basic principle in the use of extended active imagination, again very much in line with psychosynthesis, is that all aspects of the imagery, every object that emerges, every figure whether a human, animal or imaginary creature, is the product of the client's psyche and represents some meaningful aspect of their deep psychology.

Thus, when an antagonistic figure appears, such as a wicked demon on the imaginal plane or a Severe Critic subpersonality, the goal is not to rid the psyche of that figure, but to seek its transformation. Crampton points out, "to destroy a figure in the imagery is symbolically to destroy some part of oneself, and may produce reactive guilt and depression (p. 15)". Equally, where conflict becomes manifest between different parts of the personality, such as when subpersonalities are at odds, the goal is to seek reconciliation and integration.

Active imagination and will

For Martha Crampton, there is an important principle that is particular to psychosynthesis: for the wisdom available through the unconscious to bring healing to the client's soul, more is needed than simply bringing unconscious contents into the light of consciousness. It is vital to go further, and to help the client assume responsibility for what the work of active imagination reveals, and to train and use their will to integrate these insights into their life and their experience of living (Assagioli, 1973). Crampton concurs with the emphasis that Jung gave to the "ethical imperative" to live up to insights gained in working with imagery.

Crampton has a telling metaphor, "Knowledge without congruent action, just like unassimilated food, may actually be toxic to a person and stir up a backlash from the unconscious". The techniques of active imagination need to be employed hand in hand with active techniques to ground the imagery and to help the client relate their imaginal experience to their everyday life and to harness their will to change.

Active imagination and integration of personality

Crampton points out that in psychosynthesis the guide must always maintain what I term dual vision: on the one hand, the guide seeks to understand and address the client's immediate issue and help them towards a resolution; on the other hand, the guide looks beyond the immediate issue to reflect on what may be emerging in the client's psyche and what movement may be seen beyond the present stage towards higher levels of integration. "Mental imagery techniques", she writes, "provide an excellent means of getting in touch with positive and transforming symbols that point to the person's next stage of development".

During my psychosynthesis psychotherapy training, I was taught a dynamic model of the psyche, the Triphasic Model of Psychospiritual Development (Joan Evans, n.d.), which the guide uses to seek to maintain a *triple vision* of the client's unfolding psychic development. In my MA thesis (England, 1998), I summarised this model in three sentences:

Ego is built by mirroring.
"I" is attained through self-reflection.
Self is realised by the individual seeing through to the universal.

Building ego: In some cases, the images emerging in active imagination work can serve to build and strengthen a client's ego.

Attaining 'I': Just the very practice of active imagination can help a client to attain a greater sense of "I", of their personal self, and thus a capacity to be self-reflective, to be wilful, and to make conscious choices.

Realising Self: Sometimes, the images emerging, as Crampton indicates, can be transforming symbols reflecting higher values and spiritual insights and point the client beyond their individual being towards a greater oneness and the realisation of Self.

Establishing the ground rules for active imagination work

Martha Crampton discusses the importance of explaining some ground rules to a client before embarking for the first time upon a journey of active imagination work.

1. The world of imagination is very different from the day-to-day world. In the imaginal realm the normal laws of nature do not apply, so we may find we can breathe under water, speak with animals,

fly through the air, or we may encounter creatures of fantasy. In one shamanic journey that I undertook I climbed on a dragon's back. In the imaginal realm, be ready for anything to happen.

2. Attaining a relaxed state of mind is a necessary preliminary to active imagination work. It may be difficult at first to let go of the conditioning, by Western culture, to maintain tight rational control. We need to be assured that with patience, practice and mindful focus upon the breath the skill of deep relaxation can be attained, and that by letting go to our depth process "a new trust in our inner wisdom and in the power for healing and evolution at the core of our being" can be acquired.

3. Every image that emerges in an active imagination procedure, whether an object, animal, person, or figure of fantasy, represents some aspect of ourselves and is a message in image form from our deep psyche to our conscious mind.

4. Moreover, these imaginal messages are of the essence of the active imagination process. They are not simply to be interpreted by the mind—much less by the guide—but to be reflected upon intellectually and emotionally in dialogue with the guide, to be sat with and mulled over so that their insights can be absorbed into our conscious experience of life.

5. Thus, following an active imagination procedure, guide and client together need to spend some time grounding the procedure.

Grounding the imagery procedure

Crampton concurs with Virel and Frétigny in advocating that the client be asked to write an account of the imagery that unfolded and the feelings they experienced. The guide and client explore this material, so as to help the client appreciate what has unfolded and to consider how the new insights can effectively be integrated into their daily life. Virel and Frétigny advocate that the guide take note of those aspects of the imagery work coming out in discussion that the client "repressed or failed to record" in their written account, as this may indicate deeply repressed material that the guide needs to keep in mind. Subsequently, the guide has the responsibility to help the client to evoke in their daily life their will to live up to insights gained in the active imagination procedure.

Combining active imagination with other techniques

Crampton emphasises that in psychosynthesis the extended active imagination procedure is only one of a repertory of psychotherapeutic techniques available to the guide. Moreover, even within an active imagination procedure the client may spontaneously take the work in a different direction. The skill of the guide is to combine active imagination with other techniques according to the context of each client session and to be sensitive to the spontaneous flow of the session.

For me, techniques that fit well with the active imagination procedure include: brief imagery, dream work, subpersonality work, inner child work, work with the will and development of "I", and Assagioli's approach to the balance and synthesis of opposites (Assagioli, n.d.).

Resonant stories and poems

I have a collection of poems and stories that can resonate with a client and can offer a distillation of their immediate experience in their current concern. Examples of poems are "I will not die an unlived life" by Dawna Markova (2000) (reproduced in Chapter Three) and "The journey" by Mary Oliver (1986). I often use the latter with clients when they are going through a time of spiritual crisis, change, and transformation.

Examples of stories are the "Chest of Drawers" story in the Foreword and my version of the Vasilisa and Baba Yaga tale (England, 1998), which is based on the Russian story *Vasilisa the Beautiful* by Afanas'ev (1945).

The practice of active imagination

The setting

At the start of a client session, the guide listens attentively to the concerns that the client brings. If it seems to the guide that an extended active imagination procedure would address these concerns, this is offered to the client. Inviting the client to enter into the activity acknowledges their autonomy and immediately engages their will to make a choice and thereby to take responsibility for their own inner work.

It is essential to consider the setting for extended active imagination. The client needs to be comfortable on a couch or reclining chair and footstool, with cushions available and a blanket to keep them warm, with the lighting dimmed and an eyeshade available.

Relaxing the client

When the client is comfortable, they are invited to take a few minutes to relax, to clear the mind, and to follow the flow and rhythm of their breathing, without seeking to change it. Crampton places less emphasis on relaxation than Virel and Frétigny, since she considers most clients to be able to access deep and meaningful levels of experience without extensive relaxation procedures. I, on the other hand, concur with Virel's and Frétigny's emphasis on preliminary relaxation as a pathway to deeper levels of the psyche; in a deeply relaxed state of consciousness the client becomes less aware of their physical body and more identified with their "imaginal body": the inner analogue of their physical senses—sight, hearing, taste, smell and touch, together with visceral and kinaesthetic senses. By way of illustration, I made a shamanic journey in which I became a mole. Being underground without sight, I experienced my inner touch and kinaesthetic senses.

My approach is to employ directed imagery as an "induction", to help the client attain a deeply relaxed state of consciousness, using images of the breath, deep roots, and pure healing light. The client may need to practise letting go into deep relaxation and connection with their imaginal body before proceeding further with active imagination work.

Images and themes of departure

Crampton refers to images or themes of departure, such as: a meadow, climbing a mountain, following the course of a stream, visiting a house, or an ideal personality of the same gender. An image or theme of departure is the starting point of the client's journey into deeper levels of their psyche. An image of departure would be an agreed seed image with which to commence an imagery procedure. A theme of departure would be more directive, possibly to the extent of being a guided visualisation.

Some images and themes popularly used in psychosynthesis imagery work (Joan Evans, 2007) are set out below in relation to the three levels of Assagioli's model of the psyche, the Egg Diagram, which is described in Chapter Six.

Higher Unconscious images

- The Sun, Warmth, a Star, Light: these can be symbols of protection and transformation and are useful images to use alongside the rhythm of the breath for inducing a deeply relaxed state of consciousness, as well as for psychic protection.
- A mountain: travelling to and climbing a mountain can symbolise a person's relationship with higher values and with Self.
- A wise person or wise being can be a symbol of inner wisdom and a reflection of Self.
- A temple can be a symbol of interiorisation, taking the person into the dwelling of Self.

Middle Unconscious images

- A meadow can symbolise the time of innocence before any trauma was experienced. This is a neutral starting point for an imagery procedure, suggesting a return to nature and a new beginning or renewal. Also, the meadow is a place of retreat if images become too fearful and protective symbols are needed.
- The river of life represents the flow of psychic energy and the obstacles that impede its flow. Explore the depth and breadth of the river and the clarity of the water.
- A house reflects a person's perception of their own personality. Explore the contents, the size and architecture of the house and the relationship between its inner spaces.
- A horse and riding a horse can be a symbol of a person's will.

Lower Unconscious images

- A cave, or under the sea, or an old treasure chest—these are places from which to explore repressed images.

Sometimes, it is useful to suggest to a client a general image or theme of departure such as these. Sometimes, various images can be combined into a guided visualisation; for example, start in a meadow; ride a horse to a mountain; climb the mountain, where there is a temple; enter the temple; meet a wise person and ask a question about a current concern; receive a token from the wise person, an image to denote the answer; return on the horse to the meadow.

Often, however, it is less directive for the client to suggest an image of departure, maybe an image related to a concern that they have, or an image that has arisen naturally in prior therapy work, or an image that has arisen in a previous active imagination procedure that warrants further exploration.

Guiding the active imagination procedure

Flowing with the process

For Crampton, the guide needs to be sensitive and intuitive in their conduct of an active imagination procedure and be willing to flow with the process. For example, the guide may be prompted to make a response they do not rationally understand, yet it may prove effective to follow such a prompting. For example, I said to an experienced client in the middle of a session, "From what you have said I would normally do some subpersonality work with you, but I feel reluctant to do so." Immediately, the client burst into tears, said that she felt seen and heard, and so, with an increased sense of trust and confidence, the work moved to a deeper level.

At the same time, the client needs to be free to reject any of the guide's suggestions about the conduct of the procedure. As Crampton points out, clients have a way of sensing when a suggestion will steer them away from what they need to be experiencing, and this in itself may be a sign of the client's growing autonomy and increasing will and responsibility for the direction of their own process.

Flowing with the process means following the client's flow of imagery in a non-directive way. For example, when the client is pursuing a particular imagery sequence and suddenly—as happens in dreams—switches to another, this is not to be taken as avoidance, but as evidence of the psyche's wisdom in taking the client where they need to go.

Using supportive mental imagery

To alleviate any anxiety arising on the part of the client during an imagery procedure, the guide can support the client by using symbols of psychic protection, such as wrapping the client in an envelope of healing light or returning them to the meadow.

Virel and Frétigny propose measures that are context dependent: if the client is in a dark cave, the guide can suggest he has a flashlight; if the client feels in psychic danger, the guide can suggest that they have a sword; if they feel helpless, they could have a magic wand.

Not automatically rejecting an image

Because every image emerging is the product of the client's psyche, and something within the client knows the meaning of the image, it is essential not to reject any image that appears. On the contrary, the guide needs to help the client to explore the image long enough for its meaning to be revealed or for a transformation to take place. It is sometimes helpful for the client to "become" the image in order to grasp its meaning, which can be done using symbolic identification.

Using symbolic identification to aid integration

Symbolic identification means imagining one is the image in order to see things from the image's perspective. Crampton asserts that identifying with protagonists in the imagery, especially frightening or powerful figures, serves in transforming negative energy and integrating psychic elements. Crampton provides an illustration (p. 20):

> One student saw an image of his mother sixty feet tall and made of cement. He was unable to find a way to reach her as long as he remained in his own skin. His voice did not carry that far and the elevator he tried installing did not function. It was suggested in this case that he actually become the mother. In doing this he connected with the mother's pain. She was humanised in his eyes and gradually became smaller until she was human size.

When the client is silent for a long period

A guide's sensitivity, intuition and tact are probably stretched to the limit when a client does not communicate for a protracted period. This is particularly the case during an active imagination procedure, if the client is expected to be giving a running commentary on their experiences, images, and feelings.

Crampton tends not to allow a client's silence to drag on too long, unless she feels the client is experiencing a particularly intense and moving experience that they need time to absorb. Otherwise, where she feels the client has lost focus or has hit resistance, she will ask a neutral question such as, "What are you experiencing now?" or "What is happening now?" in order to help the client to refocus. If she feels the client has become fatigued, she will terminate the active imagination part of the session.

When threatening beings emerge in the imagery

Crampton considers the situation where a threatening or aggressive figure emerges in the imagery. On the principle that everything emerging in the imagery is the product of the client's psyche and represents some meaningful aspect of the psyche—and to destroy such a figure would be to destroy some part of themselves and may produce reactive guilt and depression—Crampton's approach is to seek reconciliation and integration of the threatening figure. She suggests interventions such as, "Is there a way you could establish communication with this creature?" or "Is there anything that either of you wants to express to the other?"

Equally, negative feelings towards something appearing in the imagery need not be suppressed but rather acknowledged and expressed, otherwise the imagery becomes shallow and its flow becomes blocked. The principle of trusting the wisdom of the creative unconscious means that whatever emerges in the imagery is revealed for a purpose and needs to be received and accepted positively and its meaning made the subject of reflection and exploration.

When confrontation arises between antagonistic elements

On a related issue, Crampton regards it as a major challenge to the guide when confrontation arises between figures in the imagery. She advocates reminding the client of the principle that everything emerging in the imagery is the product of the client's psyche, and actively intervening to direct the work towards achieving communication and integration between the conflicting figures.

For me, such active intervention means following the principle of combining the active imagination procedure with such other techniques as are helpful in working with conflicting figures, such as subpersonality work and Assagioli's method for the balance and synthesis of opposites (See his paper, "The balancing and synthesis of the opposites"), which involves searching for a place of synthesis that transcends the opposites whilst including their essential qualities.

Terminating an active imagination procedure

Throughout the imagery procedure the client may remain in a deeply relaxed state of consciousness. For me, it is important for the guide to be slow and gentle in bringing the client back into normal consciousness. This means letting the client know the imagery procedure is coming to an end so they can round off the imagery in their own way. Then, after a pause, and if it is relevant, to suggest they return to the place from which they began; in a guided visualisation this is likely to be the meadow. After another pause, invite them, in their own time, to come back into the room and own their eyes. Allow a further pause before any discussion of whatever transpired, making sure the client has returned to normal consciousness.

The guide and the client need to discuss and agree when the client is going to write their account of the imagery procedure. Ideally, this account is best completed within the session whilst still fresh.

Crampton considers it desirable for the active imagination procedure to last no more than 45 minutes. I think this is too long, if the client's account is to be completed within the session. However, 45 minutes still leaves time in the session to do at least some grounding work and to round off the session in a positive way; this means conferring with the client before the end of the session to ensure that they feel there has been adequate discussion and grounding of whatever emerged, at least until the next session.

Grounding an active imagination procedure

Grounding the imagery procedure involves the guide helping the client to search for what is meaningful for them in whatever unfolded, to relate their understanding of the material to their daily life, and to evoke their will to make choices about how to bring the new insights into their life. Crampton suggests the use of the "as if" technique in which the client imagines themselves acting as if they possessed desired qualities suggested by the imagery, then affirming these qualities with a firm voice.

Furthermore, I consider it is of particular benefit to the client for the guide to maintain triple vision, as discussed above, during the grounding process as guide and client review the emerging images. Here is an illustration:

Ego is built by mirroring:

> A client, Rhiannon, in a young adulthood crisis, enters therapy feeling vulnerable and anxious, with persistent and groundless fears that her boyfriend will be unfaithful and abandon her. After a few weeks in therapy building trust and creating a sense of safety for Rhiannon, she says that when her boyfriend fails to respond promptly to her texts she goes into "meltdown". I invite her to put "meltdown" on a cushion and say what she sees: a nine-year-old-girl curled up in a ball feeling sad and dejected and wanting to be loved.
>
> After two years of therapy, Rhiannon is feeling vulnerable despite a good holiday in Morocco with her boyfriend. I invite her to do an active imagination procedure, a journey through a meadow, riding to a mountain, meeting a wise person in a temple at the top of the mountain, receiving a gift. Though I have suggested the journey, my interventions are minimal.
>
> The horse Rhiannon rides is black and shiny. She meets a tall wise man a few years older than her. He leads her around the temple, which is all made of mirrors. For his gift to her, he hands her a hand mirror.
>
> In the grounding, Rhiannon observes how she normally doesn't like to see herself in a mirror, but in the temple it is fine. We discuss the crucial importance of mirroring for a small child. She recalls the people in her life who have been authentic mirrors for her. She speaks of no longer feeling vulnerable but of feeling powerful.

"I" is attained through self-reflection:

> After a two year gap, Rhiannon returns to therapy. For several weeks we mainly work with her inner child, Tiny. Then, she speaks of finding her present office job unsatisfying and unfulfilling. I invite her to repeat the active imagination procedure, climbing a mountain to meet her wise person. This time, the wise person gives her two tokens, a golden globe and an empty notebook.
>
> In the grounding work, first Rhiannon speaks of training in Reiki, being interested in an employment that exercises her intuitive and personal skills.

Her first impulse, then, seems to be to leap straight into thinking about a new career without first fully exploring her sense of purpose implicit in the imagery.

As we open the wise person's gifts, the meaning they have for her emerges: the golden globe offers a world of opportunities to shine, and the empty book is for her to write the unfolding story of her life. The golden globe and the empty notebook together represent a purpose for her life at a high level, to discover her unique calling at this point in her life.

Her continuing psychological work involves developing her self-reflective awareness, so as to become mindful of various ways this purpose might be given practical meaning; developing her "I", to equip her to apply her will to choose a vocation in accordance with her sense of purpose and values (for more about this process, see Assagioli's The Act of Will).

Self is realised by the individual seeing through to the universal:

Rhiannon has made good use of her two periods of psychotherapy in the way she recognises the need for change and so has developed psychologically and spiritually. Rhiannon is still a young woman. I feel confident that with her self-understanding and her capacity for self-reflection she will continue to grow psychologically and spiritually. So that when she reaches a spiritual crisis later in her life, she will again recognise the need for change and be willing to see beyond her individual being towards a greater oneness and the realisation of Self.

Communication between conscious and unconscious levels of the mind

The active imagination procedure provides an effective approach to the integration and improved communication between conscious and unconscious levels of the psyche, because in their deeply relaxed state of consciousness during the procedure the client has simultaneous access to both levels. The client can be in contact with products of the deep psyche, including higher values and spiritual experience, whilst with their conscious mind and will they can act upon these products.

Thus, the realm of imagination, "one of the highest forms of psychic activity", provides a bridge across which "the conscious and unconscious personality [of the client] flow together into a common product in which both are united", serving as a powerful element in the development and integration of the client's personality.

Dreams

Discussing the best way of working with the contents of the deep psyche, Mulhern quotes Jung as saying that dreams are unsuitable or difficult to make use of, because the demands on the client are too great. I take this point. These demands clearly are that the client is required to remember and record their dreams for use in therapy. Moreover, although recording and reflecting upon one's dreams can be insightful, Mulhern points out that many visionary experiences of the inner world may not fully reach consciousness; on awakening we remember little of our dream world. Thus, for Mulhern, however interesting and insightful dream work can be, as a therapeutic tool it is also random and hit and miss.

On the other hand, recording and reflecting on my own dreams has provided me with significant insights into my inner world. At the height of a spiritual crisis, I kept a dream journal charting the progress of this time of turmoil and change. I was able to take my dreams into my personal psychotherapy. A sequence of dreams from this period is quoted below, as recorded at the time, unedited, in chronological order, together with my subjective and psychospiritual interpretations, in some cases interpretations contemporary with the dreaming.

I include this material here in order to demonstrate just how insightful dream work can be, because I aim to show in the next chapter how the shamanic journey provides a technique for simulating a dream state with the advantages of consistency and focus: a shamanic journey can be undertaken in a client session whenever appropriate; the "dream" is entered with a clear intention of exploring a specific issue; the client enters a focused, conscious state—albeit an "altered state"; the client is able to report their experience of the journey immediately afterwards, enabling the journey to be a source of reflection while still fresh.

Personal dream record

Here is my dream record as my dreams unfolded during my spiritual crisis:

> I dream that I am visiting a coastal town. I am being shown around the town by a man, someone I do not know outside the dream. Between the buildings, down side streets off the main street, I can see waves. We are near the sea.

One wave is huge, a tidal wave. The man tells me to run. We run away from the sea, with the tidal wave catching up behind us. We run down a wide street at right angles to the main street. There are benches fixed to the ground, a little bent. The man tells me to grab hold of one of the benches and let the wave roll over. He says I will be all right. I run towards the bench. The dream ends before I am engulfed.

Subjective interpretation now: I am in danger of being overwhelmed. I am advised by a wise person, an inner part of myself, who tells me to turn from my present path and run at right angles, where I can be grounded enough to survive engulfment. *Psychospiritual interpretation now:* I am directed and guided by Self.

I dreamed I was on a journey. At a railway station. I did not know whether I was travelling by air or train. When I got to the ticket desk, I could not remember where I was going. When I woke I felt panic.

Subjective interpretation now: This type of frustrated travel dream was common at this time. It speaks to the inner turmoil and uncertainty about the way my life needed to go. In this dream, I am alone, with no wise person to help me. *Psychospiritual interpretation now:* The inescapable inner turmoil is, in and of itself, the movement towards Self-realisation.

Travel problems. I vaguely remember a railway station. Then I am in this street in an old part of the town. All the buildings are old. Some are more or less knocked down. I am to meet someone. There is a particular place, a street or house, involved in this meeting. I think that is where we are to go after meeting. I cast about looking for this place. It is around here some-where, but I cannot find it. I am anxious. I do not find the place. I wait. Within the dream, I know: *I am trying to find myself.* It is not easy. I feel the panic.

I am met and taken down a subway. We emerge from the subway into another land, another state of being, like heaven, with lots of colourful peo-ple enjoying themselves. It is like a carnival. It is entered through an arch, into a great bowl of enjoyment.

Subjective interpretation now: This begins as another frustrated travel dream. The state of the old buildings speaks to the state of my psyche, in need of renewal. The telling insight within the dream is "I am trying to find myself". Then, there is a turning point. My inner wise person meets me and takes me via a subway into the Higher Unconscious, to show me another state of being that I might attain, which is vividly realised in the dream.

Psychospiritual interpretation now: The admission, "I am trying to find myself", at the turning point of the dream, indicates the will to align with Self, and a vision of the life that my renewed psyche might experience living.

> Dream. Old building. I am in an old building. I work there. Everything is very decrepit. It is late. I am going soon. There is a box I am working on. I am going to take it with me. To get out I know I have to go down an old staircase, steep, to a back door. I see it in my mind in the dream.
>
> Before I leave, I have to set some kind of old burglar alarm with an ancient bell. I feel confusion about the setting of the alarm. Anyway, I pick up the box and walk out of the door of the office. Instead of the old stair and door, I am in a wide concourse with many people walking purposefully through it. It is in a huge building of grey stone, with a high roof supported on massive classical columns. It too is an old building, but in a good state, spacious, cool, clean.
>
> The stone is grey, the people in grey clothing, but the place feels good, wholesome, busy, purposeful. *I am part of them. They are part of me.* At this point I wake up. I get up, go to my desk, and write brief notes. Then back to bed and sleep. It is 5:20am.

Subjective interpretation then: The building is my present life, run down. But there is something I want to take with me, something I have worked on and learnt. I am frightened of leaving—the procedures I have to go through, the appalling stair and door. But when I determine to do it, it is not like I imagine.

Psychospiritual interpretation now: I knew it was coming, this wilful act of walking out of the door into a good, new place within myself, experienced so powerfully in the dream: spacious, cool, clean, wholesome, busy, purposeful—a place of higher values. The words "I am part of them. They are part of me" show a deep disidentification from what was decrepit in my psyche and an identification with this good, new place. Even more than this, with the presence of other people in this place, the statement "I am part of them. They are part of me" seems to touch upon the collective unconscious.

Dream. I am with Bob in a town. We are looking for the same old building. We work there. There are streets of terraced houses. We drive through the town. We stop at a house, and walk up a staircase. It is a long, wide, straight staircase, old and ruinous, and there are doors off to the right and left, but I fail to find the doorway I am looking for. I am concerned.

At this point, Bob produces a company brochure that he has prepared. We are suddenly by the side of a river, on the embankment, by the wall. Bob rests the brochure on the wall, and the brochure gives us access to our new office, very smart and modern, with pine walls, pine chairs, and a pine coffee table.

There is a group around the coffee table, colleagues. There is animated discussion about what work people should do. There is argument and the expression of disappointment.

I am distracted by another brochure Bob has done. It is a fold out. On the front there are drawings of luggage. It is some kind of Quality Assurance brochure aimed at wives. It says on the front "How you can plan your vacation without the pressure of dates", and an arrow that goes over the page to the words, Plan Ahead. The dream is enormously detailed, even down to the printer's logo on the brochure.

Subjective interpretation then: More searching. More looking for myself. In the end, I am taken. I cannot get there by my own efforts alone. The new office is a good place to be, but there is conflict, a reminder of my inner conflict. This is my conflict. The brochure is about quality, the quality of life, the preparation for travel, the enigmatic message, Plan Ahead.

Psychospiritual interpretation now: Whilst still sixth formers, my friends and I looked up to our friend Bob, who already had a salaried job in aerospace. Hence, in the dream, Bob is the one who knows the way, who can direct and guide me to the good, new place. He has even published a magical guidebook! How transpersonal is that? In response to some continuing inner conflict, Bob directs me to the importance of quality—of being fit for purpose—and to focusing on my future, "Plan Ahead". Oh, yes, so what about the "brochure aimed at wives"? I can only think it refers to the feminine side of me, much overlooked up to that time.

Two nights ago, a dream. I am walking down a wide street. I believe it to be my home town. The buildings are very old and magnificent. They are in a luxuriant Rococo style on the outsides, like nothing I have ever seen, except perhaps inside Italian churches. They are grand buildings, in stone, with flamboyant gold decoration, encrusted, like gold flame rising from the first floor to the flat roofs of the buildings.

All the buildings are being renewed. Some have barely started, and still look shabby, but very fine. Others have been completely renewed, with their gold work shining bright.

I am walking down the wide street, looking closely at the renewed buildings. On the outside their magnificence is restored. On the inside they have been completely rebuilt. The outsides do not feel like facades. Inside and outside harmonise. They seem to be business premises, busyness I feel, renewed and vigorous.

The drawing: My interpretation then: Now, I draw one of the buildings, with its gold encrusted decoration. Then I realise that the buildings are not decorated "like gold flame". What I see in the dream *are* flames. This is one of my mind's processed images. The yellow flames are reduced to a still image, enveloping the top part of the building.

It fascinates me that the mind presented a processed image, a static representation of flames, which I did not recognise in the dream, but which my cognitive processes were able to interpret when I was in a conscious state. What I see in the dream is the process of renewal, the burning out of the old, leaving a renewed, harmonised whole. This is working in me. But I am unconscious of it, except through this dream. The pain of it is remote, dispersed.

I dreamed another frustrated travel and buildings dream. I was travelling in a town. I was on a town road, not a motorway. It had intersecting streets and shabby old houses. I do not know where it was, except it was called Lily Road and it ended in a dead end with heaps of garbage cans. Just before I reached the end, I made a right turn into another road, a different road. Here there were tall, stately old buildings.

Subjective interpretation then: "'Why Lily Road?'" What comes into my mind is "lily livered road". Straight to the rubbish tip. I need a different road, a courageous road. Lilies are for death. *Psychospiritual interpretation now*: This is like a recapitulated summary of the previous dreams. The psyche is rapidly on its way to the rubbish tip, until just in time, as in the first dream about the tidal wave, a right angle puts the psyche on a different path, in this case a courageous road to the good, new place with tall, stately old buildings, the identification and alignment with Self.

The thrusting energy of dreams

I was immersed in my dream world during that period of turmoil and change. I find it interesting now to revisit the reflection below, which I wrote at the time in my dream journal, with its conclusion that dreams in their raw, unconscious form consist of a thrusting energy.

Night before last, two dream sequences that seemed to merge, though their content is quite different. In the first sequence, I was on some sort of sales visit with a colleague. All I remember is walking through a shopping mall, then being in a building. All I remember in the building is interminable corridors and elevators. I have dreamed of passages and elevators before. I remember a dream set in a department store which had an elevator at each corner.

In the second sequence, I am walking to my original home, after work. I am pushing something, a pram, but there is no baby in it. I am walking up a road that I think I know, and reach an area I think I know. It looks different. So, I ask a man where I am. He tells me where I am, and it is miles from where I think I am. He mentions a place called Chapel something. It strikes me that I have walked (from work is in my mind) in the wrong direction, still pushing the pram. I feel humiliation and shame.

I immediately awake, feeling awful. It is 5:20am. I am so affected that I am unable to get up on the alarm, and stay in bed until 7:00am.

While writing this, more memories come of other dreams. One where I cross and re-cross a city of huge stately buildings—I wrote "I city", then corrected it—another where I make long journeys by bicycle. I had these dreams some time ago, months I think. I wonder whether these are memories of past dreams, or whether they are momentary dreams I am having now. The sense I have, the image, is that the dream I am describing "touches a nerve", which runs down and activates other memories, maybe feelings, which I then experience.

So, there is a pattern of repeated dreams, or images of repeated dreams, with the same content, in different settings. Corridors and elevators. Travelling by bicycle or on foot or across "I city". There is an underlying theme, or structure, a bundle of energy, which is transformed into images as it crosses the edge of my consciousness. In its raw, unconscious form, it is not images, nor "seen through a glass, darkly". It is a thrusting energy.

Revisiting this reflection, I realise what a good insight this is, and a profound metaphor—the deep psyche as pure thrusting energy, working upon itself in a way that is directed and focused, and translating this energy into images that communicate with the conscious mind. The metaphor of pure thrusting energy resonates with Assagioli's concept of a spiritual essence, Self, which serves to direct the integration of the personality over time.

CHAPTER NINE

Approaches to the deep psyche: soul retrieval

Introduction and scope

This chapter, like the previous chapter, looks at four ways of using imagination to approach the deep psyche. Active imagination and dreams were discussed in the previous chapter. The shamanic journey and soul retrieval are discussed in the present chapter.

The shamanic journey

The shamanic journey has much in common with the extended active imagination technique discussed in the previous chapter; in particular, the principles of active imagination apply equally to the shamanic journey:

- The wisdom of the creative unconscious needs to be recognised.
- Every image is to be treated as part of the psyche. The exception to this principle is where trauma has resulted in an "attachment" (see Chapter Six); the handling of an attachment is discussed later in the present chapter.

- The client needs to be helped to assume responsibility for what the shamanic journey reveals.
- With shamanic work being about the integration of personality, the guide needs to maintain *triple vision*:

  Developing ego: ego is built by mirroring;
  Expanding personal self : "I" is attained through self-reflection;
  Realising Self: Self is realised by the individual seeing through to the universal.

- Ground rules need to be established with the client before undertaking a shamanic journey.
- Grounding is as important as the shamanic journey itself. The guide and client need to explore whatever emerged, so as to help the client appreciate what has unfolded and to consider how it can effectively be integrated into their daily life. Combining a shamanic journey with other techniques or introducing a relevant story or poem is often a beneficial part of the grounding process.

Ritual

The first distinguishing character of the shamanic journey is the use of a ritual setting.

Opening the door into the realm of imagination: Whilst Crampton (Crampton 2005 [1974]) places less emphasis on preliminary relaxation, I emphasise the value of using ritual to frame a shamanic journey in order to deepen the client's relaxation and intensify their experience.

In his book *Passages of the Soul, Ritual Today*, James Roose-Evans (1994) lends support to this approach. He sees ritual as a key that can open the door into the realm of imagination, and he writes, "To have imagination is to enjoy a richness of interior life, an uninterrupted flow of images. Without imagination we are cut off from the deeper reality of life, from our souls (p. 1)".

Seeing "spirituality" as the development of our innermost self, Roose-Evans says that ritual "works on two levels, that of the psychological and that of the spiritual. ... A ritual can resolve, at a deeper level than the intellect, some inner conflict, thereby releasing the individual from a psychological block (p. 9)".

Creating the Space: The first element of ritual for a shamanic journey involves dimmed lighting, with a candle burning as the client enters the space. I like the soft blush of a tea light in a Himalayan salt crystal holder. The burning candle offers to the client the experience of entering into a sacred, liminal space: the threshold of the depths of a human soul, which is always deserving of reverence.

Clearing the space: Having greeted the client, the next step is the ritual symbolic "clearing the space" of any residual negative energies. Traditionally, this is done by smudging the space around the client with burning dried sage. However, I prefer to use Tibetan cymbals, called tingsha, or a Nepalese singing bowl. The clear tones of these instruments symbolise a clarity and purity of space within which the journey is to be conducted.

A supportive presence: At this point, unless we have done this preparation work in a previous session, I quietly explain the ground rules; in detail for an unfamiliar client, in summary for an experienced client. We agree the intention of the journey. Then, I invite the client to take their place on a reclining chair and footstool, and to make themselves comfortable using cushions and a blanket. There is more to this than comfort. The client and I are no longer sitting opposite each other in dialogue. Although I shall be providing a supportive presence and beating the drum for the journey, the client will be journeying alone.

The induction: When the client is comfortable, I begin speaking the words of the induction, to help the client to feel secure and safe and to achieve a state of deep relaxation. Throughout the induction, I beat a slow rhythm on my medicine drum, further helping the client to relax. In this part of the ritual, both symbolically and experientially, the client turns from their customary external world to the threshold of their depth of soul.

The journey accompanied by the drum: The induction culminates in the client crossing the threshold, setting out from their place in nature to begin their journey. I increase my drumbeat to about 240 beats per minute, a frequency that serves to induce and maintain a simulated dream state in which the client's controlling ego is quiescent, allowing images to flow freely. Put another way, the drum is the "shaman's horse", symbolically carrying the client on their journey. Other than playing the medicine drum, I remain silently attentive throughout the client's journey, simply and symbolically holding the space.

The return: The next piece of the ritual is the change in drumbeat, calling the client back from their journey to their place in nature. Here, if I have briefed the client to bring back a token from their journey, I use my rattle to rattle the token, ritually and symbolically, into their heart. Finally, I gently invite the client, in their own time, to open their eyes and be present in the room.

The ritual nature of the shamanic journey suggests the use of the term "ceremony" rather than the more clinical term "procedure". Hence the expressions, shamanic journey ceremony, soul retrieval ceremony and soul deliverance ceremony are used in this book.

The shamanic psychological model of the psyche

The second distinguishing character of the shamanic journey is the shamanic universe. In her work on active imagination, Crampton refers to the use of an image or theme of departure as the starting point of the client's journey into deeper levels of their psyche. The equivalent of a theme of departure for a shamanic journey, in addition to its intention, is the shamanic universe.

There is a close kinship between the shamanic universe (Figure 9.1) and Assagioli's (1965) model of the psyche, the Egg Diagram (Figure 9.2), as discussed in Chapter Two and Chapter Six. Taken together, these models form a composite shamanic model of the psyche. They have in common the Lower World/Lower Unconscious, the Middle World/ Middle Unconscious, and the Upper World/Higher Unconscious. The Egg Diagram contributes the essential elements of Self and "I" or personal self.

Figure 9.1. The shamanic universe: our inner world.

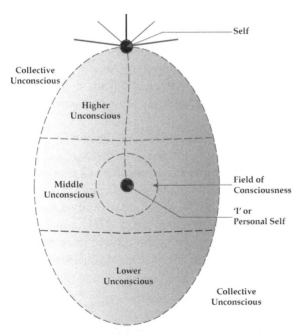

Figure 9.2. Assagioli's Egg Diagram: model of the psyche.

The imaginative theme running through this model is the presence of allies who accompany and support the client during their shamanic journey. In the Lower World/Lower Unconscious, the client's instinctual energies are typically personified as animal allies. In the Upper World/Higher Unconscious, the client's intuitive energies are typically personified as wise beings. Thus, the power of imagination is employed to recruit the client's natural positive psychic energies to support them throughout their journey. As they cross over from the deep psyche into consciousness, these energies are translated into images of animal allies and wise persons to communicate with the conscious mind.

This imaginative theme, with its images of supporters, animal allies and wise beings, appearing during the journey as images unfold, serves to provide an inner safety and security system—drawn from the client's natural, healthy psychic resources—to protect the client throughout their journey. Such protection is important because it is not possible to predict what will emerge during a journey and where an intention will lead; the intention may lead to the emergence of fearful creatures, the personified images of negative energies residing in the psyche. The supporters serve both to protect the client from such creatures and to help the client deal with them.

When a client becomes experienced in journeying, they often become familiar with their supporters, though they can still be surprised by the appearance of an unfamiliar supporter. An experienced traveller will often retain their relationship with, and rely on, their supporters in their day-to-day lives—these are, after all, an expression of their own positive psychic resources.

An introduction to the composite shamanic model of the psyche, animal allies and wise persons, and the importance of these, is an essential part of establishing clear ground rules prior to a shamanic journey. The concept of the composite shamanic model could be seen as imposing a structure or a constraint on the imagination. Rather, it is an imaginative theme of departure; once the client has met an animal ally or wise person, they have the limitless space and time of imagination in which to travel together wherever they need to go to fulfil the intention.

Soul retrieval

Soul retrieval is a way of communicating with the deep psyche in psychospiritual therapy. The client journeys into their inner world of imagination to meet with personified elements of their unconscious mind. In psychological terms, when a child is traumatised they typically remove the unbearable memory and/or experience of trauma through dissociation. The effect of dissociation is also to remove something of the child's vital essence, such as their sense of innocence or self-esteem. Instead, the child, and later the adult, is likely to feel, for example, a diffuse guiltiness or low self-esteem, even though they may have either no memory of the trauma or no memory of the feelings surrounding the trauma.

In shamanic terms, "dissociation" is called "soul loss", meaning loss of part of the person's soul energy and vital essence. A soul retrieval is a shamanic journey that has the specific intention of retrieving a lost part of the client's soul energy and restoring their vital essence, in the above example their sense of innocence or self-esteem. The psychotherapeutic value of soul retrieval is this:

> The journey into the imagination to retrieve what the client consciously lacks—their sense of innocence or self-esteem—offers an oblique route towards the underlying unconscious trauma, should the psyche in its wisdom accept the offer to reveal its secrets, often in the form of telling images.

When it is about exploring the past, the soul retrieval is typically a journey to the Lower World. In the journey, an animal ally escorts the client wherever they need to go to retrieve the client's lost soul energy. A soul retrieval may also be about exploring what the client's life might be—the meaning and purpose of their life. This is typically a journey to the Upper World. In the journey, the client meets with and receives guidance from a wise being. A Lower World journey is illustrated by the following case study.

Lionel is an intelligent, single man in his mid twenties. He is a registered social worker.

Lionel's father was verbally abusive, selfish, controlling, and intrusive. He opened Lionel's mail and listened in to his phone calls. He constantly shouted at him for imagined misdemeanours. Lionel speaks of the fear he felt of his father, and of his mother's chilling words, "Wait till your father gets home." Lionel's mother was utterly compliant and appeasing in relation to father.

Lionel presents for psychotherapy with depression. He says he feels ugly, uncomfortable in his own skin, worthless, inadequate, hopeless, and despairing. When faced with a social occasion, he collapses into a pit of despair and intolerably low self-worth, and withdraws into himself.

After a year in weekly psychotherapy, Lionel has learnt to be self-reflective and this has provided him with much greater self-awareness. He has insight into the childhood origins of his depression, yet he remains profoundly stuck and unable to connect with his will to change. Beneath his depression he suffers poor self-confidence, low self-worth, and most of all a limited sense of identity.

We agree to do a soul retrieval, with the intention of retrieving Lionel's lost sense of identity. I explain the ground rules. I guide Lionel through the induction and invite him to enter his safe place in nature, a sandy beach. I invite him to move to the portal and state his intention three times: "My Intention is to journey to the Lower World to retrieve my lost sense of identity." Then he begins his journey, entering the tunnel to the Lower World.

Emerging in the Lower World, Lionel looks around for his animal ally, a Lion, Lionel's namesake. He greets Lion. Lion escorts him to the house where Lionel grew up, where he observes a scene from his childhood, a scene that has never emerged before in the psychotherapy: after some minor misdemeanour, Lionel's father becomes enraged and embarks on a demeaning punishment. He removes all of Lionel's toys, takes down Lionel's posters and school art work from his bedroom wall. He even strips the Dennis the Menace duvet cover from his bed. He leaves only old worn clothes for Lionel to wear. He removes every last trace of Lionel's presence from the house, except for Lionel himself, and sends him to Coventry.

His mother does nothing to help Lionel and is forbidden to speak to him or even acknowledge his presence. He is given food and made to eat alone. Now, Lionel watches as his mother and father scream abuse at his younger self, until with a wave of the paw Lion silences them. The journey to retrieve Lionel's sense of identity has revealed to Lionel the underlying, dissociated traumatic experience that took away his sense of identity.

Lion reassures Lionel that his ordeal is over, and offers him a gift to symbolise his restored sense of identity and his transformation, a shining star. Lionel places the shining star in his heart.

The change of drum beat signifies the return from the journey. Lion and Lionel travel back to the mouth of the tunnel. Lionel thanks Lion and they bid one another goodbye. Lionel returns via the tunnel to the beach, where

I rattle the shining star firmly into his heart. Then he returns to the therapy room with the shining star, his restored sense of identity, in his heart.

In the next week's session, Lionel tells how, for several days after the soul retrieval, he had felt grief for what had happened to him as a child, a sadness that he realises he needs to feel. He has a sense both of something ending and something new, a change taking place. He feels genuinely in good spirits, not just a bounce back after feeling down. He says he has a new core feeling, a new experience of himself. He feels he can now contain the varied feelings of sadness and happiness, with a sense of his consistent self. He has a new experience of self-worth, grounded in his new sense of identity, a new sense of being.

As Lionel enters the therapy room for the following week's session, I am immediately struck by the difference in his whole looks and demeanour from how he had been just a few weeks earlier, before we had carried out the soul retrieval. He is visibly more upright, confident, and mature. His physical appearance radiates a grounded self-worth and sense of who he is.

Soul deliverance

An "attachment" is an alien energy lodging in the unconscious as a consequence of trauma—in psychological terms it is typically a projective identification that has been ingested into the psyche. Sometimes, the alien energy appears in a dream or the simulated dream state of a shamanic journey. As it crosses over from the deep psyche into consciousness, the alien energy is translated into images of nightmare creatures—scary monsters or demons that have form, character, and the power of speech.

In some cases an alien energy will intrude into a person's life in a tangible form; for example, a sexually traumatised client was troubled and frightened when she experienced an alien creature behind her, its hot breath on the back of her neck.

Just as recognition of what a client consciously lacks—their sense of innocence or self-esteem— offers an oblique route towards the underlying unconscious trauma, so the appearance of a demonic creature when in a dream state offers an oblique route towards the underlying attachment lodging in the deep psyche.

A principle in the use of active imagination is that each aspect of the imagery, every figure that emerges, is a product of the client's psyche, and the goal is not to rid the psyche of that figure, but to seek its transformation. Part of a guide's work, however, is to distinguish between a subpersonality, which is part of the client and capable of transformation, and an attachment that needs to be removed. "Soul deliverance" is a ceremony for removing an attachment; the soul is delivered from the grip of the attachment.

Mircea Eliade (1964), in his anthropological survey of shamanistic practices, refers to the practice of including both soul retrieval and "expelling the demons" as necessary to restoring a person to health.

> The cause of illness can be the intrusion of a magical object into the patient's body or his 'possession' by evil spirits; in this case, cure consists in extracting the harmful object or expelling the demons. Sometimes disease has a twofold cause—theft of the soul aggravated by 'possession' by evil spirits—and the shamanic cure includes both searching for the soul and expelling the demons.

Soul deliverance is illustrated by the following case study, in which a variation of the shamanic journey is employed. Walter was born into a poor working-class family. On leaving school, he apprenticed as a miller. Now, at fifty years old, he is the manager of a flour mill. Coming into psychotherapy, Walter describes his issues as, "Depression, anger, heavy drinking, mental confusion, and marital problems". This is an account of his psychotherapy work leading up to and including the soul deliverance:

> As we work through Walter's history and background, he tells me about his elder brother and sister. Then, as an afterthought, he says, "Oh yes, and I had a little brother, but I don't remember him, he died when I was very young." This has a strong impact on me, like a loud bell ringing in my head, and I feel convinced his little brother is far more important than Walter apprehends. I do not say this or give any hint about what I sense. Walter's mother grieved for his little brother Johnny for a long time. Though she provided for Walter's physical needs, she was emotionally unavailable, consumed by grief.
>
> There is a repeating pattern throughout Walter's adult life. Normally, he has a clear and astute mind and a positive attitude to life, "Onwards and upwards!" But, when he feels he has reached a plateau, the symptoms of depression, anger, heavy drinking, mental confusion and marital problems return. I wonder to myself if Walter's life is spent unconsciously competing with Johnny for their mother's love.

After six months of weekly psychotherapy, Walter describes a recent nightmare, "I am walking along a road when a ghost appears, keeping pace with me. I feel terrified and fear that somehow I shall be swallowed up by the ghost."

As we work with the dream, the ghost turns out to be a child, whom Walter calls Little Walter. My unspoken thought is about Little Johnny. In subsequent sessions, Walter speaks about Little Johnny more and more. Finally, he says, "I lost Johnny, then I lost my mother." Walter has no conscious memory of Johnny's death, yet is seems as if the death involved a trauma for little Walter. I wonder to myself if he witnessed his little brother's death.

We are doing more imaginative work around the dream, when Walter says he sees a box and hears a voice from the box saying, "Look what you have done." He is keen to see who is in the box, as well as feeling apprehensive about this. We agree to do a shamanic journey in the following session, with the intention of exploring who is in the box. Walter decides on a wise person as his supporter. I explain the ground rules, that I will guide him on the journey, and that Walter will need to give me a running commentary.

In the following session, we do the planned ceremony. Walter is very emotional throughout. Without using the drum, I guide Walter through the induction to the point where he meets the wise person. Walter invites the wise person to stand behind him, and Walter feels his supportive hand on his shoulder. Walter sees the box.

Through Walter, I ask whoever is in the box, "Are you willing to speak to me?" "Yes," is the reply, which Walter relays to me. I say, "Thank you."

I ask, "What would you like me to call you?" I ask three times, with short intervals between, before I receive an answer, "Johnny." I thank Johnny.

I ask Walter if it is all right for him to open the box. Walter tells me he is reluctant to open the box. He is feeling very emotional. Then, Walter opens the box just a little. When Johnny says, "Yes," Walter opens the box fully.

I ask, "How did you come to be in the box?" It is Walter himself who replies, "I put him there. He hurt me." I ask Johnny, "Is that so, Walter put you in the box?" He replies, "Yes."

I ask Johnny, "Are you willing to come out of the box and say sorry to Walter?" He says, "Yes."

I ask Walter, "Are you willing to say sorry to Johnny for putting him in the box?" He says, "Yes."

I ask them to say sorry to one another. They do so.

I ask Johnny, "Are you willing to go into a place of light where you can be with your relatives?" He answers, "Yes."

I ask Johnny, "Who would you like to come and escort you to the place of light?" He replies, "My mother."

Walter sees their mother coming from the place of light and Johnny going up to meet her. This is very moving for Walter.

Walter sees the box disperse.

I ask Walter to thank his wise person for their support and to let them go. He does so.

I visualise healing light flowing in, filling the space within Walter where Johnny and the box were, and filling any other empty space within Walter. I invite Walter to return and gently come back into the room. We end by simply going over what happened during the journey.

The following session is the grounding session. Straight away, Walter says he feels differently since we released Johnny: he feels like a millstone has fallen from around his neck; he is noticeably less angry and more mentally alert; he is more willing to coast rather than feeling he has to be going onwards and upwards; he no longer feels depressed and is no longer drinking heavily. Last night he explained to his wife what had been happening to him and told her of the renewed warmth and affection he feels for her.

The grounding work is about affirming Walter in the change he recognises in himself. With the soul deliverance having delivered Walter from the alien energy and its influence on his personality and behaviour, it is neither necessary nor desirable to go back into the imagery or explore the image of Johnny in a box. In subsequent sessions, the work is about consolidating the change and the task for Walter of moving forward with his life.

Points about soul deliverance

There are some points to add about soul deliverance: sometimes the client is reluctant to be delivered from the attachment. They may want to hold on to what is familiar, or be fearful of what change will mean for their lives, or not want to give up their behaviour. All the guide can do then is to wait until the client's will to change emerges.

An attachment is sometimes reluctant to leave and needs to be persuaded. This is achieved in a more extended dialogue between the guide and the attachment, via the client, than in the above case study. Soul deliverance is a gentle process involving respect for the attachment, which is persuaded to leave rather than being driven out. This is quite different from the traditional, more violent, practice of exorcism or driving out demons. Violence, even towards an alien attachment, is not helpful to the client.

The symbolism of sending the attachment to the place of light, and of filling the space that the attachment occupied with healing light, symbolically emphasises to the client that the attachment has gone; there is nowhere for it to return to, and it is not going to return.

CHAPTER TEN

Psychotherapy and counselling with soul

Introduction and scope

In his inspired and inspiring book *Healing Intelligence*, Alan Mulhern (2012) sets out the kind of "psychospiritual psychotherapist" whom I aspire to be in using the term "psychotherapy with a spiritual dimension (p. 1, p. 86)". In his approach to psychotherapy, Mulhern acknowledges an affinity with the approach of Roberto Assagioli (1965 & 1973), the originator of psychosynthesis. Mulhern writes that his four stage approach to psychotherapy with a spiritual dimension is "close to that envisaged by Assagioli (p. 2)".

The first part of this chapter summarises what, from Alan Mulhern's book, I have received and made my own, from a psychosynthesis stance, in relation to what he aptly describes as "healing intelligence". In the second part of the chapter, I set out my approach to psychospiritual therapy—psychotherapy and counselling with soul—building upon Mulhern's approach by incorporating the shamanic psychology and practice described in the present volume.

My approach to psychospiritual therapy is based on Mulhern's four stages of psychotherapy with a spiritual dimension, which are summarised as follows:

1. *Containment and comprehension*: The therapy seeks to contain the client such that they "feel held, appreciated and understood at an emotional level", and that their "real nature is in some sense being recognised, valued, and reflected back to them (p. 3)".
2. *Analysis of character*: The therapy seeks to understand the presenting issue and to "comprehend the presenting symptom in the context of the character of the client", as well as gain "a clearer understanding of the psyche, its suffering, vulnerabilities, defences, and strengths (p. 3)".
3. *Alignment with the deep psyche*: The therapy seeks "to help the client orientate the ego to the deeper psyche", by means of "light trance states which bypass the ego and lie between the state of wakefulness and sleep (p. 5)".
4. *Integration and emergence of a new centre to the personality*: The therapy seeks to integrate and transform the personality to the extent that the transforming personality may shift "from its original position to a new one which is some way between the Self and the ego (p. 6)".

Healing intelligence

Self as inner directing centre

Mulhern writes of an "inner directing centre, a guidance system" in the unconscious, "capable of directing and developing personality", a "subtle yet powerful healing intelligence that permeates the psyche". Mulhern makes clear that in his book he uses the term "Self" in the sense of "the inner director, the organising principle" and "an inner directing centre within the deep psyche". This is the same sense in which the term "Self" is used in the present volume. Self is our source of life energy supplied through the I–Self relationship, our inner guidance system that directs and develops personality, and our healing intelligence within the deep psyche.

Participation of the conscious with the unconscious

Mulhern adopts the reasonable supposition that, "whatever process happens in the outer world to promote healing, it must stimulate some inner, largely unconscious, process in the inner world that brings it about". This is the "twofold vision" discussed in Chapter Seven; the context of therapy is not just about addressing the client's existential issues but is about healing their primal wound.

The unconscious communicates indirectly and often in the form of images. I suggest the reason for this is that these images depict activity in the client's inner world, not the client's conscious reality. So, for a guide to maintain twofold vision it is vital for them to be able to have all their senses open to whatever the client's inner world is indirectly seeking to express—analysis of character is not enough. Guide and client together need a way in which they can consciously receive intelligence from the client's unconscious and grapple with the meaning that it conveys for the client. And, in this way, the conscious participates with the healing intelligence operating within the unconscious.

So, what might this way be? This "union of the conscious with the unconscious"?

Union of the conscious with the unconscious

The most obvious way of participating with healing intelligence within the unconscious is through dream work. Recording and reflecting on dreams can provide significant insights into one's inner world, as I demonstrate in Chapter Eight. Generally, however, dream work is unreliable, lacks immediacy, and makes too many demands on a client's capacity to recall their dreaming. Instead, Mulhern offers "hypnogogic states"—visionary states relating to the state of consciousness just before one is fully asleep.

In the course of his book, Mulhern suggests a variety of methods for contacting the unconscious, including: active imagination, experiential focusing, meditation techniques, and chakra work. He comes to the very threshold—which this book sets out to cross—of suggesting shamanic techniques, "Shamanistic techniques are among the most ancient healing and spiritual practices we know of. As practitioners become aware of the long healing traditions they may learn more from them (p. 48)". Indeed, commenting on a case study using chakra work, the advantages he cites would apply equally to the shamanic healing technique of soul retrieval (p. 109):

> The inner world, experienced in such visionary states, consists of images, symbols, stories, and metaphors which are identical to the dream world. They are indeed the world of phantasy: dramatic, over-determined, humorous, apparently absurd or nonsensical

but on closer inspection full of meaning. One can interpret them in exactly the same way as dream images. However, the vital difference is that visionary, inner states allow the activation of inner awareness which is a direct participation of a part of consciousness in the drama.

I couldn't have put it better. It supports my contention that the shamanic journey provides a way of simulating a dream state, which moreover is reliable, has the quality of immediacy, and being a state of consciousness can readily be recalled afterwards. More than that, during a soul retrieval the client is on a journey into their inner world, is engaged imaginatively with the psychic energies that inhabit that world, and is participating in their drama. Participation with the unconscious continues as client and guide work on grounding the soul retrieval and unravelling for the client the meaning of their experiences during the journey.

Psychic humour

Mulhern includes "humour" among the attributes of the "world of phantasy". During a shamanic journey that I made, a punning dragon commanded me "Scale!" to tell me to scale its scales. Here is another example of the often surprising psychic humour, which might equally be described as "absurd or nonsensical" and even "full of meaning"!

Early in my shamanic training, we undertook an upper world journey as an exercise. After the usual induction and my entry into trance, I found myself at the foot of a ladder to the Upper World. As I began to climb I saw I was not alone on the ladder, for above me was a scruffy old witch dressed in voluminous black. I was not pleased about this and told her to clear off, to which she took not one wit of notice but continued to climb.

When we reached the top of the ladder she balanced on one of the uprights and I balanced on the other. Then she spoke, "We don't have to stand here, we can drift around." So, we held hands and drifted around for a bit, before being joined by a younger, motherly looking woman in normal dress. The three of us held hands and drifted around for a bit more.

Then, I realised something, "I get it, you're the Crone and you're the Mother, so where's the Virgin?" The two women began to cackle, and after they'd cackled for a bit they said, "You're the Virgin." And, of course, being new to journeying, so I was.

The spiritual journey and the I–Self relationship

In the context of the participation of conscious with unconscious, Mulhern has a metaphor in which ego and Self sit at opposite ends of an axis, where the "centre of personality" is located in the ego. The effect of therapy is to shift the centre of personality along the axis, away from the ego and closer to Self, where, from this "new centre of awareness" that transcends the ego, it can "listen to both positions" and "build a ladder to the Self (pp. 14–15)".

Assagioli (1965) has a similar metaphor, in which "I" shifts along the I–Self axis closer to Self, penetrating into the Higher Unconscious, the realm of "higher intuitions and inspirations" and "latent … spiritual energies (pp. 17–18)".

Here is my version of this axis metaphor. Each of us has latent qualities—talents, values, intuitions, insights—and unacknowledged creative potential. Each of us is on an axis, or rather a path, which runs from thick-skinned narcissism to Self-realisation. We can choose to move up the path because we are guided and shown the direction by Self and because energy for life and will to move are supplied to us through the I–Self relationship.

Why "spiritual"?

The word "spirit" can be used to refer to the human spirit, or to the New Age idea of an ephemeral spirit world distinct from the concrete world of reality, or to the world of imagination and in particular the inner world of the psyche. It is the latter usage that is employed in the present context. When we consciously bring into our life experience a previously latent quality we might refer to this as bringing spirit into matter, like the man who surprised himself by his discovery, "I realise I can do plumbing."

The path is a "spiritual" journey because it unfolds as spirit comes into matter, or, put another way, as our latent qualities and creative potential are realised. As we move up the path, including more and more of our spirit, realising more and more of our qualities and creative potential, we grow psychologically, we enrich our experience of being alive, we expand our soul—James Hillman's (1975) evocative term is "soulmaking". As "I" aligns ever closer with Self, we realise more and more who we truly are. This is the spiritual journey towards Self-realisation.

A spiritual journey all the way

Psychotherapy with a spiritual dimension embraces "both ends of the spectrum, engaging in the solid task of character analysis while searching for transformational, spiritual energy as well as promoting integration". In other words, it is a spiritual journey all the way, and as a guide I need to maintain twofold vision just as much in Stages One and Two of therapy as in Stages Three and Four, as these two cases portray:

> *Building Ego:* Janice was a psychotherapy client. Her husband poured verbal abuse upon her, telling her at extreme and obscene length that she was a horrible person. Having weak psychic boundaries, Janice believed everything he said about her, until in the therapy she learnt to protect herself and maintain her integrity by imaginatively building a wall around herself. Then she learnt to allow within the wall those whom she chose. When it came to a final showdown with her husband, in the rigours of a courtroom, she held her ground and prevailed. In therapy, whilst dealing consciously with her existential issues, Janice was unconsciously, at a psychic level, building a strong, protective ego.

> *Attaining "I":* A coaching client, Bill, was a senior manager at a utility company going through major reorganisation. With his own job on the line, he swept through life delivering orders to his staff, never offering thanks or giving praise for their efforts. He was taken up short when he realised he never praised his own children for their sporting achievements and never gave himself any credit. We discussed self-reflection, or his lack of it; he said he didn't know what the words mean. After some months working together, Bill phoned me in great excitement, "I've realised what self-reflection is." After this, his attitude to his staff was so utterly changed that on completion of the reorganisation he was promoted, and he said to me, "I couldn't do this new job without recognising how I have a whole group of effective decision-makers reporting to me." Ostensibly, the coaching work was about how to maintain business as usual whilst in the throes of a major organisational change. At a psychic level, it was about differentiating a self-reflective "I" from the trappings of personality.

Recognition that psychospiritual therapy is a spiritual journey all the way, as much through Stages One and Two as through Stages Three and Four, has an important corollary that is easily lost sight of. Working in therapy through the symptoms of developmental trauma is walking a leg of the client's spiritual journey, because it carries them further along the path.

By the same token, Stages Three and Four of the therapy are just as much about healing developmental trauma, healing the primal wound, and repairing the fractured relationship with Self as are Stages One and Two. So, psychospiritual therapy is, at one and the same time, a spiritual journey all the way and a journey of healing the primal wound all the way.

Each step we take along the path towards Self-realisation is a paradigm shift, providing us with new perspectives, a broader world view, and a deeper self-concept. The woman who had an abusive husband sees a safer world where she can stand her ground and maintain her boundaries. The self-reflective senior manager sees a world where people are to be valued, including himself, and where genuine regard, thanks and praise can be bestowed. Each paradigm shift brings a new perspective on the therapy, new ground to be explored, and new insight into the interaction between conscious and unconscious in preparation for a further step along the path.

What is meant by "healing"?

With the psyche impaired by primal wounding, the personality founded upon the wounded psyche is also impaired—hated child, abandoned child, owned child—and soul is diminished.

Working in therapy at the level of personality with twofold vision, the gradual healing of the primal wound brings about the gradual healing of the personality, promoting spiritual development, soulmaking, and the "unconscious state of wholeness we call health". This is what "healing" means in this context: the gradual healing of the primal wound and the gradual healing of soul, bringing health and wholeness, "so as to lead a more fruitful and fulfilled life".

Psychotherapy and counselling with soul

This part of the chapter discusses the union of shamanic psychology and practice with the insights of contemporary psychology to provide an integrated approach to psychospiritual therapy. I refer to the psychotherapeutic practice described here as "psychotherapy and counselling

190   SOULFULNESS

Figure 10.1. The cycle of psychotherapy and counselling with soul.

with soul", because the thrust of the work is helping the client towards enriching their experience of being alive and the expansion and healing of soul as they move around this spiral path towards Self-realisation. This is soulmaking.

The approach described is based on Mulhern's four stages, with the proviso that the four stages are cyclical rather than sequential, as shown in Figure 10.1. For each paradigm shift along the spiritual path, each turn of the spiral, there are new vistas, a new world view, and at the same time the return of familiar existential issues at another level and the opportunity for further soulmaking and the healing of soul.

The spiritual cycle and spiral of life: the spiritual context of therapy

Whilst psychospiritual therapy needs to be deeply concerned with healing the present—existential symptoms of past wounding throughout all four stages—its primary context is the healing of soul, the movement of the client along the spiral path towards Self-realisation.

This means that, throughout all stages of therapy, the contextual question that, as a guide, I need to keep at the forefront of my mind is, "What is emerging in the client's life?" (Figure 10.2). And, the corollary to this question is another question, "Where is the client on the unfolding of the spiritual spiral of life?" (Figure 10.3).

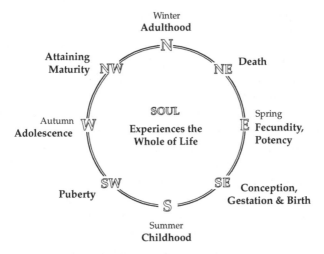

Figure 10.2. The cycle of seasons: the cycle of life.

Figure 10.3. The spiritual spiral of life: "seven year" cycle.

Each direction on the cycle of life represents a paradigm shift along the path towards Self-realisation, and within that context each direction on the spiritual spiral of life presents particular changes and challenges that the client needs to work through with the support of their guide.

The four stages of psychospiritual therapy

Below I discuss the evolution of the relationship between the client and the guide through the four stages of psychospiritual therapy, and how at each stage something new is added to the relationship whilst including all that has gone before.

At Stage One, "Containment and comprehension", the guide's primary role is to create for the client a sense of safety and trust, in order to move towards establishing a psychotherapeutic alliance. Most important is the guide's quality of mirroring, for it is by offering the client an authentic mirror that they can come to see and know something of their "real nature" and know they are in the presence of someone who is attentive and empathic towards them in the suffering that brought them into therapy. At Stage One there is a marked division of roles between the professional helper and the one seeking help to alleviate their suffering, often a "doctor/patient" distinction in the eyes of the client.

At Stage Two, "Analysis of character", with the emergence of a psychotherapeutic alliance comes the recognition by client and guide that they can make common cause in addressing the client's existential issues and furthering the client's psychological growth. The guide's role emerges more clearly as being the care of Soul, as outlined in Chapter Two. Whilst still providing an authentic mirror, the guide's role is to hold the space for the client, supporting them in broadening and deepening their present, whole, lived experience of themselves, expanding their soul as they grow in self-worth and self-esteem, self-awareness and self-will, as they pursue their soul journey towards the realisation of who they truly are.

At Stage Three, "Alignment with the deep psyche", whilst remaining an authentic mirror and carer of Soul, the guide is most truly a guide along the client's path towards Self-realisation. They can serve the client by opening gates for them along the client's path, being one who has passed along a similar road, even though they may be barely a whisker ahead. The guide can open gates for the client by being willing to share whatever is relevant of their own spiritual journey.

At Stage Four, "Integration and emergence of a new centre to the personality", whilst remaining an authentic mirror, a carer of Soul, and a gatekeeper, the guide is a fellow traveller along the path. By Stage Four, client and guide have a great deal of common ground, both in terms of a psychological understanding and appreciation of the maps and models and familiarity with and experience of the practice of psychotherapeutic endeavour. They can now work as a team on the client's project of drawing closer to Self and through Self with the wider world. The guide remains an authentic mirror, a carer of Soul, a gate-keeper, and a fellow traveller as the client spirals around the four-stage cycle of psychotherapy and counselling with soul.

Subpersonality work

A particular concern at Stage One, "Containment and comprehension", is to help the client develop their self-awareness, to recognise their habitual moods and patterns of behaviour. I find work with a client's subpersonalities to be particularly effective. An account of subpersonalities is provided in Chapter Six, as illustrated by the example of Martin, who comes to recognise different subpersonalities, "It's like it's another person; it's me but it's not me." (Note: further reading about subpersonalities can be found in Assagioli (1965) and Rowan (1990).)

I might have thought that Martin was deeply depressed through and through had he not spoken one day in a way that was more animated than usual about a tennis match he had played the previous weekend. Then, we began recognising the tennis player part as well as the customary withdrawn and depressed part and drawing out the differences between them. The work at this stage is for the client to become aware of, to differentiate, and to accept their subpersonalities.

A subpersonality often emerges quite naturally in the therapy. For example, when the client says, "I don't feel myself today," the guide can reflect the part they normally feel like and the part they feel like today. Having identified a pair of subpersonalities, one approach is to explore the elements of the client's personality from a subpersonalities point of view; their body, feelings, mind, and spirit. For example:

> When Martin is identified with his withdrawn and depressed part, he sees his body withdrawn inside a protective armour, he feels depressed and threatened by the outside world, his mind is ever watchful for any external offence or threat, and he is morose, dispirited, and stuck.
>
> When he is identified with his tennis player, on the other hand, he sees himself as taller and more athletic, he experiences an intensity of feeling, a rapport with his partner, he is not depressed, his mind is outwardly focused in a positive way, and he is more lively and engaged.

Subpersonalities and the Choreography of Energy

The Choreography of Energy map is an effective vehicle for exploring a subpersonality's energetic use of its body, feelings, mind and spirit, helping the client to increase their awareness and understanding of themselves in the way they employ their energy. For example: a person sometimes cannot distinguish their feelings from their thoughts—answering a question about feelings with a thought—or they think feelings are in the mind rather than seated in the body.

As in Martin's case, the use of energy can vary widely between the client's different subpersonalities. The Choreography of Energy map can be used to enhance a client's self-awareness by exploring each of their subpersonalities. Here is an example:

May has a subpersonality that she calls Dark Cloud. When identified with Dark Cloud May is overwhelmed by her feelings, often weeping throughout a session; in her body she suffers panic attacks; and she cannot think because she says her mind is foggy.

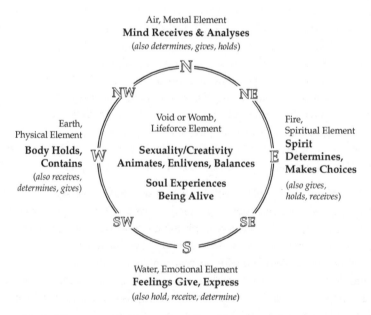

Figure 10.4. Elements of personality: the Choreography of Energy.

May works as an alternative therapist, offering reiki and sound healing, and has another subpersonality that she calls The Healer. When identified with The Healer, her feelings are calm, she is grounded in her body, and her mind is outwardly focused on the needs of her client and receptive to whatever her body is informing her about her client.

Working with the Choreography of Energy map enables May to become more aware of herself, as she comes to recognise her subpersonalities in the different ways they use energy and understands how this controls her behaviour.

When May is identified with Dark Cloud, it feels to her like this anxiety-ridden, suffering person is all she is, and when I remind her of The Healer she replies that she can't remember; her mind is too foggy. Assagioli (1965) recognises this experience of a dominant subpersonality: "We are dominated by everything with which our self becomes *identified*. We can dominate, direct and utilise everything from which we *disidentify* ourselves (p. 22)". Assagioli provides an exercise and a practice for disidentification along the following lines (pp. 116–119):

> *I* have a body, and *I* am not my body. *I* have feelings, and *I* am not my feelings. *I* have thoughts, and *I* am not my thoughts. *I* am a centre of awareness and will.

My addition to this disidentification practice, as May might employ it, is:

> *I* have a Dark Cloud, and *I* am not my Dark Cloud. *I* have a Healer, and *I* am not my Healer. *I* am a centre of awareness and will.

The operative word in this disidentification practice is "I". The practice serves to transcend identification with the body, feelings, and thoughts, and with subpersonalities, to the level of "I". This links with the Choreography map; transcending to the level of "I" frees the mind to receive and be aware of bodily sensations, feelings, and thoughts, and frees the spirit to exercise will and make a choice about where to identify next. As a guide, time and patience are often required of me before a client is able to disidentify from a dominant subpersonality like May's Dark Cloud.

Development of subpersonality work

The concern at Stage One, "Containment and comprehension", is to help the client to recognise they have subpersonalities, to get to know them using the Choreography map, to accept them as part of their personality, and to learn to disidentify from them. Not infrequently, a subpersonality is identified that the client then sees as the source of their difficulties, and responds by saying, "I want to get rid of that part." As a guide, I need to allow time and exercise patience before the client is able to accept the subpersonality as part of their personality.

Subpersonality work has a double benefit: the client understands themselves better and at the same time can feel seen, understood and valued by the guide. There are four key questions to ask and to work with:

What is this part's behaviour? This emerges from working with the
    Choreography map.
What does this part want? Meaning what the part would *like* to have.
What does this part need? Meaning what the part *must* have.
What quality or gift does the part bring to the personality?

By slowly and carefully drilling down—from external behaviour to an inner quality—it is possible to reach a quality of Self that this subpersonality seeks to express, which the client can then acknowledge, and the guide can affirm.

The concern at Stage Two "Analysis of character", having achieved recognition and acceptance of subpersonalities, is to begin the process of integrating pairs of subpersonalities by encouraging dialogue between them, as discussed in Chapter Six. The work focuses on fostering a right relationship between the parts—not dissimilar to right relationships between people—mutual respect, acknowledging difference, being open, non-judgemental, and willing to work together, and perhaps most of all each appreciating the quality of Self that the other brings to the personality. As the dialogue proceeds over a period of time, the Choreography map provides a gauge to show changes in the subpersonalities in terms of their use of energy.

The concern at Stage Three, "Alignment with the deep psyche", having achieved a right relationship between subpersonalities, is the integration of personality—pairs of subpersonalities becoming able to work together on some task, as in the following example:

> Jason saw himself as a super-salesman, with his stripy suit and lightweight aluminium briefcase. Before entering the office of a potential customer, he would pause to go over his sales pitch. When he sat across the desk from the customer a change came over him. He felt himself to be a ten-year-old boy sitting across from his overbearing father. He forgot his sales script, became tongue tied, and let the customer do all the talking, achieving nothing.
>
> On a psychosynthesis-based personal development programme, Jason came to recognise and differentiate his super-salesman and ten-year-old boy subpersonalities, so that these two could enter the customer's office hand-in-hand and work together. Instead of a sales pitch, the ten-year-old boy listened carefully to what the customer was saying and assessed his needs, so that the super-salesman could respond with a proposal to match the real needs of the customer.

Integration doesn't mean merging, it means the union of subpersonalities, bringing together and contributing their individual gifts and qualities, and thereby aligning more closely with Self. Here is a personal example:

> During my psychotherapy training, when learning about subpersonalities mine turned out to have animal form. Frog, the feeling part of me, sits on a water lily leaf, alone, isolated, and at the same time watchful. Raven, the thinking part of me, with his sharp beak and glasses on the end of his nose, is analytical and articulate. When I began to practise psychotherapy, I came to realise how much the union of the watchful Frog and the Raven's wits serve me in my work.

The concern at Stage Four, "Integration and emergence of a new centre to the personality", is with the synthesis of the whole personality, transcending and including both individual subpersonalities and the union of subpersonalities. Stage Three to Stage Four is a move along the path from the intrapersonal to the transpersonal and interpersonal, which is very much about Self being realised by the individual seeing through to the universal; Stage Four is about the client's relationship with the wider world, their love for humankind and for the natural world, their realisation that no man or woman is entire of themselves:

> No man is an island,
> Entire of itself,
> Every man is a piece of the continent,
> A part of the main.

> (John Donne)

At Stage Four, the guide's work is to help the client realise what this means in a practical, grounded way.

The shamanic journey and soul retrieval

At Stage One, "Containment and comprehension", simple journeys suffice. I avoid too much explanation or anything unfamiliar like the use of the medicine drum, though a reclining chair is helpful to relaxation. The simplest form of shamanic journey that can be undertaken is a relaxing visit to a quiet place in nature familiar to the client. There is no need to speak of trance states; this is simply about relaxation. The client is invited to make themselves comfortable, then to focus on their breathing, and when they are relaxed they are invited to enter their quiet place in nature and enjoy being there until invited to return.

Showing the client how to relax helps to contain the emotional suffering that brought them into therapy. It teaches them how they can relax at home. Being able to relax in the therapy room helps to build trust. This simple journey also serves quietly to introduce the experience of a shamanic journey to the client and to develop their confidence.

Later, another simple journey might be undertaken (again focusing on the breath), such as a visit to a familiar place or situation to see it with inner eyes and experience it with all their inner senses. There is no need to explain that this is a simple form of a journey into the shamanic Middle World. The client is guided simply to observe with their senses, not to become involved. This introduces the client to the experience of visiting their inner world. It helps them develop their observer self. It helps them develop "I" and the capacity to be reflective. It also, incidentally, provides a useful tool for assessing a social or business situation, with the important proviso that the person remains an uninvolved observer during the journey, seeing but not being infected by the energies swirling around the situation.

At Stage Two, "Analysis of character", a twenty minute shamanic journey can be introduced, with all its ritual elements, along the lines variously discussed in previous chapters. To begin with, the intention of these journeys might be a journey to the Lower World to meet an animal ally or a journey to the Upper World to meet a wise being. Such shamanic journeys enable the client to become familiar with the land-scapes of the shamanic universe and introduces them to healthy instinc-tive and intuitive elements of their psyche, which may prove helpful in subsequent shamanic journey and soul retrieval ceremonies.

Whilst not being overtly analytical, the therapy at Stage Two never-theless illuminates aspects of the client's personality that can then be addressed. As therapy unfolds, issues will arise concerning the client's personality that indicate soul loss, specifically low self-worth or self-esteem or self-confidence, or the lack of a clear sense of innocence or identity or sexual power. Work with the Choreography map may reveal a lack of feeling or emotional control or concentration, or a poverty of spirit or a lack of the power to change. The issue, whatever has arisen, can be formed into an intention for a soul retrieval ceremony. The soul retrieval and subsequent grounding serve to advance the client's heal-ing and thereby affect their personality for the good.

Should the guide judge that there is an alien energy attached to the psyche, they may, with the client's consent, undertake a soul deliver-ance ceremony to remove the attachment. Soul retrieval and soul deliv-erance are described and illustrated in some detail in Chapters Five, Seven, and Nine.

By Stage Three, "Alignment with the deep psyche", the client is familiar with the landscapes of the shamanic universe, is used to travelling into these imaginative realms of their inner world, is well acquainted with animal allies and wise beings, and is accustomed to the subsequent grounding, to the unravelling of what the images mean for them, and how this can make a difference to their life. Stage Three is about aligning the personal self with the deep psyche, so while sha-manic journey and soul retrieval ceremonies continue, these are now less about retrieving lost soul energy and more about connection and communication with the client's allies in the deep psyche in the form of animals and wise beings.

The journeys can be longer (say up to forty minutes) and deeper. For example, the client may journey with the intention of consulting with their allies about:

- The balance between their feelings, body, mind and spirit, in relation to the Choreography map.
- The relationship between pairs of elements, such as between feelings and mind.
- How the relationship between a pair of their subpersonalities might become more harmonious.
- Their behaviour in particular social or business situations.
- How they are benefited and limited by a particular trait of character.

With both client and therapist maintaining twofold vision, journeys with these kinds of intention help the client to set out from known territory to explore unknown territory, in order to make known something of what is unknown, such as a subpersonality deep-seated in the psyche.

Some subpersonalities can exist wholly in the Lower or Upper Unconscious. Such a subpersonality may be encountered in some imaginative form during a shamanic journey, thus bringing the subpersonality into consciousness. The client, being familiar with subpersonalities, may engage in dialogue with the subpersonality during the journey, as well as work with it during the grounding, in order to bring further into consciousness the way in which the unconscious subpersonality has affected their personality. In this way, by means of the journey, the conscious collaborates with the unconscious.

In the practice of psychospiritual therapy, throughout all four stages, the enduring contextual questions are:

"What is emerging in the client's life?" (Figure 10.2, p. 191)
"Where is the client on the unfolding of the spiritual spiral of life?" (Figure 10.3, p. 191)

This is never more so than at Stage Four, "Integration and emergence of a new centre to the personality", which is overtly concerned with the shift to a new position on the path towards Self-realisation. From the client's position on the cycle of life:

- The four non-cardinal directions on the spiritual spiral—South East, South West, North West, North East—represent periods of transition and change, a turning of the wheel, a movement along the path.
- The four cardinal directions on the spiritual spiral—South, West, North, East—represent periods of consolidation and affirmation of the new position.

At Stage Four, the client can make a shamanic journey with the intention, at a non-cardinal direction, of enjoying the support of their allies during the challenges of a transition and change, or, at a cardinal direction, of gaining insight into their new perspectives.

A shamanic journey: the dragon's gift

This is an example of a shamanic journey at Stage Three, "Alignment with the deep psyche", which I undertook at a late stage in my shamanic training:

I am about to make a shamanic journey. The shamanic guide invites me to choose where I shall begin the journey—a place in nature that is important to me—and to decide my intention. I shall begin my journey at a stone circle on Bodmin Moor that I call "The Healers", beside a central stone I call the "Shaman Stone". My intention is to meet an animal ally and to receive a gift from them.

I lie in a darkened room with my head on a cushion and a blanket over me. The shamanic guide uses relaxing words whilst slowly beating her drum, then invites me to stand at the entrance to my journey and to state my intention three times, which I do. The guide's drumbeat increases as I begin my journey.

There is a stone in the circle that I call the Herbalist. The Herbalist peals off from her stone, takes me by the hand, and leads me into the woods to a glade where we sit facing each other. All my animal allies and spirit guides come and sit with us; they are just there to support me in the journey.

The Herbalist says I need to go deeper into the woods alone. I feel anxious that I won't recognise my animal ally, as I can see many animals in the woods and fish in its streams. I hear the voice of the Herbalist, "Follow the drum." When I follow the sound of the shamanic guide's drum my anxiety falls away. My body is shivering, alive with emotion.

I find myself in a desert place. I see a snake, which becomes a dragon. It looks forbidding. I look at its scales. The dragon speaks, saying "Scale!" to tell me to scale its scales, so I climb onto the dragon and sit astride its soft back.

I follow an impulse to listen to the drum, which I realise is the dragon's heartbeat. I follow an impulse to align my heartbeat with that of the dragon and to take the dragon into my heart. This is the dragon's gift to me.

As soon as I take the dragon into my heart, the shamanic guide's drumbeat changes to call me back from my journey.

I return with the dragon in my heart.

Dragon heart: the psychological power of the image

I gave no further thought to my dragon heart until I chose to include here the above example of a shamanic journey, which I had made over a year earlier. Soon after, I received strong signs that a lost friendship might be restored. It lifted my heart. I woke in the night with feelings of elation and a powerful connection with my dragon heart.

When my hopes were dashed, I felt bereft. My confused mind needled around a groove of repetitive words of explanation and justification. For two days I was unable to work, yet all the time I felt the beat of my dragon heart, leading me towards clarity of thought, allowing of what I did not know of the other, compassion for them, a capacity both to be with and to contain my feelings of hurt and anger and also to admit, restrain and calm the urge in me to react.

During the shamanic journey, I had entered a deep part of my psyche—deeper into the woods—from which arose the image of my dragon heart. Images drawn from deep in the psyche have the power to bring about change; the image of my dragon heart entered and enlarged my soul and was ready and waiting to guide me out of a repetitive cycle of explanation and justification, back to secure psychological ground.

The Circle of Mirrors

This section describes and illustrates the Circle of Mirrors ceremony, whereby a client is guided first around the dark mirror and then around the light mirror. The climax of the dark mirror circle is to the East, where the client is confronted by the payoff for a life of illusion and fantasy before the dénouement, which is to face their imperfect concept of Self to the South East. Here, the client is invited to visualise

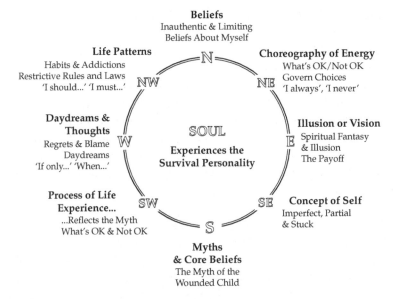

Figure 10.5.   The Circle of Mirrors: the dark mirror.

Figure 10.6.   The Circle of Mirrors: the light mirror.

a gift that their wounded self needs from them. This gift provides the starting point for the second cycle, the light mirror. The gift their wounded child needs serves as "the myth of the whole child", to the South of the light mirror.

When employing the Circle of Mirrors model in psychospiritual therapy, the dark mirror (Figure 10.5) relates to Stage Two, "Analysis of character". Chapter Four shows the results, in terms of a life narrative, first of analysing the formation in childhood of client Peter's survival personality, then of analysing Peter's survival personality, with its particular model of the world, as it exists in adulthood. The present section illustrates the application of the dark mirror using the same example of client Peter.

The light mirror (Figure 10.6) relates to Stage Three, "Alignment with the deep psyche". Moving around the light mirror, as set out in the Chapter Three section "The myth of the whole child and the light mirror", the client has the opportunity to reflect on what their life might be, having received the gift and acquired the myth of the whole child as their core belief. The light mirror illuminates their path towards Self-realisation and what closer alignment with Self might mean for their life. Application of the light mirror again uses the example of client Peter.

The ceremony for working with The Circle of Mirrors has the following ritual elements:

Creating the space: The first element for the dark mirror ceremony is dimmed lighting with a candle burning in the space. A Medicine Wheel, with the eight directions marked by stones, is set out, with a cushion in the centre for the client. If space is limited, the Medicine Wheel can be set out on a low table.

Clearing the space: Having greeted the client, the next step is the symbolic ritual of "clearing the space" within the room and around the guide and the client of any residual negative energies, either by smudging or by using cymbals or a singing bowl.

The client is asked two questions, inviting them to affirm their commitment before proceeding with the ceremony:

Guide: Are you willing to die to what no longer serves you?
Guide: Are you willing to speak your truth to the best that you are able?

The client is invited to take their place within the Medicine Wheel facing South. If a table is used, the client sits facing the table to the South. The guide sits outside the circle, or across the table, facing the client. As the dark mirror dialogue proceeds, client and guide move around the circle clockwise to each direction in turn, until they return to the South.

The dark mirror dialogue then proceeds as illustrated below. The guide does not speak during the dialogue, except to ask the set questions, so as to maintain the client's focus. (Note: I am indebted to Dawn Russell of Eagle's Wing for permission to reproduce the carefully crafted dark mirror and light mirror questions.)

The light mirror dialogue immediately follows on, as illustrated below. Again, the guide does not speak during the dialogue, except to ask the set questions. The light mirror dialogue begins with the gift that their wounded self needs, which serves as the myth of the whole child.

At the end of the ceremony, the client is invited to take some time to reflect before being invited to step out of the Medicine Wheel. The ceremony needs to be followed by grounding work, which may take several more sessions, to discuss and evaluate what emerged during the dialogue. My practice is to take verbatim notes of the dark mirror and light mirror dialogues, which can then be copied for the client and referred to in subsequent sessions.

Although The Circle of Mirrors ceremony is essentially cognitive, with the client being asked a series of set questions, its ritual context serves to intensify the client's experience, helping them to delve more deeply into their inner world to find answers, which I hope Peter's example effectively conveys.

The dark mirror dialogue

The following example is the verbatim dialogue between client Peter and the guide, from which Peter's life narrative in Chapter Four was ultimately derived.

SOUTH: Myths and core beliefs
GUIDE: Speak of the core belief you have about yourself.
PETER: I am unloveable.
GUIDE: Speak of how you feel hurt by this core belief.
PETER: It hurts me that at the age of fifty-two I still feel unloveable. I've never learnt how to have an intimate relationship with

women. It's like my body, my feelings and my sexuality have never properly joined up. I miss the deep connection with another that I see others enjoy.

SOUTH WEST: Process of life experience

GUIDE: How was this reflected in your everyday life?

PETER: I never felt any intimacy with my mother; the idea would have horrified me. I always recoiled from her. I still do. I think she resented me because my father was going away all the time and she'd had to give up her business career when I was born.

My father seemed never to be home, he was a distant figure, never played with me. It seems like I was always waiting for him to come home, but he never came home for me. He shut himself away in his office. Sad little boy. Lonely.

I suppose I spent a lot of time in my head. I was always imaginative. I thought up games to play with my friends, it gave me an in [sic]. I imagined being liked by the girls in my group.

GUIDE: How has this affected your life?

PETER: I did have a relationship once, but there wasn't much passion in it. It seems like I avoided getting too close. I never felt loved for myself. I've been alone for a long time.

It's deep-rooted, it's affected all relationships of intimacy; I've avoided them. I'm alone not out of fear but avoidance of my ideal relationship.

Before I went to school one of my friends was a pretty girl called Shirley. I liked her, but in my infantile way I always felt she preferred to play with this other boy Ivan, and it hurt—I felt left out.

I've always got on well with women socially, but looking back there have been many times when I've missed the signals that a woman is interested in a relationship with me. How could I miss the signals? Sometimes when I've got closer to someone, I start getting fearful, negative fantasies and distorted thoughts and images about her and doubt her love for me. So, I've never experiencing [sic] the intimacy of a real relationship.

Down the years I've had lots of friends, men and women, but as people move around I've never tried very hard to hang on to them—it's easy to let them go.

WEST: Dreaming and reflection

GUIDE: Speak of your "if only ..." statements.

PETER: If only I could have taken the risk—stepped out, overcome my reserve towards others—to be able to articulate my feelings and not to run away and avoid women's signals and advances. I remember dancing at a university party with a voluptuous, powerful, young and remarkable woman, then distancing myself. It's gut-wrenching to think of it.

If only I could express my feelings and if only I could receive what is put out by the other instead of avoiding it and if only I could have the relationship I dream of, that is fulfilling at all levels—missed that all along, a creative relationship.

GUIDE: Who does the child in you blame? (If you weren't to blame yourself, who would you blame?)

PETER: Undoubtedly my mother. A resentful woman. She was very unhappy with my father away so much, so it rebounded on me. There were some moments, like watching Watch with Mother together on the TV. I cherish these moments, but they're not comfortable.

My father was neglectful of me, wrapped up in his own business world, the only time he showed interest in me was the 11+ exam, but that was about his ambition to have his son at grammar school. I felt resentful doing old exam papers rather than playing football with my friends.

NORTH WEST: Life patterns

GUIDE: What are the familiar recurring patterns in your life that relate to this core belief?

PETER: Diffidence about expressing emotions. Avoidance of relationships. Constant longing and daydreams about the love of my life and sexual fulfilment. Envy and resentment of men who have it all.

As a child, playing out, away from my mother, as much as possible, even in the middle of winter, absorbing myself in imaginative games. As an adult, throwing myself into my creative technical work, whatever my current project might be.

I'm thought of as a quiet person, but I can be fierce, my commitment is strong. Often impulsive, swift to take foolhardy decisions without adequate forethought. Avoiding intimacy has put a lot of energy into my mental processes.

GUIDE: What are the habits and routines— "I should" and "I ought" statements—which come out of this core belief, that limit you?

PETER: The shoulds I comply with? I should conform, I should do what is expected of me, I should obey rules to a fault, otherwise I worry. I should not upset people. I suppose I'm just conservative.

Fiercely independent. Self-reliant, imaginative, determined. Combative in support of my projects, willing to fight intellectually for my ideas.

I do the things I want to do and that seem important to me, with a lot of energy and determination, but I neglect everything else. There are lots of oughts that I fail to observe and in this way I limit myself. I ought not to neglect people, but pay more attention to people and so have a better memory of them. I ought to be a much better networker and communicator. I ought to reach out to others, see other people as important, foster relations. I ought not let people come and go and make no effort to maintain contact.

In all these ways I limit myself.

I limit myself emotionally, putting a lid on my feelings, but I also limit myself physically by being unadventurous, timid even, even though my body's pretty ok. My mother was nervous, I suppose, being alone a lot, "Stay away from the river," "Stay away from the road," "Don't climb trees," as if I was a weakling, which I wasn't.

NORTH: Beliefs

GUIDE: What beliefs do you hold that support this core belief?

PETER: I believe I'm a good guy. I believe I'm a good man, loyal and kind. I believe I should do something beyond my work that contributes to society, so I'm on the Lions Club committee. I believe it's right to focus a lot of my energy and commitment on whatever my current projects happen to be. I believe in firm commitment. Yea, I think I'm ok, unusual in some ways. [sighs] So why do I still think I'm unloveable?

GUIDE: What are your beliefs about yourself and life?

PETER: Most of it is a waste of time, very interesting intellectually but as if in a bubble. Committee work with the Lions, but not really engaged with anything worthwhile.

Being good at thinking up jokes and telling them is not the same as fostering relationships, a good salesman maybe.

NORTH EAST: Choreography of Energy

GUIDE: What choices have you made that keep this core belief alive in you? (Choices made from the core belief).

PETER: How I employ my time is about things I do. I get satisfaction from a job well done.

Doing stand-up, the comedian, the performer. Presenting myself as a good person doing useful things. Kudos of being the performer so I can be liked for that.

I don't foster relationships or friendships, so I'm always a bit distant, too much in my head. I suppose I'm a bit reclusive, a lot of time alone, watching TV and reading science fiction.

GUIDE: How do you design and choreograph your life to be the way it is? This is about saying "I always ..." and "I never ..."

PETER: We've talked about this. I've realised how disconnected I am from my feelings, and yet when things aren't working out for me and I'm feeling stressed it's intensely painful. And, I've realised I'm neglectful of my body, smoking and drinking too much, eating a lot of sugar and fat, and taking no exercise.

I'm good at the technical stuff, struggling to solve problems, but I realise I am in my mind all the time. I think I'm a bit depressed.

I always tell myself I enjoy my own company, which I do, but it's still a way I avoid too much connection with other people.

EAST: Illusion or vision: The payoff

GUIDE: How does having your life this way keep you safe/stuck?

PETER: Good way to avoid pain and the difficulty and stress of the reality of real relationships. Restrict myself.

GUIDE: What aspects of your passion and spirit fail to get expressed in the way you live your life?

PETER: Passion is expressed into the things that I do. I'm passionate about my work. I'm seen as a calm person, but then my passion doesn't get expressed directly.

On stage as a stand-up comic I become almost a different person; I create magic. I know it's just a performance but my passion comes out. Then I'm the fullest I can be, with the proviso that it's only a performance—the sting in the tail. Intensity of relationship, though, with the audience or the group I'm with—this isn't love, there are elements of love.

I rarely weep.

SOUTH EAST: Concepts of Self and world view
GUIDE: How does this leave you feeling about yourself?
PETER: Sad, as if after all this I'm stuck.
GUIDE: How are you in relationship to yourself?
PETER: I feel disconnected in relation to myself, something wrong with me, as if there's another me not connected.

The light mirror dialogue

The example below is the <u>verbatim dialogue</u> between client Peter and the guide, which followed straight on from the dark mirror dialogue above.

SOUTH EAST: Concepts of Self and world view
GUIDE: What does your wounded self need from you? [Visualise. Take the client through this visualisation ...]
PETER: Image of child and presence— less defined—union of the two.
GUIDE: Close your eyes, take a few deep breaths, and receive from yourself ... [Mirror back what the client said they needed; in this case, "union of the child and presence".]
PETER: Small boy looking to the spirit. Small boy asks to be part of the flow and the spirit. And there's love there, love both ways, boy and spirit. I can see threads connecting small boy and spirit. I can feel it in my body.

Loving connection. Image of connection, intensity, feeling.
SOUTH: Myths and core beliefs
[The guide mirrors back what the client has just said, in this case, "the loving connection between small boy and spirit, the intensity of feeling".]
GUIDE: How does that now feel to receive this from yourself?
PETER: Expansive, wider than boy and presence. Not about Facebook, more direct connection with others, from the heart.
SOUTH WEST: Process of life experience
GUIDE: How does your life feel now?

PETER: Expansive opening feeling, reconnection with people, not everybody. I tend to live more in the future than the present up till now. Being present moment by moment. Ritual, simple acknowledgement of the present.

GUIDE: What are the new possibilities you now open your life to? (The dreams you are now manifesting and wish to manifest).

PETER: Metaphor, imperfections, which add character, such as a table with a repair.

The stand-up comic/performer is to be valued. More being a comedian/performing. The individual and the wider connection with the audience. More magic space. Bits, dreams coming together.

WEST: Dreaming and reflection

GUIDE: How does this affect your everyday life?

PETER: Much less reclusive, in contact on a daily basis with people. More dancing. Physical, flirting, and stirring of emotions.

Fostering existing relationships, valued even when they don't have this element of passion/life/dance. Accepting the contrast.

GUIDE: How does it feel to live this new dream?

PETER: Ok, but the boy-spirit connection needs affirming—I still feel the grip of the past. So, affirmation is needed.

NORTH WEST: Life patterns

GUIDE: What new positive practices, habits and affirming guidelines do you now hold?

PETER: Practising simple rituals to connect with myself in the present, before immersing myself in work.

It's easier to go into myself and the work I'm doing rather than going out to connect. I need the ritual, the discipline to let go.

Part of the discipline is to allow time each day for myself, meditation, physical exercise, mind, body and spirit.

In personal life, play for my joy and benefit.

NORTH: Beliefs

GUIDE: What are your (new) life affirming attitudes towards yourself and life?

PETER: I'm a genuine authentic person, imperfections and all. My feeling matching my words. I can be a worthwhile creative person. Very freeing. Not stuck. I'm ok.

NORTH EAST:	Choreography of Energy
GUIDE:	What new choices do you now make to manifest your dreams and new possibilities?
PETER:	Ritual, discipline as commitment not as slavery. Free. Open to people, sharing and compassion. Dancing and physical connection. Connection with feelings needs to be added to reconnection with body, such as dancing. More enjoyable. Being present.
EAST:	Illusion or vision
GUIDE:	How does this new way of being affect your lifeforce (sexuality) and presence in life?
PETER:	My presence in life? It just is what it is. Sexuality? Too soon to say, seems like a long stretch.
SOUTH EAST:	Concepts of Self and world view
GUIDE:	How does this leave you feeling about yourself now?
PETER:	Movement [client shows with his arms] rather than words. Expansive. The presence is that movement.
GUIDE:	How is your relationship with yourself now?
PETER:	I am with the presence now. Small boy is happy on his feet. Still a bit reserved but more "ho!"

The inner child

When a client makes a deep connection with their inner child, they are close to the trauma of primal wounding and close to the Child of Self, which means that inner child work is especially important, and often it is particularly poignant for a client to meet their young self and find them: isolated, alienated, sad, angry. A guide may sense the presence of a client's inner child at Stage One, "Containment and comprehension", maybe when the client is feeling sad.

A guided visualisation or simple shamanic journey for the client to observe their inner child playing on a beach or in a playground—what they look like, how they look, what they are wearing, how they are playing—can be a relatively gentle introduction to their young self. Sometimes, seeing their young self triggers memories of their childhood—in one case, remembering being dressed as mother wished rather than as the child wished— providing further grist to the therapy mill. In a later shamanic journey, the client can make a connection with their inner child, begin to get to know them, show their good will and love towards them, and gently work through any initial hostility from or towards their young self.

At Stage Two, "Analysis of Character", the inner child sometimes emerges quite naturally in cushion work. A cushion is placed in front of the client, who is invited to see an image on the cushion of the feeling about which they have been speaking. This helps a client to disidentify, at least to some degree, by observing their feeling imaginatively. Often, the image on the cushion represents the subpersonality with which they are identified. Sometimes, the image is of the client's inner child, allowing the client insight into the plight of their young self and possibly providing the opportunity for dialogue between their adult and young self. This can be followed up by a shamanic journey for the adult and young self to meet and get to know one another in a natural setting, perhaps somewhere they enjoyed being as a child. This work deepens a client's understanding of their adult suffering's roots in childhood, and fosters compassion for their young self.

The inner child and the Circle of Mirrors

The myth of the wounded child (Figure 10.5) is the way the Child of History articulated their experience, their pain and difficulty, in terms of what they believed was wrong with them. The myth of the whole child (Figure 10.6) is the way a client seeks to articulate what it might mean to be making the return journey to the Child of Self.

The dark mirror, relating to Stage Two, "Analysis of character", is essentially an analysis of the payoff, for a life of illusion and fantasy, founded upon the client's myth of the wounded child. The light mirror, relating to Stage Three, "Alignment with the deep psyche", is an opportunity, founded upon the client's myth of the whole child, for the client to begin envisaging what aligning with Self means for their soul; their experience of a life lived to the full with an open heart.

As the client spirals around the four-stage cycle of psychotherapy and counselling with soul, they repeatedly revisit the Circle of Mirrors, each time at a different place on the path towards Self-realisation. This is Stage Four, "Integration and emergence of a new centre to the personality". At each advance along the path, they transcend what went before, including and integrating it into their expanding soul, with each return offering a fresh perspective on their life, a renewed myth of the whole child, and bringing them closer to the Child of Self.

In the light mirror dialogue above, it is clear that Peter is speaking from a place deep within himself, and is articulating a profoundly felt experience. It is an experience that very much involves his inner child, the "small boy"; the gift to his wounded self is "Image of child and presence—less defined—union of the two", which the guide mirrors back as, "Union of the child and presence".

Articulating an intense experience—rather than clearly reporting thoughts, images, and ideas—is evident in the words that Peter uses; for example, to receive the gift from himself:

Small boy looking to the spirit. Small boy asks to be part of the flow and the spirit. And there's love there, love both ways, boy and spirit. I can see threads connecting small boy and spirit. I can feel it in my body. Loving connection. Image of connection, intensity, feeling.

At the same time, Peter's reply to the guide's question, "How does it feel to live this new dream?" is tentative, "Ok, but the boy-spirit connection needs affirming—I still feel the grip of the past. So, affirmation is needed." And, his answer to the guide's final question, "How is your relationship with yourself now?" is equivocal, "I am with the presence now. Small boy is happy on his feet. Still a bit reserved but more 'ho!'"

We might reasonably speculate that as Peter revisits the light mirror his communication with the psyche will deepen, will become more finely tuned, and he will shift more closely to Self. The light mirror charts the transcending spiritual path towards Self-realisation, as may be revealed by a few minutes of reflection on the Chapter Three section "The myth of the whole child and the light mirror".

Lest it be thought that this transcending spiritual path simply leads to a mystical union with Self, it needs to be said that mystics are practical, down-to-earth people. An Indian Hindu monk and a disciple of the Indian mystic Ramakrishna, Swami Vivekananda (see Toyne, 1983), who introduced the Indian philosophy of Vedanta to the Western world in the late nineteenth century, expressed the idea of a firmly grounded spirituality in fine Victorian prose, "My ideal indeed can be put into a few words and that is to preach unto mankind their divinity and how to make it manifest in every movement of life". And, the Christian mystic Saint Teresa of Ávila was such an energetic and determined reformer that she even fell foul of the Spanish Inquisition.

"Self is realised by the individual seeing through to the universal" means not only loving and honouring ourselves, but also recognising how much we are part of a much wider and interdependent network, such that we are called to love, honour and serve other people and the natural world.

Summary

"Healing energies are a natural intelligence within the psyche, promoting the unconscious state of wholeness we call health"

"At its most natural, healing in the psyche is an unconscious issue"

"In many [cases], the inner sense of wholeness is dependent on someone or something outside of oneself"

"There is a special quality when a practitioner helps to mobilise, focus, and augment this natural healing energy within the sufferer".

Alan Mulhern makes the above statements in the Introduction to his book *Healing Intelligence* (2012), setting the agenda for a style of psychotherapy that is spiritual from the outset; that involves participation of the conscious with healing intelligence within the deep psyche and employs to this end "light trance states" that "help the client orientate the ego to the deeper psyche" and "activate and stimulate" healing intelligence by the client's "*inner awareness*". In the present chapter, I have set out to show how this agenda might be fulfilled through the marriage of shamanic and contemporary psychology and practice.

In this marriage, several points of creative union have been identified:

- The spiritual cycle of life serves to clarify the unfolding psychospiritual, therapeutic context of a client's therapy.
- The shamanic journey, besides extending the scope of active imagination techniques, affords a way of cooperating with healing intelligence within the unconscious that is reliable, immediate, in a state of consciousness, and thus readily recalled, and can provide significant insights into a client's inner world.

- Soul retrieval enables a client to be engaged imaginatively with the psychic energies that inhabit their inner world, such as to "allow the activation of inner awareness which is a direct participation of a part of consciousness in [their] drama".
- Inner child work brings a client close to the trauma of primal wounding and to the Child of Self. The Circle of Mirrors offers to a client a way of facing up to their early wounding, which led to their adoption of a false belief about themselves and to the consequences this has had for their life, and then a way of redeeming their life and making the return journey towards the Child of Self.
- In the psychospiritual, therapeutic use of The Circle of Mirrors, the dark mirror affords a systematic and comprehensive method of analysing a client's character in relation to their early wounding. The light mirror charts the spiritual path towards Self-realisation and at each step illuminates the client's way.

AFTERWORD

In praise of mothers

Contemporary psychology gives mothers a bad press. Yes, I know,
a child's primary attachment, caregiver, maternal environment, and all
that. But, it's mothers who take the brunt. I see mothers in action at
Dance Camp. I see the way they are constantly alert to the needs of
their children, whilst allowing them to roam within the safe environment of the camp; the caring way they hold, attend and respond to their
children when they come to share their joys and woes; the quiet way
they organise their lives so as to be available to their children throughout the day, whilst still playing a full part in camp life; the calm way
they negotiate disagreement with their children, neither over-strict nor
over-lenient, taking time to coax out a resolution that esteems a child's
spirit.

Part of me thinks I'm being condescending by writing these words,
but it feels important to me to redress the balance by expressing my
heartfelt praise, honour and respect for mothers.

Relational being

I am not claiming all mothers to be saints; this is not the point. The point is this: it is an irony that even the best of mothers suffer lapses, moments of inattention, times of sadness, grief, pain, sickness, anger, or preoccupation—just being human. At those times, the holding and mirroring of their infant may become peremptory or lacking. With an infant's finely tuned sensibility—an infant for whom the only time is now—each lapse is a wound to soul.

The irony is not simply that lapses occur, that soul is wounded, but that *it cannot be otherwise*. A human being is relational, and so *must* relate, *must* be involved in humankind in all its variety, complexity, difference, and discord, for as human beings we are all different, each with our own history, wounding, world view, and thus our discordant beliefs, wants, needs, motivations, values, and cruelties, as well as our innate gifts and our gradual attainment of growth, insight, and wisdom.

As Joan Evans says, Self, immanent throughout, aims towards the realisation of its own specific and unique "goals". This is Self-realisation. And this is the deepest irony: only when human beings are willing to be involved in humankind, with all its mess of difference and discord, and to make the soul journey towards Self-realisation, with all its pains and pitfalls, does Self become manifest in the world and its goals become realised.

It cannot be otherwise. The human being is relational and at the deepest level this relationship is between "I" and Self. And, because the human being is relational, Assagioli in his wisdom places Self on the Egg Diagram at the porous outer boundary with the collective unconscious; the relationship between "I" and Self is a relationship reaching out from the individual to the collective, from each person to all people, from all people to the natural world. Self *serves* us throughout our life's journey as a source of vitality and as a womb of boundless creativity, insight, and inspiration. *Service* is the essence of *Self*. Thus, the call to Self is a call to service, a moral imperative to engage with, love, honour and serve other people, every condition of man or woman, and to love, honour and serve the natural world.

Without relationship, without engaging with the world, without love, the psyche would be an unfertilised egg.

Love and will

I have written little about "love" specifically in this book. "Love" is a tricky word, with its confusing variety of meanings and connotations. Bowlby sought precision by introducing the word "attachment", rather than using the word "love", to denote an infant's tie to its mother. Yet, love infuses every page of this book, the love of mother for child, child for mother, love of oneself, love for Self, love of Self, love for other people, for humanity, for the natural world, love of therapist for client, client for therapist, our love of ideas, the love we hold of our dreams and our callings. So, I feel I need finally to pin down what I mean by "love" in the context of this book.

We speak of unconditional love, yet I wonder how much love is truly unconditional. Parental love, for example, is often conditional on a child conforming to parental expectations. A child's love for parents cannot be separated from their dependency. Certainly, love exists within a therapeutic relationship. A supervisor of mine used to say "Clients pay for therapy, the love comes for free", but even here, a therapist might see their client through modality-tinted spectacles.

Dependency is also often part of marital love. To add to the confusion, love is often thought of simply as a feeling, so problems arise when feelings change, and furthermore the comingling of love and sex can be difficult to untangle. The Choreography of Energy map can help provide clarification. Sex is part of the lifeforce (Centre), the instinctive urge that serves to propagate the species. And, in the process creates change, even chaos; the sexual urge can be so strong that it overpowers rational thought (North) and permeates the feelings (South) with a craving for bodily release (West).

In a committed sexual partnership, the instinctive sexual urge can transpose into feelings of desire to have children and into sustained energy to nourish the children throughout their childhood and beyond, which is called marital love. Such sustained energy entails a determination to remain committed to the family unit. Determination, the choice to sustain commitment, is a function of spirit (East). Love is an act of will.

I offer the view that this principle applies not only to a sexual partnership, but to the sustaining of any creative relationship or creative endeavour: love is not simply a feeling, love is an act of will. Our response to a call of Self, a call to service, is a choice, "yes" or "no", and to say "yes" demands both love and will for its fulfilment: love of the creative relationship or endeavour to which we are called; sustained will to overcome any obstacles necessary to see it through. In a delightful and little known sonnet "The Penalty of Love", Sidney Royse Lysaght (1923) expressed this principle most poignantly:

> If love should count you worthy, and should deign
> One day to seek your door and be your guest,
> Pause! ere you draw the bolt and bid him rest,
> If in your old content you would remain,
> For not alone he enters; in his train
> Are angels of the mist, the lonely guest
> Dreams of the unfulfilled and unpossessed,
> And sorrow, and Life's immemorial pain.
> He wakes desires you never may forget,
> He shows you stars you never saw before,
> He makes you share with him for evermore
> The burden of the world's divine regret.
> How wise you were to open not! and yet,
> How poor if you should turn him from the door!

Quite often, I share this poem with clients, when they face a critical choice.

Soulfulness

In writing this book, I have set out to present the ancient wisdom of shamanic theory and practice in a form that is fit for use within the mainstream of twenty-first century psychotherapeutic endeavour, and have included an extensive explanation of shamanic psychology and a practical description of the ceremonies of the shamanic journey and soul retrieval.

I have reflected on key aspects of contemporary psychological thinking—infant and adult attachment patterns, developmental trauma and the survival personality from various theoretical perspectives, work with imagination and dreams, the spiritual dimension in psychotherapy and counselling—and in extended discussion I have set out to relate these subjects to the maps and models of shamanic psychology, the practice of shamanic journey and soul retrieval ceremonies, and the psychotherapeutic application of both.

I have brought everything together by offering, in the final chapter, a practical approach to the integration of psychotherapy and counselling practice with a present-day form of shamanic practice, when working with developmental trauma. The resulting marriage of shamanic and contemporary psychology and practice I have called "Soulfulness".

Footnote

Finally, I should like to share with you the words that my reader, friend and fellow writer Jessica Nelson wrote to me when she read this Afterword:

> It is a lovely piece and much appreciated. I'm sure many mothers will thank you for it, along with me. It made me cry, actually! I think it is the most painful and most creative aspect of all human experience that the people we love the most (our significant/(m)others) are sometimes those who cause us the most hurt and anguish. This duality must underpin all our relationships and inspire most of our stories. Blessed are those who can hold together the joy and the pain, the shadow and the light, the euphoria and the hopeless depths of Love!

REFERENCES

Afanas'ev, A., & Norbert, G. (Trans.) (1945). "The Bold Knight, the Apples of Youth, and the Water of Life". In: A. Alexeieff, *Russian Fairy Tales.* Copyright © 1945 by Pantheon Books [renewed Random House LLC, 1973]. Used by permission of Pantheon Books, an imprint of the Knopf Doubleday Publishing Group, a division of Penguin Random House LLC. All rights reserved.

Ainsworth, M. D. S. (1978). *Patterns of Attachment: A Psychological Study of the Strange Situation.* New Jersey: Lawrence Erlbaum Associates [republished Psychology Press, 2014].

Assagioli, R. (n.d.) The balancing and synthesis of the opposites. European Federation for Psychosynthesis Psychotherapy (available on their website).

Assagioli, R. (1965). *Psychosynthesis: A Manual of Principles and Techniques.* Wellingborough: Turnstone Press.

Assagioli, R. (1973). *The Act of Will.* The Synthesis Center [reprinted New York: Penguin, 1974]

Bettelheim, B. (1976). *The Uses of Enchantment.* Thames and Hudson [Reprinted Penguin Books, 1991].

Bowlby, J. (1953). *Child Care and the Growth of Love.* London: Penguin.

Boyesen, G. (1980). *Collected Papers on Biodynamic Psychology.* London: Biodynamic Psychology Publications.

223

Bradshaw, J. (1990). *Home Coming (Reclaiming and Championing Your Inner Child)*. London: Piatcus [reprinted 2012].

Coleridge, S. T. (1817). *Biographia Literaria*. [republished CreateSpace Independent Publishing Platform, 2014].

Couzyn, J. (1978). *House of Changes*. London: Heinemann Educational Books.

Crampton, M. (1969). The use of mental imagery in psychosynthesis. *Journal of Humanistic Psychology, 9*(2). (Available at the European Federation for Psychosynthesis Psychotherapy website.)

Crampton, M. (1974). Guided imagery: A psychosynthesis approach: History and manual for practitioners. Quebec Center for Psychosynthesis. [second revised edition published by The Synthesis Center, 2005]. (Available at the European Federation for Psychosynthesis Psychotherapy website.)

Crampton, M. (1975). Answers from the unconscious. *Synthesis, 1*(2): 140–152. (Available at the European Federation for Psychosynthesis Psychotherapy website.)

Davis, J. (1996). *Jacqueline Bouvier: An Intimate Memoir*. Hoboken, NJ: Wiley.

Dawkins, R. (2010). *Enemies of Reason*. Channel 4 TV programme.

Eliade, M. (1964). *Shamanism: Archaic Techniques of Ecstasy*. Pantheon Books [republished Arkana, 1988].

Eliot, T. S. (1944). *Four Quartets*. London: Faber and Faber Limited. Reprinted with permission.

England, D. (1998). Telling Tales. MA Thesis. London: The Institute of Psychosynthesis Library. [The story "Vasilisa and Baba Yaga" can also be found on David England's storytelling website.]

England, D., & Bailey, J. (2014). *Lancashire Folk Tales*. Stroud: The History Press.

England, D., & Bilbé, T. (2013). *Berkshire Folk Tales*. Stroud: The History Press.

Evans, J. (n.d.). *The Triphasic Model of Psychospiritual Development*. London: The Institute of Psychosynthesis Training Manual.

Evans, J. (Ed.) (2005). *Foundation in Psychosynthesis*. London: The Institute of Psychosynthesis Training Manual. Anamcāra Press.

Evans, J. (Ed.) (2007). *Core Principles in Psychosynthesis Psychology*. London: The Institute of Psychosynthesis Training Manual. Anamcāra Press.

Evans, R., & Russell, P. (1990). *The Creative Manager*. London: HarperCollins.

Fairbairn, W. R. D. (1952). *Psychoanalytic Studies of the Personality*. London: Routledge and Kegan Paul [reprinted 1986].

Firman, J., & Gila, A. (1997). *The Primal Wound: A Transpersonal View of Trauma, Addiction and Growth*. New York: State University of New York Press.

Freud, S., & Riviere, J. (translator) (1949). *Introductory Lectures on Psycho-analysis*. London: Allen and Unwin.

Gendlin, E. T. (1978). *Focusing*. Everest House [reprinted London: Rider, 2003].

Hammarskjöld, D. (1964). *Markings*. London: Faber and Faber.

Herbert, G. (1633). *The Temple: The Poetry of George Herbert* [republished Paraclete Press, 2001].

Herodotus, 460–420 BCE, *Histories Book II*.

Hillman, J. (1975). *Re-Visioning Psychology*. New York: Harper Perennial.

Hillman, J. (1983). *Inter Views: Conversations With Laura Pozzo*. Woodstock, CT: Spring Publications.

Ingerman, S. (1991). *Soul Retrieval: Mending the Fragmented Self*. New York: HarperOne.

Jaynes, J. (1976). *The Origin of Consciousness in the Breakdown of the Bicameral Mind*. London: Allen Lane.

Johnson, R. A. (1986). *Inner Work: Using Dreams and Active Imagination for Personal Growth*. HarperSanFrancisco.

Johnson, S. (1994). *Character Styles*. New York: W. W. Norton.

Jung, C. G. (1921). *Psychological Types*. Princeton University Press, 712–714.

Kalsched, D. (1996). *The Inner World of Trauma: Archetypal Defences of the Personal Spirit*. London: Routledge.

Killick, S., & Taffy, T. (2007). Telling tales: Storytelling as emotional literacy. Blackburn: Educational Printing Services.

Koskuba, E., & Koskuba, K. (2007). *Tai Chi for Every Body*. New York: Reader's Digest.

Lawrence, D. H. (1950). *D. H. Lawrence: Selected Poems*. London: Penguin Books. Reprinted with permission.

Levine, P. (1997). *Waking the Tiger: Healing Trauma*. Berkley, CA: North Atlantic.

Lysaght, S. R. (1923). *Poems of Today: Second Series*. London: Sidgwick and Jackson for the English Association.

Main, M., & Goldwin, R. (1984). *Adult Attachment Scoring and Classificatory System*. Berkeley: University of California.

Markova, D., PhD. (2000). *I Will Not Die an Unlived Life: Reclaiming Purpose and Passion*. Berkeley, CA: Conari Press. Reprinted with permission. Dr Markova's website: www.ptpinc.org.

Masterson, J. F. (1990). *Search for the Real Self: Unmasking the Personality Disorders of Our Age*. New York: Free Press.

Merchant, J. (2011). *Shamans and Analysts: New Insights on the Wounded Healer*. London and New York: Routledge.

Mulhern, A. (2012). *Healing Intelligence: The Spirit in Psychotherapy—Working with Darkness and Light*. London: Karnac.

Nin, A. (2010). *Seduction of the Minotaur*. Texas: Sky Blue Press.

O'Brian, F. (1967). *The Third Policeman*. Publisher's Note. London: Picador.

Oliver, M. (1986). *Dream Work: The Journey*. The Atlantic Monthly Press.

Parkes, C. M. (2006). *Love and Loss: The Roots of Grief and its Complications*. London and New York: Routledge.

Roose-Evans, J. (1994). *Passages of the Soul: Ritual Today*. Shaftsbury: Element.

Roszak, T., Gomes, M. E., and Kanner, A. D. (Eds.) (1995). *Ecopsychology*. San Francisco: Sierra Club.

Rowan, J. (1990). *Subpersonalities: The People Inside Us*. London and New York: Routledge.

Rutherford, L. (2008). *The View Through the Medicine Wheel*. Winchester and Washington: O Books.

Smith, S. (2000). *Inner Leadership: Realize Your Self-Leading Potential*. London: Nicholas Brealey.

Stauffer, K. A. (2010). *Anatomy and Physiology for Psychotherapists: Connecting Body and Soul*. New York: W. W. Norton.

Storm, H. (1994). *Lightningbolt*. New York: Ballantine Books.

SwiftDeer Reagan, H. (1980). *Shamanic Wheels and Keys*. Deer Tribe Metis Medicine Society.

Thomas, D. (1937). *The Poems of Dylan Thomas*. New York: New Directions.

Toyne, M. (1983). *Involved in Mankind: Life and Message of Vivekananda*. Bourne End: Vedanta Press.

Virel, A. (1965). *Histoire De Notre Image*. Geneva: Editions du Mont Blanc.

Winnicott, D. W. (1987). *Babies and Their Mothers*. Boston, MA: Addison-Wesley.

Winnicott, D. W. (1988). *Playing and Reality*. London: Penguin [republished London and New York: Routledge, 2005].

Winnicott, D. W. (1996). *Maturational Processes and the Facilitating Environment: Studies in the Theory of Emotional Development*. London: Karnac.

APPENDIX

A reflection on the Russian folktale by Aleksandr Afanas'ev

The Bold Knight, the Apples of Youth, and the Water of Life

The shamanic world, like the world of the folktale, is a world of imagination, an inner world, a world of the psyche, of soul. This Appendix introduces the landscape of this "psycho-shamanic" world by means of a sequence of reflections on a traditional Russian folktale from the collection of Aleksandr Afanas'ev (1945), "The Bold Knight, the Apples of Youth, and the Water of Life".

These reflections are meant to be chewed over and digested slowly. Hence, they are scattered in bite-sized pieces throughout the Appendix. The reflections provide a musing, and occasionally mildly amusing, counterpoint to the main text of this book. The Bold Knight folktale both implicitly reflects the shamanic landscape and has a powerful psychological resonance. For the reader, the Bold Knight's journey can be a journey into the depths of soul. Please keep in mind that these reflections—like folktales, like life—are not in sequential time.

The intention of the journey

A CERTAIN KING grew very old and his eyes began to fail. He heard that beyond the ninth land, in the tenth kingdom, there was a garden with the apples of youth, and in it a well with the water of life; if an aged man ate one of those apples, he would grow young, and if a blind man's eyes were bathed with that water, he would see. That king had three sons. So he sent his eldest forth on horseback to find that garden and bring him the apples and the water, for he wanted to be young again and to see.

Reflection: journey of the soul

The story is a journey. The journey has a clear intention from the outset. It is to obtain the apples of youth and the water of life for the king. We are told, "if an aged man ate one of those apples, he would grow young, and if a blind man's eyes were bathed with that water, he would see". So, the end of the story is where we start from. We are already outside of normal, sequential time. Here, time runs in a circle.

Apples of youth and water of life: the story speaks to the soul about inner youthfulness and insight, the spiritual qualities of vitality and wisdom. The story, as we shall see, is for Everyman, male and female; for you the reader and me the writer. It is about kingship in the sense of self-mastery, being master of our own will. Like the story, a shamanic journey is a voyage of discovery beginning with a clear intention.

Death at the crossroads

The eldest son set out for the distant kingdom; he rode and rode and came to a pillar. On this pillar three roads were marked: if he followed the first, the marker said, his horse would be sated and he himself would be hungry; if he followed the second, it said, he would lose his own life; if he followed the third, it said, his horse would be hungry and he himself sated. He thought and thought and finally took the road that promised food for himself.

Reflection: the void or an adventure

The young knight is at a crossroads. No doubt he has enjoyed the companionship of peers, full of bold idealism and grand plans, convinced of his own immortality. Now, the king has sent him out alone to look the future in the face, only to see there the reality of all those adult pressures, dread responsibilities, struggles. Naive mistakes, failures, delusions, and fantasies. Times of heartbreak and despondency.

It was a simple thing, I dropped a glass onto the kitchen floor and as I swept up the shards I thought of all those future times when I shall smash a glass on the kitchen floor and have to clear it up, and I felt that touch of pure despair. It's hard for young men and women to be faced with such adult pressures before they have gained the wit and wisdom to handle them. It's a critical time. As a psychotherapist I sometimes help young people over the hump from being teenagers to accepting themselves as mature adults walking into an unknown future.

When a young person fails to receive the help they need, tragedy can follow. According to a recent report by The Lancet Commission, self-harm is the largest cause of death among 20–24 year old young people in the UK; in 2013, 329 people in their early twenties died from a self-harm related injury. Part of the problem for young people is the lack of any clear rite of passage in Western society. We need to discover a straightforward shamanic rite of passage.

There at the crossroads, contemplating the options of death, hunger, or fullness, what the young knight sees most of all is the inevitable, overwhelming, all-pervading reality of death. He could turn back, into the void of non-being: it is not death but non-being that the suicide desires; giving up on life is giving up on being. Or he could choose a half-life, starved of vitality, withdrawn, avoiding risk, intensity, engagement, adventure.

Or else he could grasp hold of life in all its fullness, with all its pressures, responsibilities, struggles. Its naive mistakes, failures, delusions, and fantasies. Its times of heartbreak and of despondency. Even of death! As well as all its adventures, strivings, successes, insights. Its times of ecstatic joy and love. And to do it with relish. When the young knight chooses to go forward into life, this is when he takes the mantle of Bold Knight.

Falling deep underground

The bold knight approached a beautiful house, opened the gates, and without doffing his cap nor bowing his head galloped into the yard. The owner, a widow who was not very old, called to him: "Welcome, dear guest!" She plied him with viands and heady drinks. He regaled himself and lay down to sleep on the bench. She said: "It is not fitting nor honourable for a gallant man to lie alone! Lie with my daughter, beautiful Dunia." He was pleased with this proposal. Dunia said, "Lie closer to me, so that we will be warmer." He moved toward her and fell through the bed. In the cellar into which he fell he was compelled to grind raw rye all day long and he could not climb out.

Reflection: the dark mirror

I feel for the lad, he is cocky and cocksure, arrogant and self-centred. He has no respect or regard for others, and is so innocent of the world that he is at the mercy of the worldly wise widow. It is easy for her to bend his will to hers, to seduce him from his task of bringing the apples of youth and the water of life. When she offers him her beautiful daughter Dunia, he seems to be on to a good thing; "Dunia" means "seemingly good" in Russian. He falls prey.

Deep underground, he is "compelled to grind raw rye all day long", and cannot climb out. These words powerfully evoke the daily grind of being stuck in an interminable, vicious cycle. As Flann O'Brian (1967) put it, "Hell goes round and round. In shape it is circular and by nature it is interminable, repetitive and very nearly unbearable". This is just how I often felt during a long period of feeling depressed and stuck. As long as my ego was immature, I was trapped in a vicious cycle that limited my emotional and psychological growth, narrowed my soul.

The psychological term for a vicious cycle is a "maintaining cycle", because it is a stable, self-maintaining structure within the psyche. The shamanic term for a vicious cycle is a "dark mirror". In the main text there is a description of the dark mirror and a method for use by a shamanic guide to help a client break the dark mirror and realise a self-sustaining and soulful "light mirror". The dark mirror/light mirror model is based on the shamanic Medicine Wheel.

Life underground

In vain the king waited and waited for his eldest son to come back. Finally he gave up waiting. Then he sent his second son to get the apples and the water. This bold knight took the same road and suffered the same fate as his elder brother, falling deep underground where he is compelled to grind raw rye all day long.

Reflection: the Lower World

There are strong parallels between this underground place, the shamanic "Lower World", and Assagioli's "Lower Unconscious". The
figure shows Assagioli's Egg Diagram model of the psyche.

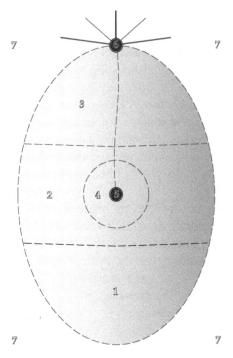

The components of the model
are:

1. The Lower Unconscious
2. The Middle Unconscious
3. The Higher Unconscious
4. The field of consciousness
5. The personal self or "I"
6. The Higher Self
7. The collective unconscious

Assagioli's Egg Diagram: model of the psyche.

The Lower Unconscious represents a person's psychological past and
their pre-personal struggle to gain a sense of their individuality. It is
the place where we repress the memories of traumas that our conscious
mind is unable to cope with. For example, referring to the "Chest of
Drawers" story, when the child says, "Mummy, Mummy, look at my
picture of myself," and she repeatedly replies, "Not now, I'm busy," the
child's unbearable feelings of rejection, hurt and disappointment are
repressed into the Lower Unconscious.

   This place where the bold knight resides—deep underground, compelled to grind raw rye—is the past. He is trapped in the past. We infer

that the earliest and strongest female impression upon this man's soul was made by his mother. He carries her image within him, and if he experiences in a woman—or projects onto her—qualities that seem to match what is present in his own soul, then he sees his object of attraction as his soulmate, falls subject to her will, and suffers the daily grind of being trapped in a repetitive, maintaining cycle. The wily widow is really a tyrannical part of himself.

Being alone with my mother between the ages of two and six left an enduring impression on my soul. She was wracked with fears, characterised by my memory of lying in bed with her listening to the engine of a flying bomb. Then, when the engine stopped, we listened to the silence, waiting for the bang. Even now, though I vividly remember the incident and am surprised that my young self knew so much about flying bombs, I nevertheless have no recall of the fear I must surely have felt. Even more surprisingly, I have always remembered this incident. Despite many years in therapy, I only realised how I had repressed the fear when I wrote this piece.

Living with my mother in an oppressive atmosphere of fear, I found the closeness between us so unbearable that I was unable to use the word "we". The word "we" implied an intimacy that to my young self was excruciating. I created a barrier against intimacy that persisted into my adult life. This was my maintaining cycle. My young child cut himself off from the insufferable agony of a sustained trauma, and buried it deep "underground". However, the trauma still had the power to distort my adult life and to narrow my soul.

In the tale, a powerful metaphor is offered in that both mother and object of attraction are present together. The mother repeatedly—one brother after another—seeks to initiate sexual intimacy with one who is "seemingly good"—that is, who matches his soul image. One meaning of "grind" is "sexual intercourse": the mother has certainly caught the man in a sexual trap.

Psychotherapists and counsellors may recognise how certain men, carrying their soul image within them, seem repeatedly to marry their own mothers, and how certain women seem repeatedly to marry their own fathers. This is life underground, survival at the cost of being subject to the mastery of past traumas and an inner tyrannical mother.

Blessing for the journey

From long waiting for his sons, the king became very sad. Now the youngest son began to beg his father's permission to go forth to seek the garden. But his father refused to let him go, saying, "A curse is on you, little son! Your older brothers perished on this quest and you, who are still a tender youth, will perish even sooner than they." But the youngest son kept imploring his father and promised him that he would bear himself more bravely for the king's sake than any brave knight. His father thought and thought and finally gave the boy his blessing for the journey.

Reflection: maturing ego

In the symbolism of the story, the three sons comprise a composite individual at different stages of maturity, the arrival of each son representing a later psychological stage. Thus, the youngest son, being the latest, is the most psychologically advanced. The story messes around with sequential time.

The king will not let his "little son" go on the quest because he is "still a tender youth". The curse that is upon him, as his brothers have shown, is the lack of psychological maturity to equip him for the task. It takes time, much thought, persistence and courage to overcome the curse of naivety and to make the act of will necessary to win the blessing of his master the king.

We learn more about the king. It is the king who is the initiator of the quest to gain the apples of youth and the water of life. It is the king who is the recipient of these qualities. It is the king who is the seer and overseer of the journey. Psychologically, the king represents the "Higher Self", "a deeper source of being beyond the conscious personality" (Firman & Gila, 1997), the conscious personality being represented by the bold knight.

In the story, the king's restraining hand prevents the youngest son from starting on the quest too soon, lest he perish. Likewise, as psychotherapists and counsellors know, the soul in its wisdom prevents us from learning traumatic secrets before we are psychologically ready to contain them in consciousness, lest we be re-traumatised.

A bath and a beating

When the youngest son reached the widow's house, she said to him, "It is not fitting for a knight nor honourable for a gallant man to lie alone! Lie with my beautiful Dunia." But he answered: "No, little aunt! A visitor must not do that without first making certain preparations. Why don't you heat up a bath for me? And let your daughter lead me to the bathhouse."

So the widow prepared a very, very hot bath and led him to the bathhouse with the beautiful Dunia. Dunia was just as wicked as her mother; she made him go in first, locked the door to the bath, and stood in the hall. But the bold knight pushed open the door and dragged Dunia with him into the bathroom. He had three rods—one of iron, one of lead, and one of cast iron—and with these rods he began to belabour the young girl.

She wept and implored him to stop. But he said: "Tell me, wicked Dunia, what you have done with my brothers!" She said that they were in the cellar grinding raw grain. Then only did he let her go. They came back to the main room, tied one ladder to another, and freed his brothers.

He told them to go home; but they were ashamed to appear before their father, because they had lain down with Dunia and had failed in their mission. So they wandered about in the fields and woods.

Reflection: masculine and feminine split

By the time the third son reaches the widow's house, he has gained enough psychological maturity and sense of self to equip him to deal with her attempts to seduce him from his mission. He is no longer dominated by an image of a tyrannical mother. He distances himself by referring to the widow as "little aunt".

The bold knight belabours Dunia with three rods to get the truth out of her. Multiplicity in folktales denotes emphasis, so excessive force is signified by the knight having three rods with him. In my first draft, I was so shocked and appalled by this scene of callous, premeditated brutality by the hero of our tale towards this young woman that I left it out.

However, it would be wrong to ignore the phenomena of violence, oppression, possession, mutilation, injustice, disregard and denial of basic human rights that men worldwide inflict upon women. There seems to be a massive split in the collective psyche of our human species that serves to repress and deny the power, wit, dignity and nobility that women possess.

When I read this passage to my friend Bernadette, she responded, "It sounds to me like you are acting out the split by putting women on a pedestal, to be knocked down." Ah!

The scene is meant to shock: to command our attention and force us to reflect on the split in our own soul between masculine and feminine. As Bernadette's response reveals, the split is subtle and insidious.

For much of my adult life the masculine held sway, not by using physical force, but by using the force of my ambition, facility with words, leadership ability, and a capacity to take risks. I split off and denied the feminine side of my nature, being thoughtful yet not self-reflective, passionate yet far from feelings, an effective communicator yet unreceptive, intelligent yet without insight. We shall return to this most important theme of feminine and masculine before this tale is done.

After forcing Dunia to tell him what has happened to his elder brothers, the bold knight releases them by lowering a long ladder deep into the underground cellar. We shall, for the moment, leave the elder brothers to wander about in the fields and woods in shame, while we follow the bold knight on his journey.

The maiden's question

The knight went on; he rode and rode till he came to a farmhouse. He entered; there sat a pretty young girl weaving towels. He said: "God bless you, pretty maiden!" And she answered: "Thank you! What are you doing, good knight? Are you running away from an adventure or are you trying to find one?" "I am trying to carry out a mission, pretty maiden," said the knight "I am going beyond the ninth land, to the tenth kingdom, to a certain garden, where I hope to find the apples of youth and the water of life for my aged, blind father." She said to him: "It will be hard, very hard, for you to reach that garden."

Reflection: the call to a life of adventure

Beginning the next phase of the story, when the young man meets the first of three sisters, an extraordinary volume and precision of meaning is condensed into a few words. He greets the pretty young girl who is weaving towels, and she replies with a highly pertinent question, "Are you running away from an adventure or are you trying to find one?"

We are told she is weaving towels: this allusion, to those three powerful maidens who weave the fates of men like him, shows the manner of woman she is. I see her toying with her towel as she asks her astute question, leaving him in no doubt she is a power he must reckon with. So must we. We may all confront her question at some point in our lives: "Am I running away from an adventure or am I trying to find one?"

When I feel called to something, there is for me no more challenging question. By holding the question, the powerful maiden holds the fate of my soul in her hands. Because nothing is predestined, because I have free will, the choice is mine. It is the *question* that is my destiny. How I *respond* determines the fate of my soul. This makes the question deeply spiritual: my response to the question is crucial to my soul, how willing am I to experience myself fully and to engage with the adventure of life?

The young man's answer to the maiden's question is to affirm his intention, but with some ambivalence: he is "*trying* to carry out a mission", "I *hope* to find the apples of youth and the water of life." It means he might still run away from the adventure. Far from encouraging or reassuring him—as friends might easily do—the maiden makes his choice more stark, "It will be hard, very hard, for you."

Following a calling is not a once-for-all choice. When we find obstacles in our path, our intention is challenged. Then we need to think carefully, to consult our intuition; because our chosen way may not be the right path after all and we may need to allow space for a change of direction. On the other hand, the moment is crucial, because we could so easily betray ourselves and run away. If we have chosen the right path, then we need to affirm our intention clearly, with all the resolution and courage needed to overcome any obstacle. This is soulmaking and the way of Soulfulness.

Responding to a call means we engage more deeply in the adventure of life, in a small way perhaps, or maybe it means our lives are changed beyond recognition. Here is a personal story:

My father was a head teacher, he was on the education committee, he set up and ran the school's music festival and the teacher's centre, as well as many other educational endeavours. One of my enduring images is of him doing the National Union of Teachers accounts on the dining table. It left him little time for his sons and it left me determined to have nothing to do with the field of education, until some decades later, when I felt the pull to go into schools to tell stories.

I put the call to the test and offered to tell stories for no fee. The children and I enjoyed the storytelling, but in some of the schools I felt so unwelcome and unappreciated by the staff that I thought this work was not for me; I had been right to think that I should have nothing to do with education. Faced with an obstacle, I ran away.

Three years later, I attended a telling workshop with Malcolm White, at the Society for Storytelling Annual Gathering. I had been thinking vaguely about trying telling stories in schools again. At the end of the workshop, I said, "I have a project." The call was back, marked by other signposts, such as: discovering Steve Killick's and Taffy Thomas' (2007) book about storytelling with children; friend and fellow storyteller Alan Woollard speaking to me about the educational value of his storytelling work in schools; and hearing of a newly opened Children's Centre and receiving a booking.

Now, as a professional storyteller, storytelling with primary and early years children, and listening to their stories, is both affirming and brings joy to my soul.

Each time we are faced with the question, "Am I running away from an adventure or am I trying to find one?", it's almost like we have circled back to the crossroads, until we realise we are not looking at a signpost but a milestone. We discover what free will is really about: going forward down the road or turning back.

Receiving the maiden sisters' guidance

The first sister told the bold knight, "Continue on your way. Soon you will come to the house of my second sister. She knows better than I how to find the garden and will tell you what to do."

He rode and rode till he came to the house of the second sister. He greeted her just as he had the first, and told her who he was and where he was going. She bade him leave his horse with her and ride on her own two-winged horse to the house of her older sister, who would tell him what to do—how to reach the garden and how to get the apples and the water.

Reflection: interdependency between feminine and masculine

Previously, the young man relied on crude, masculine force to beat the truth out of Dunia and rescue his brothers. Now, he needs to submit to the guidance of the three sisters to enable him to complete the present phase of his journey. There is a recurring motif in powerful Russian folktales like this one, the masculine relying upon the feminine, the feminine upon the masculine, in the business of soulmaking. Attaining interdependency between feminine and masculine is essential for the young man, for any of us, to become whole.

I remember a time when I felt admiration for what I perceived as "strong women". I saw in them something I thought was lacking in myself. Eventually, I came to realise that what I lacked was connection with the feminine side of my own being. In raising a barrier against my mother, and hence against intimacy with women, I had also cut off from my own feminine side. (I only saw clearly how I had done this as I wrote these words!)

A life crisis caused me emotional turmoil and precipitated change, though lasting psychological change only came about gradually. First, I began to connect with my feelings, to experience them and be able to give them names. These feelings had, of course, been there all along. I realised, when I replayed my mind's memory tapes of my life, I simply had not been aware of my feelings, and ironically had only experienced feelings as something unbearably painful, full of angst, anger and resentment.

I remember a time when I scoffed at the idea of intuition. Some time after starting to connect with my feelings, I began to know things I didn't know I knew, and gradually came to acknowledge the reality of intuition as a useful guide. In my work as a psychotherapist, I increasingly found myself saying things that came to me by grace from a deeper part of my being.

In my foundation year, prior to my psychotherapy training, I was introduced to "subpersonalities" and found images for these different facets of my personality, all of them animals: Frog, Bear, Raven, Eagle, and Stag or Herne the Hunter. I was also introduced to shamanism, and found to my surprise that my animal subpersonalities fitted the shamanic Medicine Wheel.

These are my animal allies, as they sit around the Medicine Wheel:

Direction	Element	Element of Personality	Animal ally
South	Water	Feelings	Frog
West	Earth	Body	Bear
North	Air	Mind	Raven
East	Fire	Spirit	Eagle
Centre	Void	Lifeforce	Stag or Herne the Hunter

The third sister's warning

So he rode and rode till he came to the house of the third sister. She gave him her four-winged horse and told him: "Be careful. In that garden lives our aunt, a terrible witch. When you come to the garden, do not spare my horse. Spur him strongly, so that he clears the wall in one bound; for if he touches the wall, the strings with bells that are tied to it will sing out, the bells will ring, the witch will awaken, and you won't be able to get away from her! She has a horse with six wings; cut the tendons under his wings so that she cannot overtake you."

Reflection: the Upper World

At the start of the tale, the king "heard that beyond the ninth land, in the tenth kingdom, there was a garden with the apples of youth, and in it a well with the water of life". The words "beyond the ninth land, in the tenth kingdom"—some tales reach even further, "beyond thrice-nine lands, in a thrice-tenth country"—provide a common motif in Russian folktales, signifying a fairy tale land far from the world where the tale begins. I see the young man soaring higher and higher, first on a two-winged horse then on a four-winged horse, to reach the garden in the kingdom of the sky.

There are strong parallels between this sky garden, the shamanic "Upper World", and Assagioli's "Higher Unconscious" (see Figure above). Where the Lower Unconscious represents a person's psychological past, the Higher Unconscious represents their psychological future. It is the source of intuition and insight, higher values, creative potentiality, moral imperative and call to service, and of wisdom and understanding.

The Higher Unconscious is also the place where we repress the wounding to our sense of self. When the child in the "Chest of Drawers" story says, "Mummy, Mummy, look at my picture of myself," and she repeatedly replies, "Not now, I'm busy," the child experiences these aspects of his self-expression and creativity as unacceptable to the mother and so they are repressed in the Higher Unconscious—repression of the sublime.

In a workshop that I attended, led by John Firman and Ann Gila, they referred to repression in the Lower and Higher Unconscious respectively as "opposite sides of the same wound". The negative aspect of the wounding, the rejection and hurt, are repressed in the Lower Unconscious. The positive aspect, the unacknowledged self-expression, is repressed in the Higher Unconscious. Both constitute soul loss.

So, the garden to which the bold knight ascends is the future. He aspires to spiritual qualities that he does not yet own—wisdom and vitality, insight and inner youthfulness. The boy in the "Chest of Drawers" story, by cutting himself off from the insufferable agony of trauma and hiding it deep underground, also cut himself off from that bright spiritual quality of creativity, to the impoverishment of his soul. He consigned his potentiality for creativity to an uncertain future, hidden in the sky garden.

The young man's task in journeying to the sky garden is to retrieve the spiritual qualities of wisdom and vitality, insight and inner youthfulness, and restore his soul.

Incidentally, there's something about shamanic journeys: while you lie in a relaxed state of consciousness with the drum beating, the journey simply unfolds. People who are used to journeying speak of the different ways they travel between the Worlds. The commonest ways are by ladder and by flying horse, both appearing in the story, or through a vortex. These are representations of the "World Tree", which connects the three worlds of the shamanic universe: the Lower World, the Middle World, and the Upper World.

Retrieving the apples of youth and water of life

He did as she bade him. He flew over the wall on his horse, but his horse lightly touched one string with his tail; all the strings sang and the bells rang, but softly. The witch awoke but did not clearly distinguish the voice of the strings and the bells, so she yawned and fell asleep again. And the bold knight galloped away with the apples of youth and the water of life. He stopped at the houses of the sisters, where he changed horses, and darted off to his own kingdom on his own horse.

Reflection: the transpersonal call

Psychologically, where the Lower World represents the pre-personal struggle to individuate, the Upper World represents the transpersonal call, intuitively perceived, to align with higher values of sacrifice and service and to gain spiritual wisdom. Here is an example of a response to a transpersonal call, written by Dag Hammarskjöld (1964), then UN General Secretary (p. 169):

> I don't know who—or what—put the question, I don't know when it was put. I don't even remember answering. But at some moment I did answer Yes to Someone—or Something—and from that hour I was certain that existence is meaningful and that, therefore, my life, in self-surrender, had a goal.
>
> From that moment I have known what it means 'not to look back', and 'to take no thought for the morrow'.

Dag Hammarskjöld had set his course and knew there could be no looking back.

No wonder there is something implacable about the three sisters. They are open, honest and frank with the young man in his quest for the apples of youth and the water of life—the spiritual qualities of wisdom and vitality, of insight and inner youthfulness—but they demand the same openness, honesty and frankness from him. If he fails to do as they bid and hold to his quest on behalf of the king, then he will awaken their aunt, a "terrible witch", and he "won't be able to get away from her". Implacability is equally true of the aunt, but provided he is open, honest and frank she is willing to overlook a minor infraction. As in other powerful Russian folktales, these goddess-like spiritual beings are uncompromising but also fair.

What this means is that opening ourselves to spiritual qualities and a transpersonal call is fraught with moral and spiritual hazard. It seems like the terrible witch is forever seeking to lure us from the heights into a pit of self-deception, spiritual pride and ego inflation: she is forever taunting us to embrace the thought, "I am not as other people are".

All we can do in the face of this spiritual hazard is to heed the third sister's warning and remain alert to the danger; to remain open, honest and frank, most of all with ourselves; to stay grounded in our spirituality; to seek to remember that "the only wisdom we can hope to acquire is the wisdom of humility" (Eliot, 1944), and that everything we gain is a gift of grace from our Higher Self; to retain our dignity. This is soul-making and the way of Soulfulness.

Returning to the bold knight's own kingdom

On his way home, the bold knight stopped at the houses of the sisters, where he changed horses, and darted off to his own kingdom on his own horse.

The witch mounted her six-winged horse and pursued the bold knight and almost overtook him, but he had reached his own land and no longer feared her: there she dared not enter. She only looked at him and in a voice hoarse with spite said: "You are a fine little thief! You have succeeded very well in your mission! You got away from me, but nothing will save you from your own brothers." Having thus foretold his fate, she returned home.

Our bold knight went on his way in his own land, and found his vagabond brothers sleeping in a field. After he has freed his brothers, the youngest son had told them to go home, but they were ashamed to appear before their father, because they had lain down with Dunia and had failed in their mission. So they wandered about in the fields and woods.

The bold knight did not awaken his brothers, but lay down beside them and fell asleep. The brothers awoke, saw that their brother had returned to his own land, softly took the apples of youth out of his breast pocket, and threw him, still sleeping, over a precipice.

Reflection: the Middle World

The young man heeds the third sister's warning and gets out quickly, darting off towards his own kingdom on his own horse.

At the beginning of the story, the king heard that beyond the ninth land, in the tenth kingdom, there was a garden with the apples of youth, and in it a well with the water of life, so he sent his son on horseback to find that garden and bring him the apples and the water. Now, via the underground world and the sky garden, the bold knight has returned to his own kingdom on his own horse. Here he is safe from the witch, because all the action in the story happens in the Upper World or the Lower World. All the action—that is—except "normal things", which happen in the "normal world", like being thrown over a precipice.

There are strong parallels between this normal world—called the bright world in the story—the shamanic "Middle World", and Assagioli's "Middle Unconscious" (see above Figure). Where the Lower Unconscious represents a person's psychological past, and the Higher Unconscious represents a person's psychological future, the Middle Unconscious represents a person's psychological present, the flow of sensations, images, thoughts, feelings, desires and impulses, the shifting contents of our consciousness, and the personal struggle to attain worldly wisdom and personal power.

The Middle Unconscious represents everything accessible to consciousness, everything we can bring to mind or imagine ourselves doing. So, the Middle Unconscious is not the same as the physical world in which we live, but is analogous to it. Julian Jaynes (1976) speaks of, "The analogue 'I', the metaphor we have of ourselves, which can 'move about' vicariously in our 'imagination', 'doing' things we are not actually doing". Thus, "I" exist in the physical world, whilst my analogue "I" exists in the Middle World.

Journeying into the Middle World enables us to wander in imagination throughout the world we inhabit, so as to gain a greater understanding of the energy surrounding the places and persons that we encounter in our daily life, and a deeper insight into the way we animate our daily life. As Goethe is supposed to have put it so poetically:

> Whatever you can do,
> or dream you can, begin it.
> Boldness has genius,
> power and magic in it.

The Middle World abounds with folktales of mortal men and women, bold heroes and heroines, undertaking heroic journeys and impossible tasks, aspiring to become kings and queens imbued with worldly wisdom and power. Often these heroes and heroines are aided by helpful beings, respectively Lower World animal allies and Upper World wise guides.

The two elder brothers, by the way, had been too ashamed to go home. Shame is often one of the baffling symptoms of trauma: we feel ashamed and guilty for what the maternal environment has inflicted upon us, and for what our internal, tyrannical, wily widow continues to inflict.

Revisiting the Lower World

The bold knight fell for three days, till he reached the dark kingdom, where a maiden was given to the seven-headed dragon every month. Now it was the turn of the underground king's daughter, Paliusha. When our bold knight heard this, he said to the underground king, "I will save your daughter from the dragon, but later you must do for me whatever I ask of you." The king was overjoyed, promised to do anything for him, and to give the princess to him in marriage. The next day Paliusha was led to a three-walled fortress on the edge of the sea and the knight went with her, bearing an iron rod that weighed about two hundred pounds.

While he and the princess waited for the dragon, he told her about his adventures and said he had the water of life with him. Then the bold knight said to the beautiful princess, "Pick the lice out of my head, and should I fall asleep before the dragon comes, waken me with my rod—otherwise you will not arouse me!" He laid his head in her lap. She looked for lice in his hair. He fell asleep.

The dragon circled above the princess. She tried to shake the knight awake, but did not hit him with his rod for she did not wish to hurt him. She could not waken him and began to weep. A tear dropped on his face and he woke up exclaiming, "Oh, you have burned me with something pleasant!" Meanwhile the dragon had begun to swoop down on them.

The knight took up his two-hundred pound rod, swung it, and at one stroke knocked off five of the dragon's heads. He swung back a second time, and knocked off the remaining two. He gathered up all the heads, put them under the wall, and cast the monster's trunk into the sea.

Reflection: redeeming and trusting the feminine

The bold knight has fallen asleep, a metaphor for going unconscious, falling into the Lower World, that dark kingdom into which he has been thrown. The bold knight may have visited the Upper World, but now he is made to confront unfinished business in the Lower World. He has journeyed in a circle. Or rather, revisiting the Lower World is a turn of the spiral.

While the bold knight has been busy in the Upper World, the wily widow, the inner tyrannical mother, has gained strength and become a seven-headed dragon. Why should this be so? In psychological terms, because the Higher and Lower Unconscious are opposite sides of the same wound, work on one side has the effect of also opening the other.

Thus, the bold knight must journey more deeply into the Lower World—falling for three days—in order to redeem the feminine side of his nature. He faces a difficult task, to decapitate the seven-headed dragon, put the beautiful princess in her rightful place, and bring her out of the dark kingdom into the bright world, into consciousness. His task is to retrieve and redeem the feminine side of his nature and restore his soul.

At this moment, the image of the bold knight falling asleep in the lap of the princess fills my eyes with sudden tears—burning me with something pleasant—just as hers fill with tears when she cannot waken him. It is such a powerful metaphor: in the face of the seven-headed dragon our bold knight places his trust in the maiden princess and enters even more deeply into the dark kingdom of his unconscious.

The princess attends to him and cares for him gently, not wishing to hurt him, for she is both his lover and the compassionate mother he never had. Yet she was always there, safely hiding in his innermost soul, until the moment he finds her, when she awakens him with her passionate tears. After this, he deals with the dragon in two strokes.

"So, what about the lice?" I hear you cry. Well, they are parasitic bloodsuckers, they suck the life out of you, devour you, just like the seven-headed dragon would do, like the inner tyrant does. The bold knight needs help from the princess to get the lousy tyrant out of his hair.

The bold knight dismembered and restored

An envious fellow saw all this, stole lightly around the other side of the wall, cut off the knight's head, cast it into the sea, and bade the Paliusha tell her father he had saved her, or else he would strangle her. When she told the king this fellow had saved her he was enormously happy and set about preparing for the wedding feast. Guests arrived from foreign lands, and all of them drank and amused themselves. The princess secretly shed burning tears for her bold knight.

She asked her father to send fishermen to catch fish in the sea. They cast a net and dragged out the head and trunk of the bold knight. Paliusha found a phial with the water of life in his breast pocket, placed the head on the body, wet it with the water from the phial, and he came to life. She told him how she loathed the man who wanted to take her. The knight comforted her and told her he would come and set things right.

The knight asked the king, "Who saved your daughter?" The king pointed out the envious fellow. "Well, king," said the knight, "let us go to the fortress. If he can find the dragon's heads, I will believe he saved Paliusha." They all went to the fortress. The fellow could not find even one head. But the knight found them all. Then the princess told the whole truth about who saved her.

Reflection: spiritual emergency

What is it about heads? The knight knocked off all seven of the dragon's heads and put them under the fortress wall. Then, the envious fellow stole lightly around the other side of the wall, cut off the knight's head, and cast it into the sea, to join the monster's trunk. I can understand the symbolism of knocking off the dragon's seven heads. Multiplicity in folktales denotes emphasis, and seven heads signifies especial emphasis, so silencing seven internal tyrannical talking heads makes sense.

But what about the knight's head? I suggest that the symbolism has several tangled threads: what is being enacted here is the ancient ritual of purification by immersion. The knight once again descends more deeply into the dark kingdom of his unconscious, where work is done. The knight is brought from the water renewed and reborn, is reassembled, and is restored by the water of life. This is a profound act of transformation. The monster's trunk on the other hand has gone forever.

From a slightly different perspective, at a time of spiritual crisis and change, it is common for us to suffer a fantasy of sickness, disintegration and death, as the soul in its expansion bursts through our muscle-bound mental structures. We cannot go back to the way things were, there is "something broken, twisted, hurting, *forcing reflection*" (Hillman, 1983). We begin the work of imagining ourselves and our lives differently. Something does indeed die in us as something new is born, so that we know ourselves anew and see our world in a different light.

At such a time of spiritual crisis, I felt like a man with no bones, a pool of a man—this was my image of myself, and I couldn't bear to see curtains closed or apples still in their paper bag. This fantasy of dismemberment and entombment lasted for three days. Then, standing in my kitchen, I felt a strange, spontaneous, astonishing influx of energy, lasting maybe a second or an hour. A couple of days after this restorative trance, in the ambulatory of Beverley Minster, on a memorial tablet, I read the word "resurgam", I am risen. I felt thrilled and knew it was true for me. I am risen.

The bold knight is dismembered and thrown into the sea, and is later restored by the water of life. Mircea Eliade (1964) describes the ceremony to determine an initiate shaman's vocation as comprising, symbolically, of suffering, death and dismemberment, and then resurrection. The initiate's life transition is only accomplished by experiencing in trance his death and dismemberment and his restoration to a new life.

Just as in the story, the bold knight cannot complete his transformation and life transition—redeeming the feminine by bringing the beautiful princess out of the dark kingdom into the bright world of consciousness—without suffering death, dismemberment, then restoration by the princess herself with the water of life.

Riding the spoonbilled bird

The underground king wanted to marry the bold knight to his daughter. But the knight said: "No, king, I don't need anything from you. Only take me back to our bright world; I have not yet finished my mission for my father—he is still waiting for me to bring him the water of life, for he is blind." The underground king did not know how to take the knight up to the bright world; and his daughter did not want to part from him, she wanted to go up with him. She told her father that there was a spoonbilled bird that could take them there, provided she had enough to feed it on the way. So Paliusha had an ox killed and took it with her as food for the bird. They said farewell to the underground king, sat on the bird's back, and set out for the bright world.

Reflection: animal allies, instinctive wisdom

In shamanic journeys, a variety of conveyances are used to travel between Worlds. Ways of travel used in the story are by ladder, by flying horse, by falling, and in this instance by spoonbilled bird. One of the few Russian spoonbill class of birds is the sacred ibis. The story goes, according to Herodotus:

> At the beginning of spring, winged serpents from Arabia fly towards Egypt, and the birds called sacred ibises meet them at the entrance of this country and do not suffer the serpents to go by, but kill them.

After killing the seven-headed dragon, a sacred ibis is thus a worthy mount on which the victorious bold knight and princess journey from the underground world up to the bright world.

In the story the spoonbilled bird is an "animal ally". Animal allies feature strongly in folktales. Equally, animal allies are a significant aspect of shamanic journeying, where they are generally seen as creatures of the Lower World, because they represent our physicality and instinctive wisdom. When we begin to learn to journey, one of our earliest journeys is to go to the Lower World to meet an animal ally and start to get to know them. When we journey frequently we become familiar with our animal allies and learn to rely on them. Sometimes, so that we don't become too set in our ways, old allies will leave us and new allies will appear.

The underground king wants the bold knight and princess to marry, but the bold knight said, "No, king!" Nevertheless, romance is in the air.

Feeding the spoonbilled bird

When they gave more food to the bird, it flew upward faster; thus they used up the whole ox to feed it. Now they were perplexed and afraid lest the bird should drop them down again. So Paliusha cut off a piece of her thigh and gave it to the spoonbill; the bird straightway brought them up to this world and said, "Throughout our journey you fed me well, but never did I taste anything sweeter than that last morsel." Paliusha showed the bird her thigh. The bird moaned and spat out the piece, still whole. The knight put it on Paliusha's thigh, wet it with the water of life, and healed the princess.

Reflection: masculine, feminine and the Medicine Wheel

On the face of it, this is a perplexing and rather horrific part of the story, but to my mind it is about the subtle interplay between the masculine and feminine sides of our nature, which we shall now refer to as "Prince" and "Princess", in which the Princess in the tale is a strong and vital player, as we shall see.

Our "Prince and Princess" are sometimes described psychologically, though not in a gender-specific sense, as the "penetrating masculine" and the "receptive feminine". For me, this is far from being the whole story. To explain this I need to bring in the shamanic Medicine Wheel. The Medicine Wheel teaching is about the following four levels:

The four directions	West	South	North	East
relate to the four elements	Earth	Water	Air	Fire
which relate to four levels of the person	Body	Feelings	Mind	Spirit
whose primary roles or functions are	Holding	Giving	Receiving	Transforming

and each of the four levels has the three remaining functions as a secondary role.

We might acknowledge intuitively how astute this formulation is, except that the Western mind has difficulty with Mind Receiving. Our mind sees *itself*, egoistically, rather than our spirit, as assertive and transformative. However, it can be seen that the mind has the ability to input a volume of information, to sort it, process it, analyse it, and produce a coherent conclusion. Hence, our mind's primary function is to receive information, in order to make sense of it, and its secondary function is to give its evaluation.

We can now put: "Mind Receives" alongside "penetrating masculine" and "Feelings Give" alongside "receptive feminine" and thereby gain a clearer picture of the relationship between masculine and feminine aspects of soul: each gives and each receives in its own way.

The bold knight, who penetrated and forced the truth out of Dunia, briefly seeks to assert himself, bluntly rejecting the underground king's talk of marriage—"I don't need anything from you. Only take me back to our bright world"—because he is focused solely on completing his mission for his father and determined to do it on his own. Which he cannot do, as is plainly apparent to the attentive, receptive Princess, because he doesn't know how to return to the bright world any more than her father does.

The Princess quietly takes charge. She is strong in the knowledge that the Prince cannot refuse her going with him. Because she is intimately receptive to her intuitive animal nature she is wise to the ways of the spoonbilled bird. She tells her father of this, not willing to humiliate the Prince with her superior wisdom. The Princess has an ox slain to feed the bird on the journey and all is arranged by her.

When the bird's food runs out and the couple fear the flight will stall, the Princess, being committed and loyal, gives of her sweet self lest the Prince should fail in his mission. He responds by healing her wound. Using the water of life, the Princess had first healed the Prince, restoring his transformed head to his body. The Prince is now able to heal the Princess.

Here again is the recurring motif in powerful Russian folktales, the masculine relying for healing upon the feminine, the feminine upon the masculine. Interdependency between Prince and Princess having been thus attained, they are ready to go home for the final scene of the tale.

Homecoming

Then they went home. The father, the king of the land in our own world, met them and was overjoyed to see them. The knight saw that his father had grown younger from having the apples, but that he was still blind.

The knight at once anointed his father's eyes with the water of life. The king began to see; he embraced his son, the prince, and the princess from the dark kingdom. The prince told how his brothers had taken his apples and thrown him into the nether world. The brothers were so frightened that they jumped into the river.

And the prince married the princess Paliusha and gave a most wonderful feast.

Reflection: The sacred marriage

Now we have the gathered soul:

The King	the Higher Self
The Prince	the personal self
The Princess from the dark kingdom	the feminine side of the personality
The other brothers	other parts of the personality

The gathered soul portrays the personality's glorious multiplicity and complexity.

As a composite person, the elder brothers bring home for the king the apples of youth and the younger brother the water of life—inner youthfulness and insight, the spiritual qualities of vitality and wisdom. The Prince has gained these qualities during the rigours of his soul journey, and at the same time can receive them only from the King. The personal self can only receive spiritual qualities when aligned with the Higher Self, when the King embraces his son the Prince.

To my mind, the spiritual quality that the Prince gains on his soul journey and brings to the bright world is the Princess from the dark kingdom, his feminine side, without whom he can never be whole and never know deep wisdom and vitality. Thus, the culmination of the tale is the sacred marriage, Prince with Princess, masculine with feminine, the harmonisation of opposites.

So, what about the brothers, jumping into the river? The tale doesn't tell us they drowned. The brothers descend into the dark kingdom of the unconscious, where work is done, for "there's a work going on all the time, a fire burning, something elemental happening, the Soul's way of working on itself" (Hillman, 1983). The tale continues.

The folktale "The Bold Knight, the Apples of Youth, and the Water of Life" is a masculine rite of passage story involving the Prince bringing the Princess out of the dark kingdom into the bright world. The folktale "The Singing Tree and the Talking Bird", also from the collection of Aleksandr Afanas'ev (1945), is a parallel folktale, in that it is a feminine rite of passage story involving the Princess bringing her brothers out of the dark kingdom into the bright world by sprinkling them with the water of life. I entreat you, the reader, to seek out this story, to reflect upon it, and to make of it what you will. Perhaps someone reading this will one day write a parallel reflection on the tale "The Singing Tree and the Talking Bird".

Completing the circle

I dined and drank mead with them, and their cabbage was toothsome. Even now I could eat some!

Reflection: self-mastery, a soul journey

So we complete the circle and return to the beginning. The tale is about kingship in the sense of self-mastery, being master of our own will. Self-mastery is a soul journey, the gradual way of becoming free from the distorting effects of trauma, of aligning with the will of Higher Self, of embracing the King. At the tail of the tale, the storyteller identifies with the story, "I dined and drank mead with them, and their cabbage was toothsome," and its enduring relevance, "Even now I could eat some!"

So, the folktale ends on this prosaic note, reminding us that the tale is for Everyman, everyone who has a soul to nourish—man and woman, you the reader, and me the writer.

INDEX